The Speaker's Treasury
of Quotations

The Speaker's Treasury of Quotations

Maxims, Witticisms and Quips for Speeches and Presentations

Compiled by
MICHAEL C. THOMSETT *and*
LINDA ROSE THOMSETT

McFarland & Company, Inc., Publishers
Jefferson, North Carolina, and London

ALSO BY MICHAEL C. THOMSETT (AND PUBLISHED BY MCFARLAND)

*The German Opposition to Hitler: The Resistance, the Underground,
    and Assassination Plots, 1938–1945* (1997; softcover 2007)
A Treasury of Business Quotations (1990)
Insurance Dictionary Illustrated (1989)
Musical Terms, Symbols and Theory: An Illustrated Dictionary (1989)
Real Estate Dictionary (1988)
Investment and Securities Dictionary (1986)

BY MICHAEL C. THOMSETT AND JEAN FREESTONE THOMSETT
(AND PUBLISHED BY MCFARLAND)

*Sex and Love Quotations: A Worldwide Dictionary of Pronouncements
    About Gender and Sexuality Throughout the Ages* (1995)
*Political Quotations: A Worldwide Dictionary of Thoughts and Pronouncements
    from Politicians, Literary Figures, Humorists and Others* (1994)
*War and Conflict Quotations: A Worldwide Dictionary of Pronouncements
    from Military Leaders, Politicians, Philosophers, Writers and Others*
    (1997; softcover 2008)

LIBRARY OF CONGRESS CATALOGUING-IN-PUBLICATION DATA

The speaker's treasury of quotations : maxims, witticisms and
quips for speeches and presentations / compiled by Michael C.
Thomsett and Linda Rose Thomsett.

    p.   cm.

Includes indexes.

ISBN 978-0-7864-2945-5
softcover : 50# alkaline paper ∞

1. Quotations, English.   I. Thomsett, Michael C.
II. Thomsett, Linda Rose.
PN6081.S7219   2009
081— dc22   2008054522

British Library cataloguing data are available

Cover image ©2008 Shutterstock

Manufactured in the United States of America

*McFarland & Company, Inc., Publishers
    Box 611, Jefferson, North Carolina 28640
    www.mcfarlandpub.com*

CONTENTS

Preface   1

Contents

Contents

Contents

PREFACE

Every speaker faces the problem of providing relevant and appropriate quotations within speeches and presentations. Quotations serve as icebreakers and for emphasis of major points. They may be pithy, humorous, or profound.

This book is a compilation of 2,116 quotations in 263 subject categories. Compilers have to make a series of judgments concerning inclusion of quotations in a book of this nature. The criteria used in this work include:

Complete citation: Every quotation is provided with complete source, which includes the name of the person, the source book or publication, and the date. For speakers who are asked to provide citations for their quotations, this is a valuable feature that is usually not found in books of quotations or online sources.

Applicability to speaking usage: The decision to include or exclude a quotation often rested with the judgment about whether it would be useful in the context of a speaker's needs. Accordingly, some famous quotations usually included in a more general reference may be excluded, whereas other, more obscure quotations are included because they added something of value.

Variety: Given the broad range of subject areas, one motive in selecting quotations was to provide a healthy variety of sources and observations.

There are three major sections in this book: the quotations, an index of persons, and an index of key words in context. The quotations are given with entry numbers from 1 to 2116.

The speaker may look for a quotation in three different ways. The most common method is to select a specific subject, and the book is arranged alphabetically by subject as listed in the table of contents. Within each subject area, quotations are listed in date order for the most part. A second method is to select a quotation by the person who wrote or spoke the words. The index of persons cites, for each, every subject for which there is a quotation, providing the entry number for that quotation. Finally, if the speaker knows a key word or phrase, the index of key words in context is the most valuable. Here, phrases in which the word appears are listed alphabetically and then referenced to the specific quotation by entry number.

A final word: Quotable remarks have traditionally tended to favor the use of words like "he," "mankind," and "man." The duty of compilers of books of quotations is of course to be true to the original wording, even though more enlightened usage tends to be inclusive of both sexes. Consequently, the quotations to be found herein tend to be more masculine than feminine. The compilers embarked on this endeavor with the hope that speakers will understand the limitations of historical gender usage.

THE QUOTATIONS

Ability

1   Out of my lean and low ability I'll lend you something.— William Shakespeare, *Twelfth Night*, 1598–1600

2   In spite of his practical ability, some of his experience had petrified into maxims and quotations.— George Eliot, *Daniel Deronda*, 1876

3   I never doubted my ability, but when you hear all your life you're inferior, it makes you wonder if the other guys have something you've never seen before. If they do, I'm still looking for it.— Hank Aaron, *I Had a Hammer*, 1992

Absurdity

4   The privilege of absurdity; to which no living creature is subject, but man only.— Thomas Hobbes, *Leviathan*, 1651

5   Fools invent fashions and wise men are fain to follow them.— Samuel Butler, *Prose Observations*, 1660–80

6   Wise men or absolute fools are hard to be met with, as there are few giants or dwarfs.— William Hazlitt, *Characteristics*, 1823

7   Unaware of the absurdity of it, we introduce our own petty household rules into the economy of the universe for which the life of generations, peoples, of entire planets, has no importance in relation to the general development.— Aleksandr Herzen, *From the Other Shore*, 1855

8   In the consciousness of the truth he has perceived, man now sees everywhere only the awfulness or the absurdity of existence and loathing seizes him.— Friedrich Nietzsche, *The Birth of Tragedy*, 1872

9   It is not funny that anything else should fall down; only that a man should fall down ... it is the fall of Man. Only man be absurd; for only man can be dignified.— Gilbert K. Chesterton, *All Things Considered*, 1908

10   Life is full of infinite absurdities. Which, strangely enough, do not even need to appear plausible, since they are true.— Luigi Pirandello, *Six Characters in Search of an Author*, 1921

11   People who cannot recognize a palpable absurdity are very much in the way of civilization.— Agnes Repplier, *In Pursuit of Laughter*, 1936

12   At any street corner the feeling of absurdity can strike any man in the face.— Albert Camus, *The Myth of Sisyphus*, 1942

13   Ninety-nine percent of the people in the world are fools and the rest of us are in great danger of contagion.— Thomas Wilder, *The Matchmaker*, 1954

14   Modern man must descend the spiral of his own absurdity to the lowest point; only then can he look beyond it. It is obviously impossible to get around

it, jump over it, or simply avoid it.— Václav Havel, *Disturbing the Peace*, 1986

Achievement

15　It is no great art to say something briefly when, like Tacitus, one has something to say; when one has nothing to say, however, and none the less writes a whole book and makes truth into a liar — that I call an achievement.— G. C. Lichtenberg, *Aphorisms*, 1765–99

16　The tremendous strength in men [is] the impulse to creative work in every field.— Karen Horney, *Feminine Psychology*, 1926

17　We owe most of our great inventions and most of the achievements of genius to idleness.— Agatha Christie, *The Moving Finger*, 1941

18　Dazzling achievements are possible, which can make a man's name live for thousands of years. But above this level, far above, separated by an abyss, is the level where the highest things are achieved. These things are essentially anonymous.— Simone Weil, *La Table Ronde*, 1950

19　The final wisdom of life requires not the annulment of incongruity but the achievement of serenity within and above it.— Reinhold Niebuhr, *The Irony of American History*, 1952

20　Many times I wondered whether my achievement was worth the loneliness I experienced.— Gordon Parks, in *Life*, May 31, 1963

21　Everything ultimately fails, for we die, and that is either the penultimate failure or our most enigmatical achievement.— Edward Dahlberg, *Alms for Oblivion*, 1964

22　When you're young, the silliest notions seem the greatest achievements.— Pearl Bailey, *The Raw Pearl*, 1968

23　Our achievements speak for themselves. What we have to keep track of are our failures, discouragements, and doubts. We tend to forget the past difficulties, the many false starts, and the painful groping.— Eric Hoffer, *Reflections on the Human Condition*, 1973

24　If you fear making anyone mad, then you ultimately probe for the lowest common denominator of human achievement.— Jimmy Carter, speech, November 9, 1978

25　The truth is, many things are worth doing only in the most slovenly, half-hearted fashion possible, and many other things are not worth doing at all.— Barbara Ehrenreich, *The Worst Years of Our Lives*, 1985

26　Our salvation is in striving to achieve what we know we'll never achieve.— Ryszard Kapuściński, *A Warsaw Diary*, 1985

27　What we don't need to know for achievement, we need to know for our pleasure. Knowing how things work is the basis for appreciation, and is thus a source of civilized delight.— William Safire, in *New York Times*, June 1, 1986

28　When I read great literature, great drama, speeches, or sermons, I feel that the human mind has not achieved anything greater than the ability to share feelings and thoughts through language.— James Earl Jones, *Voices and Silences*, 1993

Acting

29 The mere mechanical technique of acting can be taught, but the spirit that is to give life to lifeless forms must be born in a man. No dramatic college can teach its pupils to think or to feel.— Oscar Wilde, in *Court and Society Review*, September 14, 1887

30 Acting is a form of confusion.— Tallulah Bankhead, *Tallulah*, 1952

31 Without wonder and insight, acting is just a trade. With it, it becomes creation.— Bette Davis, *The Lonely Life*, 1962

32 The basic essential of a great actor is that he loves himself in acting.— Charlie Chaplin, *My Autobiography*, 1964

33 I adore not being me. I'm not very good at being me. That's why I adore acting so much.— Deborah Kerr, in *The Times*, December 2, 1972

34 Acting deals with very delicate emotions. It is not putting up a mask. Each time an actor acts he does not hide; he exposes himself.— Jeanne Moreau, in *New York Times*, June 30, 1976

35 The actor should be able to create the universe in the palm of his hand.— Laurence Olivier, in *New York Times*, October 26, 1986

36 The invention of film has given our generation the dubious advantage of watching our acting heroes deteriorate before our eyes.— Robert Brustein, in *New Republic*, November 3, 1986

37 Acting doesn't bring anything to a text. On the contrary, it detracts from it.— Marguerite Duras, in *International Herald Tribune*, March 28, 1990

38 Acting is not about dressing up. Acting is about stripping bare. The whole essence of learning lines is to forget them so you can make them sound like you thought of them that instant.— Glenda Jackson, in *Sunday Telegraph*, July 26, 1992

Action

39 The worst of my actions or conditions seem not so ugly unto me as I find it both ugly and base not to dare to avouch for them.— Michel Eyquem de Montaigne, *Essays*, 1588

40 Talkers are no good doers.— William Shakespeare, *Richard III*, 1591

41 The awakenings of remorse, virtuous shame and indignation, the glow of moral approbation if they do not lead to action, grow less and less vivid every time they occur.— Anna Letitia Barbauld, *An Inquiry Into Those Kinds of Distress Which Excite Agreeable Sensations*, 1773

42 The most wonderful aspect of the universal scheme of things is the action of free beings under divine guidance.— Joseph de Maistre, *Considerations on France*, 1796

43 First impressions are often the truest, as we find (not infrequently) to our cost, when we have been wheedled out of them by plausible professions or studied actions. A man's look is the work of years.— William Hazlitt, *Table Talk*, 1822

44 In our cause, mere words are nothing — action is everything.— David Ruggles, in *Liberator*, August 13, 1841

45   It is vain to say human beings ought to be satisfied with tranquility: they must have action; and they will make it if they cannot find it.— Charlotte Brontë, *Jane Eyre*, 1847

46   Men's actions are too strong for them. Show me a man who has acted, and who has not been the victim and slave of his action.— Ralph Waldo Emerson, *Representative Men*, 1850

47   The sons of Judah have to choose that God may again choose them. The divine principle of our race is action, choice, resolved memory.— George Eliot, *Daniel Deronda*, 1876

48   We are born to action; and whatever is capable of suggesting and guiding action has power over us from the first.— Charles Horton Cooley, *Human Nature and the Social Order*, 1902

49   Nothing is ever done in this world until men are prepared to kill one another if it is not done.— George Bernard Shaw, *Major Barbara*, 1905

50   Drama is action, sir, action and not confounded philosophy.— Luigi Pirandello, *Six Characters in Search of an Author*, 1921

51   If one had to worry about one's actions in respect of other people's ideas, one might as well be buried alive in an ant heap or married to an ambitious violinist.— Aleister Crowley, *The Confessions of Aleister Crowley*, 1929

52   I am one of those people who are blessed, or cursed, with a nature which has to interfere. If I see a thing that needs doing I do it.— Margery Allingham, *Death of a Ghost*, 1934

53   If you delay, it may be too late.— Daphne du Maurier, *My Cousin Rachel*, 1952

54   Hibernation is a covert preparation for a more overt action.— Ralph Ellison, *The Invisible Man*, 1952

55   A thought which does not result in an action is nothing much, and an action which does not proceed from a thought is nothing at all.— Georges Bernanos, *The Last Essays of Georges Bernanos*, 1955

56   Action without a name, a "who" attached to it, is meaningless.— Hannah Arendt, *The Human Condition*, 1958

57   Effective action is always unjust.— Jean Anouilh, *Catch As Catch Can,* 1960

58   Dreams pass into the reality of action. From the action stems the dream again; and this interdependence produces the highest form of living.— Anaïs Nin, *The Diary of Anaïs Nin*, 1966

59   The world can only be grasped by action, not by contemplation. The hand is the cutting edge of the mind.— Jacob Bronowski, *The Ascent of Man*, 1973

60   It's obvious throughout secular and church history that significant legislation follows only after dramatic action.— Carter Heyward, in *Ms*, December, 1974

61   I've arrived at this outermost edge of my life by my own actions. Where I am is thoroughly unacceptable. Therefore, I must stop doing what I've been doing.— Alice Koller, *An Unknown Woman*, 1982

62   A good history covers not only what was done, but the thought that went into the action. You can read the history of a country through its actions.— Benjamin L. Hooks, in *Crisis*, December, 1985

63   A human action becomes genuinely important when it springs from the soil of a clear-sighted awareness of the temporality and the ephemerality of everything human. It is only this awareness

that can breathe any greatness into an action.— Václav Havel, *Disturbing the Peace*, 1986

Admiration

---

64   Admiration is a very short-lived passion that immediately decays upon growing familiar with its object, unless it be still fed with fresh discoveries, and kept alive by a new perpetual succession of miracles rising up to its view.— Joseph Addison, in *Spectator*, December 24, 1711

65   A lady's imagination is very rapid; it jumps from admiration to love, from love to matrimony in a moment.— Jane Austen, *Pride and Prejudice*, 1813

66   To cease to admire is a proof of deterioration.— Charles Horton Cooley, *Human Nature and the Social Order*, 1902

67   Some people are molded by their admirations, others by their hostilities.— Elizabeth Bowen, *The Death of the Heart*, 1939

68   I yield to no one in my admiration for the office as a social center, but it's no place actually to get any work done.— Katharine Whitehorn, *Sunday Best*, 1976

Adventure

---

69   The thirst for adventure is the vent which Destiny offers; a war, a crusade, a gold mine, a new country, speak to the imagination and offer swing and play to the confined powers.— Ralph Waldo Emerson, *The Natural History of Intellect*, 1893

70   The test of an adventure is that when you're in the middle of it, you say to yourself, "Oh, now I've got myself into an awful mess; I wish I were sitting quietly at home."— Thornton Wilder, *The Matchmaker*, 1954

71   Adventure is often the unintentional result of poor planning.— Michael C. Thomsett, *The Speaker's Treasury of Quotations*, 2009

Adversity

---

72   Adversity is sometimes hard upon a man; but for one man who can stand prosperity, there are a hundred that will stand adversity.— Thomas Carlyle, *On Heroes and Hero-Worship*, 1841

73   By trying we can easily learn to endure adversity — another man's I mean.- Mark Twain, *Following the Equator*, 1897

74   No man can smile in the face of adversity and mean it.— Edgar Watson Howe, *Country Town Sayings*, 1911

75   The long dull monotonous years of middle-aged prosperity or middle-aged adversity are excellent campaigning weather for the Devil.— C. S. Lewis, *The Screwtape Letters*, 1941

76   Life is truly known only to those who suffer, lose, endure adversity and stumble from defeat to defeat.— Ryszard Kapuściński, *A Warsaw Diary*, 1985

Advice

---

77   How is it possible to expect that mankind will take advice, when they will not so much as take warning?—Jonathan Swift, *Thoughts on Various Subjects*, 1706

78 Advice is not disliked because it is advice; but because so few people know how to give it.—Leigh Hunt, *The Indicator*, 1821

79 I have lived some thirty years on this planet, and I have yet to hear the first syllable of valuable or even earnest advice from my seniors.—Henry David Thoreau, *Walden*, 1854

80 Don't abuse your friends and expect them to consider it criticism.—Edgar Watson Howe, *Country Town Sayings*, 1911

81 There is hardly a man on earth who will take advice unless he is certain that it is positively bad.—Edward Dahlberg, *Moby Dick: A Hamitic Dream*, 1964

82 Advice is what we ask for when we already know the answer but wish we didn't.—Erica Jong, *How to Save Your Own Life*, 1977

Age

83 The denunciation of the young is a necessary part of the hygiene of older people, and greatly assists the circulation of their blood.—Logan Pearsall Smith, *All Trivia*, 1933

84 The question that is so clearly in many potential parents' minds: "Why should we stunt our ambitions and impoverish our lives?"—Joseph A. Schumpeter, *Capitalism, Socialism and Democracy*, 1942

85 When I was 40, my doctor advised me that a man in his 40s shouldn't play tennis. I heeded his advice carefully and

could hardly wait until I reached 50 to start again.—Hugo L. Black, in *Think*, February, 1963

86 It is a paradox that as we reach out prime, we also see there is a place where it finishes.—Gail Sheehy, *Speed is of the Essence*, 1971

87 Old age is not a disease—it is strength and survivorship, triumph over all kinds of vicissitudes and disappointments, trials and illnesses.—Maggie Kuhn, in *New Age*, February, 1979

88 We in middle age require adventure.—Carolyn Heilbrun, *Sweet Death, Kind Death*, 1984

89 You can only perceive real beauty in a person as they get older.—Anouk Aimee, in *Guardian*, August 24, 1988

90 There are only three things that can kill a farmer: lightning, rolling over in a tractor, and old age.—Bill Bryson, *The Lost Continent: Travels in Small Town America*, 1989

91 Aging is not "lost youth" but a new stage of opportunity and strength.—Betty Friedan, in *Parade*, March 20, 1994

Aggression

92 Today there's more fellowship among snakes than among mankind.—Juvenal, *Satires*, ca. 100

93 He who would be free must strike the first blow.—Frederick Douglass, *My Bondage and My Freedom*, 1855

94 The bashful are always aggressive at heart.—Charles Horton Cooley, *Human Nature and the Social Order*, 1902

95 We kill everybody, my dear. Some with bullets, some with words, and everybody with our deeds.— Maxim Gorki, *Enemies,* 1906

Alcohol

96 I believe, if we take habitual drunkards as a class, their heads and their hearts will bear an advantageous comparison with those of any other class. There seems ever to have been a proneness in the brilliant and warm-blooded to fall into this vice.— Abraham Lincoln, speech, February 22, 1842

97 There is only one really safe, mild, harmless beverage and you can drink as much of that as you like without running the slightest risk, and what you say when you want it is, "Garcon! Un Pernod!"— Aleister Crowley, *The Confessions of Aleister Crowley,* 1929

98 Alcohol is a good preservative for everything but brains.— Mary Pettibone Poole, *A Glass Eye at a Keyhole,* 1938

99 Beer is the Danish national drink, and the Danish national weakness is another beer.— Clementine Paddleford, in *New York Herald Tribune,* June 20, 1964

100 People are broad minded. They'll accept the fact that a person can be an alcoholic, a dope fiend, a wife beater and even a newspaperman, but if a man doesn't drive, there's something wrong with him.— Art Buchwald, *Have I Ever Lied to You?,* 1968

101 No other human being, no woman, no poem or music, book or painting can replace alcohol in its power to give man the illusion of real creation.— Marguerite Duras, *Practicalities,* 1987

102 Unrecognized alcoholism is the ruling pathology among writers and intellectuals.— Diane Trilling, in *New York Times Book Review,* October 3, 1993

Alliances

103 To make war upon those who trade with us is like setting a bulldog upon a customer at the shop door.— Thomas Paine, *The Age of Reason,* 1794

104 Be my brother, or I will kill you.— Sébastien-Roch Nicolas Chamfort, in T. Carlyle, *History of the French Revolution,* 1837

105 An alliance is like a chain. It is not made stronger by adding weak links to it. A great power like the United States gains no advantage and it loses prestige by offering, indeed peddling, its alliances to all and sundry.— Walter Lippmann, in *New York Herald Tribune,* August 5, 1952

Ambition

106 All true ambition and aspiration are without comparisons.— Henry Ward Beecher, *Life Thoughts,* 1858

107 All ambitions are lawful except those which climb upward on the miseries or credulities of mankind.— Joseph Conrad, *A Personal Record,* 1912

108 A generation which has passed through the shop has absorbed standards and ambitions which are not of those of spaciousness, and cannot get away from them.— Aleksandr Herzen, *My Past and Thoughts,* 1921

109   Ambition is a commendable attribute, without which no man succeeds. Only inconsiderate ambition imperils.— Warren G. Harding, speech, May 3, 1922

110   I used to think I had ambition, but now I'm not so sure. It may have been only discontent. They're easily confused.— Rachel Field, *All This, and Heaven Too*, 1939

111   Ambition if it feeds at all, does so on the ambition of others.— Susan Sontag, *The Benefactor*, 1963

112   Ambition is a Dead Sea fruit, and the greatest peril to the soul is that one is likely to get precisely what he is seeking.— Edward Dahlberg, *Alms for Oblivion*, 1964

113   A man without ambition is dead. A man with ambition but no love is dead. A man with ambition and love for his blessings here on earth is ever so alive.— Pearl Bailey, *Talking to Myself*, 1971

114   A young man's ambition is to get along in the world and make a place for himself half your life goes that way, till you're 45 or 50. Then, if you're lucky, you make terms with life, you get released.— Robert Penn Warren, in *New York Times*, June 2, 1981

Anarchism

115   The worst thing in the world, next to anarchy, is government.— Henry Ward Beecher, *Proverbs from Plymouth Pulpit*, 1887

116   The anarchist and the Christian have a common origin.— Friedrich Nietzsche, *The Antichrist*, 1895

117   The ordinary man is an anarchist. He wants to do as he likes. He may want his neighbour to be governed, but he himself doesn't want to be governed. He is mortally afraid of government officials and policemen.— George Bernard Shaw, speech, April 11, 1933

118   We started off trying to set up a small anarchist community, but people wouldn't obey the rules.— Alan Bennett, *Getting On*, 1972

Anger

119   We are quick to flare up, we races of men on the earth.— Homer, *The Odyssey*, ca. 700 B.C.

120   Anger has overpowered him, and driven him to a revenge which was rather a stupid one, I must acknowledge, but anger makes us all stupid.— Johanna Spyri, *Heidi*, 1885

121   Rage cannot be hidden, it can only be dissembled. This dissembling deludes the thoughtless, and strengthens rage and adds, to rage, contempt.— James Baldwin, in *Harper's*, October, 1953

Appearances

122   Having a beard and wearing a shabby cloak does not make philosophers.— Plutarch, *Moralia: Isis and Osiris*, ca. 95

123   The man whose whole activity is diverted to inner meditation becomes insensible to all his surroundings. His passions are mere appearances, being sterile. They are dissipated in futile imaginings, producing nothing external to themselves. — Emile Durkheim, *Suicide*, 1897

124 Does God judge us by appearances? I Suspect that He does. — W. H. Auden, in *New Yorker*, November 21, 1977

Appeasement

125 There is no avoiding war; it can only be postponed to the advantage of others. — Niccolò Machiavelli, *The Prince*, 1513

126 So enamored on peace that he would have been glad the king should have bought it at any price. — Henry Hyde, *History of the Rebellion*, 1703

Approval

127 O, popular applause! what heart of man/ Is proof against thy sweet, seducing charms? — William Cowper, *The Task*, 1785

128 Material things aside, we need no advice but approval. — Coco Chanel, *Coco Chanel: Her Life, Her Secrets*, 1972

Argument

129 A good life is a main argument. — Ben Jonson, *Timber, or Discoveries*, 1640

130 The same arguments which we deem forcible as applied to others, seem feeble to us when turned against ourselves. — Joseph Roux, *Meditations of a Parish Priest*, 1886

131 There is no sense having an argument with a man so stupid he doesn't know you have the better of him. — John W. Raper, *What This World Needs*, 1945

Aristocracy

132 Actual aristocracy cannot be abolished by any law: all the law can do is decree how it is to be imparted and who is to acquire it. — G. C. Lichtenberg, *Aphorisms*, 1765–99

133 Democracy means government by the uneducated, while aristocracy means government by the badly educated. — Gilbert K. Chesterton, in *New York Times*, February 1, 1931

134 An aristocracy in a republic is like a chicken whose head has been cut off; it may run about in a lovely way, but in fact it's dead. — Nancy Mitford, *Noblesse Oblige*, 1956

135 It is already possible to imagine a society in which the majority of the population, that is to say, its laborers, will have almost as much leisure as in earlier times was enjoyed by the aristocracy. — W. H. Auden, *A Certain World*, 1970

Art and Artists

136 The most perfect ape cannot draw an ape; only man can do that; but, likewise, only man regards the ability to do this as a sign of superiority. — G. C. Lichtenberg, *Aphorisms*, 1765–99

137   There are only two styles of portrait painting; the serious and the smirk.— Charles Dickens, *Nicholas Nickleby*, 1838–9

138   You must treat a work of art like a great man; stand before it and wait patiently till it deigns to speak.— Arthur Schopenhauer, *Note-Books*, ca. 1850

139   Art is a jealous mistress, and, if a man have a genius for painting, poetry, music, architecture or philosophy, he makes a bad husband and an ill provider.— Ralph Waldo Emerson, *The Conduct of Life*, 1860

140   Art is not merely an imitation of the reality of nature, but in truth a metaphysical supplement to the reality of nature, placed alongside thereof for its conquest.— Friedrich Nietzsche, *The Birth of Tragedy*, 1872

141   No artist has ethical sympathies.— Oscar Wilde, *The Picture of Dorian Gray*, 1891

142   Scratch an artist and you surprise a child.— James G. Huneker, *Chopin: The Man and His Music*, 1900

143   The artistic temperament is a disease that affects amateurs. Artists of a large and wholesome vitality get rid of their art easily, as they breathe easily or perspire easily.— Gilbert K. Chesterton, *Heretics*, 1905

144   An artist is a dreamer consenting to dream of the actual world.— George Santayana, *The Life of Reason*, 1905–06

145   An artist is a man of action, whether he creates a personality, invents an expedient, or finds the issue of a complicated situation.— Joseph Conrad, *The Mirror of the Sea*, 1906

146   Art bids us touch and taste and hear and see the world, and shrinks from what Blake calls mathematic form, from every abstract form, from all that is of the brain only.— William Butler Yeats, *The Cutting of an Agate*, 1912

147   The truth is, as every one knows, that the great artists of the world are never Puritans, and seldom even ordinarily respectable. No virtuous man — that is, virtuous in the Y.M.C.A. sense — has ever painted a picture worth looking at.— H. L. Mencken, *Prejudices, First Series*, 1919

148   The attitude and reactions of artists toward their art children reveal an attitude similar to that which mothers in general possess toward their children. There is the same sensitivity to any criticism, the same possessive pride.— Beatrice Hinkle, *The Psychology of the Artist*, 1923

149   Art must discover and reveal the beauty which prejudice and caricature have overlaid.— Alain Locke, *The Legacy of the Ancestral Arts*, 1925

150   The vitality of a new movement in Art must be gauged by the fury it arouses.— Logan Pearsall Smith, *Afterthoughts*, 1931

151   The work of art, just like any fragment of human life considered in its deepest meaning, seems to me devoid of value if it does not offer the hardness, the rigidity, the regularity, the luster on every interior and exterior facet, of the crystal.— André Breton, *Mad Love*, 1937

152   There is no great art without reverence.— Gerald Vann, *The Heart of Man*, 1944

153   All art is a revolt against man's fate.— André Malraux, *Voices of Silence*, 1953

154 The creative act is not performed by the artist alone; the spectator brings the work in contact with the external world by deciphering and interpreting its inner qualifications and thus adds his contribution to the creative act.— Marcel Duchamp, in *Art News*, April, 1957

155 An authentic work of art must start an argument between the artist and his audience.— Rebecca West, *The Count and the Castle*, 1957

156 Madness is the absolute break with the work of art; it forms the constitutive moment of abolition, which dissolves in time the truth of the work of art.— Michel Foucault, *Madness and Civilization*, 1961

157 Abstract art? A product of the untalented, sold by the unprincipled to the utterly bewildered.— Al Capp, in *National Observer*, July 1, 1963

158 I think of art, at its most significant, as a DEW line, a Distant Early Warning system that can always be relied on to tell the old culture what is beginning to happen to it.— Marshall McLuhan, *Understanding Media*, McGraw-Hill, 1964

159 Generosity is a two-edged virtue for an artist — it nourishes his imagination but has a fatal effect on his routine.— Alexander Solzhenitsyn, *The First Circle*, 1964

160 All art is communication of the artists' ideas, sounds, thoughts; without that no one will support the artist.— Lionel Hampton, in *New York Journal American*, August 31, 1965

161 A primary function of art and thought is to liberate the individual from the tyranny of his culture in the environmental sense and to permit him to stand beyond it in an autonomy of perception and judgment.— Lionel Trilling, *Beyond Culture*, 1965

162 Artists love to immerse themselves in chaos in order to put it into form, just as God created form out of chaos in Genesis. Forever unsatisfied with the mundane, the apathetic, the conventional, they always push on to newer worlds.— Rollo May, *The Courage to Create*, 1975

163 The artist is an educator of artists of the future who are able to understand and in the process of understanding perform unexpected — the best — evolutions.— Saul Steinberg, in *American Artist Magazine*, November, 1977

164 Art is the triumph over chaos.— John Cheever, *The Stories of John Cheever*, 1978

165 Very few people possess true artistic ability. It is therefore both unseemly and unproductive to irritate the situation by making an effort. If you have a burning, restless urge to write or paint, simply eat something sweet and the feeling will pass.— Fran Lebowitz, in *Metropolitan Life*, 1978

166 Art is dangerous. It is one of the attractions: when it ceases to be dangerous you don't want it.— Anthony Burgess, in *Face*, December, 1984

167 To choose art means to turn one's back on the world, or at least uncertain of its distractions.— Melvin Maddocks, in *Christian Science Monitor*, April 10, 1985

168 Art is in the eye of the beholder, and in the pocket of the patron.— Michael C. Thomsett, *The Speaker's Treasury of Quotations*, 2009

Authority

169   The man whose authority is recent is always stern.— Aeschylus, *Prometheus Bound*, ca. 490 B.C.

170   To expect to rule others by assuming a loud tone is like thinking oneself tall by putting on high heels.— J. Petit-Senn, *Conceits and Caprices*, 1869

171   Every great advance in natural knowledge has involved the absolute rejection of authority.— T. H. Huxley, *Lay Sermons, Addresses, and Reviews*, 1870

Awareness

172   You must never lose the awareness that in yourself you are nothing, you are only an instrument. An instrument is nothing until it is lifted.— Kathryn Hulme, *The Nun's Story*, 1956

173   Awareness is not something we are always born with. For some it is an acquired talent.— Michael C. Thomsett, *The Speaker's Treasury of Quotations*, 2009

Bachelors

174   I will have only those manly pleasures of being very drunk and very slovenly.— William Wycherley, *The Country Wife*, 1675

175   What a life we men lead! Either bachelors or cuckolds— what a choice!— Henry Becque, *Woman of Paris*, 1885

176   Bachelors know more about women than married men. If they didn't they'd be married too.— H. L. Mencken, *A Mencken Chrestomathy*, 1949

Battles

177   Half-heartedness never won a battle.— William McKinley, speech, January 27, 1898

178   My center is giving way, my right is in retreat; situation excellent. I shall attack!— Ferdinand Foch, in G. Aston, *Marshal Foch*, 1929

179   The war has started incredibly badly. Therefore, it must be continued. — Charles de Gaulle, *Mémoires de guerre: L'Appel*, 1955

180   They've got us surrounded again, the poor bastards.— Creighton W. Abrams, in *Time*, February 16, 1968

Beauty

181   He who only or chiefly chose for Beauty, will in a little Time find the same Reason for another Choice.— Mary Astell, *Some Reflections Upon Marriage*, 1730

182   Taught from infancy that beauty is woman's sceptre, the mind shapes itself to the body, and roaming round its gilt cage, only seeks to adorn its prison.— Mary Wollstonecraft, *A Vindication of the Rights of Women*, 1792

183   The human face is the organic seat of beauty. It is the register of value in de-

velopment, a record of Experience.—
Eliza Wood Burhans Farnham, *Woman and Her Era*, 1804

184   Beauty is only the promise of happiness.— Stendhal, *On Love*, 1822

185   It is generally a feminine eye that first detects the moral deficiencies hidden under the "dear deceit" of beauty.— George Eliot, *Adam Bede*, 1859

186   I have found that all ugly things are made by those who strive to make something beautiful, and that all beautiful things are made by those who strive to make something useful.— Oscar Wilde, *The Value of Art in Modern Life*, 1884

187   In the beautiful, man sets himself up as the standard of perfection; in select cases he worships himself in it. Man believes that the world itself is filled with beauty— he forgets that it is he who has created it.— Friedrich Nietzsche, *Twilight of the Idols*, 1889

188   Beauty is all very well at first sight; but who ever looks at it when it has been in the house three days? George Bernard Shaw, *Man and Superman*, 1905

189   Everybody needs beauty as well as bread, places to play in and pray in, where Nature may heal and cheer and give strength to body and soul alike.— John Muir, *The Yosemite*, 1912

190   Let us leave pretty women to men devoid of imagination.— Marcel Proust, *Remembrance of Things Past*, 1913–26

191   No eyes that have seen beauty ever lose their sight.— Jean Toomer, *Cane*, 1923

192   It is better to be first with an ugly woman than the hundredth with a beauty.— Pearl S. Buck, *The Good Earth*, 1931

193   I can't see how any woman can find time to do to herself all the things that must apparently be done to make herself beautiful and, having once done them, how anyone without the strength of mind of a foreign missionary can keep up such a regime.— Cornelia Otis Skinner, *Dithers and Jitters*, 1937

194   Beauty is desired in order that it may be befouled; not for its own sake, but for the joy brought by the certainty of profaning it.— Georges Bataille, *Eroticism*, 1962

195   Our social realities are so ugly if seen in the light of exiled truth, and beauty is no longer possible if it is not a lie.— R. D. Laing, *The Politics of Experience*, 1967

196   Beauty is a precious trace that eternity causes to appear to us and that it takes away from us. A manifestation of eternity, and a sign of death as well.— Eugène Ionesco, *Present Past— Past Present*, 1968

197   Industrial societies turn their citizens into image-junkies; it is the most irresistible form of mental pollution. Poignant longings for beauty, for an end to probing below the surface, for a redemption and celebration of the body of the world.— Susan Sontag, *On Photography*, 1977

198   The beauty myth moves for men as a mirage; its power lies in its ever-receding nature. When the gap is closed, the lover embraces only his own disillusion.— Naomi Wolf, *The Beauty Myth*, 1990

Belief

199 With most people disbelief in a thing is founded on a blind belief in some other thing.— G. C. Lichtenberg, *Aphorisms*, 1765–99

200 I am always easy of belief when the creed pleases me.— Charlotte Brontë, *Shirley*, 1849

201 No iron chain, no outward force of any kind, could ever compel the soul of man to believe or to disbelieve.— Thomas Carlyle, *Heroes and Hero-Worship*, 1840

202 Belief consists in accepting the affirmations of the soul; unbelief, in denying them.— Ralph Waldo Emerson, *Representative Men*, 1850

203 We are born believing. A man bears beliefs as a tree bears apples.— Ralph Waldo Emerson, *The Conduct of Life*, 1860

204 Why sometimes I've believed as many as six impossible things before breakfast.— Lewis Carroll, *Through the Looking-Glass*, 1872

205 Give up the belief that mind is, even temporarily, compressed within the skull, and you will quickly become more manly or womanly. You will understand yourself and your Maker better than before.— Mary Baker Eddy, *Science and Health*, 1875

206 Perhaps his might be one of the natures where a wise estimate of consequences is fused in the fires of that passionate belief which determines the consequences it believes in.— George Eliot, *Daniel Deronda*, 1876

207 Castles in the air — they are so easy to take refuge in. And easy to build, too.— Henrik Ibsen, *The Master Builder*, 1892

208 It is always easier to believe than to deny. Our minds are naturally affirmative.— John Burroughs, *The Light of Day*, 1900

209 People only think a thing's worth believing if it's hard to believe.— Armiger Barclay, *The Kingmakers*, 1907

210 Why abandon a belief merely because it ceases to be true?— Robert Frost, *The Black Cottage*, 1914

211 A man must not swallow more beliefs than he can digest.— Havelock Ellis, *The Dance of Life*, 1923

212 I have never grown out of the infantile belief that the universe was made for me to suck.— Aleister Crowley, *The Confessions of Aleister Crowley*, 1929

213 It is always a relief to believe what is pleasant, but it is more important to believe what is true.— Hilaire Belloc, *The Silence of the Sea*, 1941

214 Mass movements can rise and spread without belief in a God, but never without belief in a devil.— Eric Hoffer, *The True Believer*, 1951

215 Confronted with the impossibility of remaining faithful to one's beliefs, and the equal impossibility of becoming free of them, one can be driven to the most inhuman excesses.— James Baldwin, in *Harper's*, October, 1953

216 We have all had the experience of finding that our reactions and perhaps even our deeds have denied beliefs we thought were ours.— James Baldwin, *The Crusade of Indignation*, in *Nation*, July 7, 1956

217 The happy ending is our national belief.— Mary McCarthy, *On the Contrary*, 1962

218   A belief may be larger than a fact.— Vannevar Bush, *Science Is Not Enough*, 1967

219   When I transfer my knowledge, I teach. When I transfer my beliefs, I indoctrinate.— Arthur Danto, *Analytic Philosophy of Knowledge*, 1968

220   As a first approximation, I define "belief" not as the object of believing (a dogma, a program, etc.) but as the subject's investment in a proposition, the act of saying it and considering it as true.— Michel de Certeau, *The Practice of Everyday Life*, 1974

221   They were so strong in their beliefs that there came a time when it hardly mattered what exactly those beliefs were; they all fused into a single stubbornness.— Louise Erdrich, *Love Medicine*, 1984

222   You may fight to the death for something in which you truly believe, but keep such commitments to a bare minimum.— Albert A. Grant, speech, May 30, 1988

Betrayal

---

223   Keep guard over your eyes and ears as the inlets of your heart, and over your lips as the outlets, lest they betray you in a moment of unwariness.— Anne Brontë, *The Tenant of Wildfell Hall*, 1848

224   It is easier to betray than to remain loyal. It takes far less courage to kill yourself than it takes to make yourself wake up one more time. It's harder to stay where you are than to get out. (For everyone but you, that is.)— Judith Rossner, *Nine Months in the Life of an Old Maid*, 1969

225   Love is whatever you can still betray. Betrayal can only happen if you love.— John LeCarre, *A Perfect Spy*, 1986

Books

---

226   While you converse with lords and dukes, I have their betters here — my books.— Thomas Sheridan, *My Books*, ca. 1730

227   There are books of which the backs and covers are by far the best parts. — Charles Dickens, *Oliver Twist*, 1837–39

228   It is not all books that are as dull as their readers.— Henry David Thoreau, *Walden*, 1854

229   Books are not made for furniture, but there is nothing else that so beautifully furnishes a house.— Henry Ward Beecher, *Life Thoughts*, 1858

230   This will never be a civilized country until we expend more money for books than we do for chewing gum.— Elbert Hubbard, *The Philistine*, 1895–1915

231   Literature is my Utopia. Here I am not disfranchised. No barrier of the senses shuts me out from the sweet, gracious discourse of my book-friends. They talk to me without embarrassment or awkwardness.— Helen Keller, *The Story of My Life*, 1903

232   The proper study of mankind is books.— Aldous Huxley, *Crome Yellow*, 1921

233   Only two classes of books are of universal appeal: the very best and the very worst.— Ford Madox Ford, *Joseph Conrad*, 1924

234   There is no reason why the same man should like the same books at eighteen and at forty-eight.— Ezra Pound, *ABC of Reading*, 1934

Boredom and Bores

235   We forgive people who bore us; never those we bore.— François Duke de La Rochefoucauld, VI, *Maxims*, 1665

236   Nobody is bored when he is trying to make something that is beautiful, or to discover something that is true.— William Ralph Inge, *Our Present Discontents*, 1938

237   Ennui, felt on proper occasions, is a sign of intelligence.— Clifton Fadiman, *Reading I've Liked*, 1941

238   By his very success in inventing labor-saving devices, modern man has manufactured an abyss of boredom that only the privileged classes in earlier civilizations have ever fathomed.— Lewis Mumford, *The Conduct of Life*, 1951

239   Perhaps the world's second worst crime is boredom; the first is being a bore.— Cecil Beaton, in *Time*, January 28, 1980

Bureaucracy

240   A bureaucracy is sure to think that its duty is to augment official power, official business, or official members, rather than to leave free the energies of mankind; it overdoes the quantity of government, as well as impairs its quality.— Walter Bagehot, *The English Constitution*, 1867

241   The art of government is the organization of idolatry. The bureaucracy consists of functionaries; the aristocracy, of idols; the democracy, of idolaters. The populace cannot understand the bureaucracy: it can only worship the national idols.— George Bernard Shaw, *Man and Superman*, 1903

242   The man who will follow precedent, but never create one, is merely an obvious example of the routiner. You find him desperately numerous in the civil service, in the official bureaus. To him government is something given as unconditionally.— Walter Lippmann, *A Preface to Politics*, 1913

243   Bureaucracy is not an obstacle to democracy but an inevitable complement to it.— Joseph A. Schumpeter, *Capitalism, Socialism and Democracy*, 1942

244   Bureaucracy, the rule of no one, has become the modern form of despotism.— Mary McCarthy, in *New Yorker*, October 18, 1958

245   A committee is organic rather than mechanical in its nature: it is not a structure but a plant. It takes root and grows, it flowers, wilts, and dies, scattering the seed from which other committees will bloom in their turn.— C. Northcote Parkinson, *Parkinson's Law*, 1958

246   Muddle is the extra unknown personality in any committee.— Anthony Sampson, *Anatomy of Britain Today*, 1965

247   The only thing that saves us from bureaucracy is its inefficiency. An efficient bureaucracy is the greatest threat to freedom.— Eugene McCarthy, in *Time*, February 12, 1979

Censorship

248   To limit the press is to insult a nation; to prohibit reading of certain books is to declare the inhabitants to be either fools or slaves.— Claude-Adrien Helvétius, *De l'Homme*, 1773

249   Only the suppressed word is dangerous.— Ludwig Boerne, *Ankündigung der Wage*, 1818

250   The best the emperor can do is to snip off the heads of men and women, who are mere mortals.— Heywood C. Broun, *Pieces of Hate*, 1922

251   The burning of an author's books, imprisonment for opinion's sake, has always been the tribute that an ignorant age pays for the genius of its time.— Joseph Lewis, *Voltaire: The Incomprehensible Infidel*, 1929

252   Books won't stay banned. They won't burn. Ideas won't go to jail. In the long run of history, the censor and the inquisitor have always lost.— A. Whitney Griswold, *Essays on Education*, 1954

Certainty

253   Uncertainty and expectation are the joys of life.— William Congreve, *Love for Love*, 1695

254   Of what use, however, is a general certainty that an insect will not walk with his head hindmost, when what you need to know is the play of inward stimulus that sends him hither and thither in a network of possible paths?— George Eliot, *Daniel Deronda*, 1876

255   Love of certainty is a demand for guarantees in advance of action.— John Dewey, *Human Nature and Conduct*, 1922

256   We can be absolutely certain only about things we do not understand.— Eric Hoffer, *The True Believer*, 1951

257   A man who has humility will have acquired in the last reaches of his beliefs the saving doubt of his own certainty.— Walter Lippmann, The Public Philosophy, 1955

258   The minute one utters a certainty, the opposite comes to mind.— May Sarton, *Mrs. Stevens Hears the Mermaids Singing*, 1965

259   With the only certainty in our daily existence being change, and a rate of change growing always faster in a kind of technological leapfrog game, speed helps people think they are keeping up.— Gail Sheehy, *Speed is of the Essence*, 1971

Change

260   Fortune is proverbially called changeful, yet her caprice often takes the form of repeating again and again a similar stroke of luck in the same quarter.— Charlotte Brontë, *Shirley*, 1849

261   To get away from one's working environment is, in a sense, to get away from one's self; and this is often the chief advantage of travel and change.— Charles Horton Cooley, *Human Nature and the Social Order*, 1902

262   The deepest definition of youth is life untouched by tragedy.— Alfred North Whitehead, *Adventures of Ideas*, 1933

263 Events are not a matter of chance.—Gamal Abdel Nasser, *Philosophy of the Revolution*, 1954

264 So often I heard people paying blind obeisance to change as though it had some virtue of its own. Change or we will die. Change or we will stagnate. Evergreens don't stagnate.—Judith Rossner, *Nine Months in the Life of an Old Maid*, 1969

265 Change for its own sake may be a variation on more of the same.—Michael C. Thomsett, *The Speaker's Treasury of Quotations*, 2009

Chaos

266 Every passion borders on the chaotic, but the collector's passion borders on the chaos of memories.—Walter Benjamin, *Unpacking My Library*, 1931

267 A schedule defends from chaos and whim. It is a net for catching days. It is a scaffolding on which a worker can stand and labor with both hands at sections of time.—Annie Dillard, *The Writing Life*, 1989

268 I believe, as Lenin said, that this revolutionary chaos may yet crystallize into new forms of life.—Mikhail Gorbachev, in *Times*, May 18, 1990

269 Everybody's a mad scientist, and life is their lab. We're all trying to experiment to find a way to live, to solve problems, to fend off madness and chaos.—David Cronenberg, *Cronenberg on Cronenberg*, 1992

Character

270 Let a man then know his worth, and keep things under his feet. Let him not peep or steal, or skulk up and down with the air of a charity-boy, a bastard, or an interloper.—Ralph Waldo Emerson, *Self-Reliance, First Series*, 1841

271 For character too is a process and an unfolding among our valued friends is there not someone or other who is a little too self confident and disdainful.—George Eliot, *Middlemarch*, 1871

272 It seems as if she had given these treasures and left him alone—to use them, or lose them, apply them, or misapply them, according to his own choice.—Dinah Mulock Craik, *The Little Lame Prince*, 1875

273 To give style to one's character—a great and rare art! He exercises it who surveys all that his nature presents in strength and weakness and then moulds it to an artistic plan until everything appears as art and reason.—Friedrich Nietzsche, *The Gay Science*, 1887

274 If we divine a discrepancy between a man's words and his character, the whole impression of him becomes broken and painful; he revolts the imagination by his lack of unity, and even the good in him is hardly accepted.—Charles Horton Cooley, *Human Nature and the Social Order*, 1902

275 No man can climb out beyond the limitations of his own character.—John Morley, *Critical Miscellanies*, 1908

276 Between ourselves and our real natures we interpose that wax figure of idealizations and selections which we call our character.—Walter Lippmann, *A Preface to Politics*, 1914

277 Parents can only give good advice or put them on the right paths, but the final forming of a person's character lies in their own hands.—Anne Frank, *The Diary of a Young Girl*, 1952

278 Character isn't inherited. One builds it daily by the way one thinks and acts, thought by thought, action by action.—Helen Gahagan Douglas, *A Full Life*, 1982

279 Character contributes to beauty. It fortifies a woman as her youth fades.—Jacqueline Bisset, in *Los Angeles Times*, May 16, 1974

Charity

280 Charity begins at home, and justice begins next door.—Charles Dickens, *Martin Chuzzlewit*, 1844

281 Charity is the power of defending that which we know to be indefensible. Hope is the power of being cheerful in circumstances which we know to be desperate.—Gilbert K. Chesterton, *Heretics*, 1905

282 Honest men live on charity in their age; the alm houses are full of men who never stole a copper penny.—Taylor Caldwell, *Dynasty of Death*, 1938

283 Charity separates the rich from the poor; aid raises the needy and sets him on the same level with the rich.—Eva Perón, address, December 5, 1949

Charm

284 The charms of women were never more powerful never inspired such achievements, as in those immortal periods, when they could neither read nor write.—Hannah Cowley, *Who's the Dupe?*, 1779

285 Only in the illusions of fancy [possession] has power to charm us.—Karl Wilhelm, Baron von Humboldt, *Limits of State Action*, 1792

286 [People] believe that the world is always contemplating their individual charms and virtues.—Elizabeth Gaskell, *Lady Cumnor*, 1866

287 A man of such obvious and exemplary charm must be a liar.—Anita Brookner, Rachel, *A Friend From England*, 1987

288 Brains, integrity, and force may be all very well, but what you need today is Charm. Go ahead and work on your economic programs if you want to, I'll develop my radio personality.—Gracie Allen, *How to Become President*, 1940

289 Charm is a glow within a woman that casts a most becoming light on others.—John Mason Brown, in *Vogue*, November 15, 1956

290 Whatever it is that makes a person charming, it needs to remain a mystery; once the charmer is aware of a mannerism or characteristic that others find charming, it ceases to be a mannerism and becomes an affectation.—Rex Harrison, in *Los Angeles Herald-Examiner*, June 24, 1978

Children

291 Children have neither a past nor a future; they enjoy the present, which very few of us do.—Jean de La Bruyère, *Les Caractères*, 1688

292 Choice [is] all that we can do with children.— Dinah Mulock Craik, *The Little Lame Prince*, 1875

293 The observation of the way in which the children pass from the first disordered movements to those which are spontaneous and ordered — this is the book of the teacher; this is the book which must inspire her actions.— Maria Montessori, *The Montessori Method*, 1912

294 A child's attitude toward everything is an artist's attitude.— Willa Cather, *The Song of the Lark*, 1915

295 Every child comes with the message that God is not yet discouraged of man.— Rabindranath Tagore, *Stray Birds*, 1916

296 No one has yet fully realized the wealth of sympathy, kindness and generosity hidden in the soul of a child. The effort of every true education should be to unlock that treasure.— Emma Goldman, *Living My Life*, 1931

297 Bringing up a family should be an adventure, not an anxious discipline in which everybody is constantly graded for performance.— Milton R. Sapirstein, *Paradoxes of Everyday Life*, 1955

298 My father had always said there are four things a child needs: plenty of love, nourishing food, regular sleep, and lots of soap and water. After that, what he needs most is some intelligent neglect.— Ivy Baker Priest, *Green Grows Ivy*, 1958

299 Today there are no fairy tales for us to believe in, and this is possibly a reason for the universal prevalence of mental crack-up. Yes, if we were childish in the past, I wish we could be children once again.— Anita Loos, *No Mother to Guide Her*, 1961

300 All of childhood's unanswered questions must finally be passed back to the town and answered there. Heroes and bogey men, values and dislikes, are first encountered and labeled in that early environment.— Maya Angelou, *I Know Why the Caged Bird Sings*, 1969

301 The care of children is infinitely better left to the best-trained practitioners of both sexes who have chosen it as a vocation, rather than to harried and all too frequently unhappy persons with little time or taste for the work of educating minds.— Kate Millett, *Sexual Politics*, 1969

Civilization

302 I have no doubt that it is a part of the destiny of the human race, in its gradual improvement, to leave off eating animals, as surely as the savage tribes have left off eating each other when they came in contact with the more civilized.— Henry David Thoreau, *Walden*, 1854

303 Civilization is merely an advance in taste: accepting, all the time, nicer things, and rejecting nasty ones.— Katherine F. Gerould, *Modes and Morals*, 1920

304 A nation or civilization that continues to produce soft-minded men purchases its own spiritual death on an installment plan.— Martin Luther King, Jr., *Strength to Love*, 1963

305 We are all born charming, fresh, and spontaneous and must be civilized before we are fit to participate in society.— Judith Martin, *Miss Manner's Guide to Excruciatingly Correct Behavior*, 1982

Common Sense

306 Common sense cannot be taught.— Quintilian, *Institutio Oratoria*, 1st c.

307 Common sense is the best distributed commodity in the world, for every man is convinced that he is well supplied with it.— René Descartes, *Discourse on the Method*, 1637

308 Common sense is not so common.— Voltaire, *Philosophical Dictionary*, 1764

309 Solid good sense is often nonsense solidified.— Leo Stein, *Journey into the Self*, 1950

Communication

310 You mistake me, my dear. I have a high respect for your nerves. They are my old friends. I have heard you mention them with consideration these twenty years at least.— Jane Austen, *Pride and Prejudice*, 1813

311 The post-office had a great charm at one period of our lives. When you have lived to my age, you will begin to think letters are never worth going through the rain for.— Jane Austen, *Emma*, 1816

312 No contact with savage Indian tribes has ever daunted me more than the morning I spent with an old lady swathed in woolies who compared herself to a rotten herring encased in a block of ice.— Claude Lévi-Strauss, *Tristes Tropiques*, 1955

313 Already we Viewers, when not viewing, have begun to whisper to one another that the more we elaborate our means of communication, the less we communicate.— J. B. Priestley, *Thoughts in the Wilderness*, 1957

Conformity

314 Conformity is the ape of harmony. - Ralph Waldo Emerson, *Journals*, 1840

315 Society everywhere is in conspiracy against the manhood of every one of its members.— Ralph Waldo Emerson, *Essays, First Series*, 1841

316 We are half ruined by conformity, but we should be wholly ruined without it.— Charles Dudley Warner, *My Summer in a Garden*, 1871

317 No one can possibly achieve any real and lasting success or "get rich" in business by being a conformist.— J. Paul Getty, in *International Herald Tribune*, January 10, 1961

318 You can't walk alone. Many have given the illusion but none have really walked alone. Man is not made that way. Each man is bedded in his people, their history, their culture, and their values.— Peter Abrahams, *Return to Goli*, 1953

319 Every society honors its live conformists and its dead troublemakers.— Mignon McLaughlin, *The Neurotic's Notebook*, 1963

320 The rest of the world cannot be expected to regulate its life by a clock which is always slow.— Georges Pompidou, in *Washington Post*, May 26, 1971

321 To me, the whole process of being a brushstroke in someone else's painting is a little difficult.— Madonna, in *Vanity Fair*, April, 1991

Conquest

322 Whoever can surprise well must conquer.— John Paul Jones, letter, February 10, 1778

323 Rats and conquerors must expect no mercy in misfortune.— Charles Caleb Colton, *Lacon*, 1820–22

324 We seem, as it were, to have conquered and peopled half the world in a fit of absence of mind.— John Seeley, *The Expansion of England*, 1883

Conscience

325 There is one thing alone that stands the brunt of life throughout its course: a quiet conscience.— Euripedes, *Hippolytus*, 428 B.C.

326 Conscience without judgment is superstition.— Benjamin Whichcote, *Moral and Religious Aphorisms*, 1753

327 At length the mind grows absolutely callous.— Anna Letitia Barbauld, *An Inquiry Into Those Kinds of Distress Which Excite Agreeable Sensations*, 1773

328 Courage without conscience is a wild beast.— Robert G. Ingersoll, speech, May 29, 1882

329 Our conscience is not the vessel of eternal verities. It grows with our social life, and a new social condition means a radical change in conscience.— Walter Lippmann, *A Preface to Politics*, 1914

330 What a man calls his "conscience" is merely the mental action that follows a sentimental reaction after too much wine or love.— Helen Rowland, *A Guide to Men*, 1922

331 Conscience: self-esteem with a halo.— Irving Layton, *The Whole Bloody Bird*, 1969

Courage and Cowardice

332 To have died once is enough.— Virgil, *Aeneid*, 19 B.C.

333 Sometimes even to live is an act of courage.— Seneca, *Letters to Lucilius*, 1st c.

334 Courage mounteth with occasion.— William Shakespeare, *King John*, 1596–97

335 The better part of valor is discretion.— William Shakespeare, *Henry IV, Part I*, 1597

336 In a false quarrel there is no true valor.— William Shakespeare, *Much Ado About Nothing*, 1598–99

337 Valor lies just half way between rashness and cowheartedness.— Miguel de Cervantes, *Don Quixote*, 1605–15

338 Cowardly dogs bark loudest.— John Webster, *The White Devil*, 1612

339 Noble deeds are most estimable when hidden.— Blaise Pascal, *Pensées*, 1670

340 The courage of a soldier is found to be the cheapest and most common quality of human nature.— Edward Gibbon, *The Decline and Fall of the Roman Empire*, 1776–88

341 There is not a more mean, stupid, dastardly, pitiless, selfish, spiteful, envious, ungrateful animal than the Public. It is the greatest of cowards, for it is afraid of itself.— William Hazlitt, *Table Talk,* 1821— 22

342 The courage we desire and prize is not the courage to die decently, but to live manfully.— Thomas Carlyle, *On Boswell's Life of Johnson,* 1832

343 Familiarity with danger makes a brave man braver, but less daring.— Herman Melville, *White Jacket,* 1850

344 A great part of courage is the courage of having done the thing before.— Ralph Waldo Emerson, *The Conduct of Life,* 1860

345 Bravery never goes out of fashion. – William Makepeace Thackeray, *The Four Georges,* 1860

346 Conquest is the missionary of valor, and the hard impact of military virtues beats meanness out of the world.— Walter Bagehot, *Physics and Politics,* 1872

347 "I'm very brave generally," he went on in a low voice, "only today I happen to have a headache."— Lewis Carroll, *Through the Looking-Glass,* 1872

348 The strongest man in the world is he who stands most alone.— Henrik Ibsen, *An Enemy of the People,* 1882

349 Everyone becomes brave when he observes one who despairs.— Friedrich Nietzsche, *Thus Spake Zarathustra,* 1883–92

350 Hatred is the coward's revenge for being intimidated.— George Bernard Shaw, *Major Barbara,* 1905

351 The paradox of courage is that a man must be a little careless of his life in order to keep it.— Gilbert K. Chesterton, *All Things Considered,* 1908

352 Courage is the price that life exacts for granting peace.— Amelia Earhart, *Courage,* 1927

353 Fighting is like champagne. It goes to the heads of cowards as quickly as of heroes. Any fool can be brave on a battlefield when it's be brave or else be killed.— Margaret Mitchell, *Gone with the Wind,* 1936

354 There is plenty of courage among us for the abstract but not for the concrete.— Helen Keller, *Let Us Have Faith,* 1940

355 Cowardice, as distinguished from panic, is almost always simply a lack of ability to suspend the functioning of the imagination.— Ernest Hemingway, *Men at War,* 1942

356 To act coolly, intelligently and prudently in perilous circumstances is the test of a man — and also of a nation.— Adlai Stevenson, in *New York Times,* April 11, 1955

357 Until the day of his death, no man can be sure of his courage.— Jean Anouilh, *Beckett,* 1959

358 Courage does not always march to airs blown by a bugle: is not always wrought out of the fabric ostentation wears.— Frances Rodman, in *New York Times,* May 13, 1961

359 It is easy enough to praise men for the courage of their convictions. I wish I could teach the sad young of this mealy generation the courage of their confusions.— John Ciardi, in *Saturday Review,* June 2, 1962

360 I'm a hero with coward's legs.— Spike Milligan, *Puckoon,* 1963

361 Life shrinks or expands in proportion to one's courage.— Anaïs Nin, *The Diary of Anaïs Nin,* 1966

Courtship

362   What makes men indifferent to their wives is that they can see them when they please.— Ovid, *The Art of Love*, ca. 8

363   Courtship to marriage is as a very witty prologue to a very dull play.— William Congreve, *The Old Bachelor*, 1693

364   It is easier to be a lover than a husband for the simple reason that it is more difficult to be witty every day than to say pretty things from time to time.— Honoré de Balzac, *The Physiology of Marriage*, 1830

365   It is most dangerous nowadays for a husband to pay attention to his wife in public. It always makes people think that he beats her when they're alone.— Oscar Wilde, *Lady Windermere's Fan*, 1892

366   I don't know anything that braces one up like finding you haven't got to get married after all.— P. G. Wodehouse, *Jeeves in the Offing*, 1960

Creativity

367   Precisely due to their feeling of playing a relatively small part in the creation of living beings [men are impelled] to an overcompensation in achievement.— Karen Horney, *Feminine Psychology*, 1926

368   Work on good prose has three steps: a musical stage when it is composed, an architectonic one when it is built, and a textile one when it is woven.— Walter Benjamin, *One-Way Street*, 1928

369   All men are creative but few are artists.— Paul Goodman, *Growing Up Absurd*, 1960

370   Whoever undertakes to create soon finds himself engaged in creating himself. Self-transformation and the transformation of others have constituted the radical interest of our century, whether in painting, psychiatry, or political action.— Harold Rosenberg, *The Tradition of the New*, 1960

371   Human salvation lies in the hands of the creatively maladjusted.— Martin Luther King, Jr., *Strength to Love*, 1963

372   Create, and be true to yourself, and depend only on your own good taste.— Duke Ellington, *Music is My Mistress*, 1973

373   Creativity arises out of the tension between spontaneity and limitations, the latter (like the river banks) forcing the spontaneity into the various forms which are essential to the work of art or poem.— Rollo May, *The Courage to Create*, 1975

374   Creativity comes from trust. Trust your instincts. And never hope more than you work.— Rita Mae Brown, *Starting From Scratch*, 1988

375   Americans worship creativity the way they worship physical beauty — as a way of enjoying elitism without guilt: God did it.— Florence King, *Reflections in a Jaundiced Eye*, 1989

Criticism

376   The true critic is he who bears within himself the dreams and ideas and feelings of myriad generations, and to whom no form of thought is alien, no emotional impulse obscure.— Oscar Wilde, in *Speaker*, March 22, 1890

377   When a man spends his time giving his wife criticism and advice instead of compliments, he forgets that it was not his good judgment, but his charming manners, that won her heart.— *Helen Rowland, Reflections of a Bachelor Girl,* 1903

378   Criticism is the art wherewith a critic tries to guess himself into a share of the artist's fame.— George Jean Nathan, *The House of Satan*, 1926

379   Book reviewing is a profession in which those who flunk the course get to teach the class.— Dagobert D. Runes, *Treasury of Thought*, 1966

380   Asking a working writer what he thinks about critics is like asking a lamppost what it feels about dogs.— John Osborne, in *Time*, October 31, 1977

381   Criticism is a misconception: we must read not to understand others but to understand ourselves.— Emile M. Cioran, *Anathemas and Admirations,* 1986

382   One gets tired of the role critics are supposed to have in this culture: It's like being the piano player in a whorehouse; you don't have any control over the action going on upstairs.— Robert Hughes, *Publishers Weekly*, December 12, 1986

383   Criticism, even when you try to ignore it, can hurt. I have cried over many articles written about me, but I move on and I don't hold on to that.— Diana Ross, *Secrets of a Sparrow*, 1993

Culture

384   Culture is properly described not as having its origin in curiosity, but as having its origin in the love of perfection; it is a study of perfection.— Matthew Arnold, *Culture and Anarchy*, 1869

385   Culture is the name for what people are interested in, their thoughts, their models, the books they read and the speeches they hear, their table-talk, gossip, controversies, historical sense and scientific training, the values they appreciate.— Walter Lippmann, *A Preface to Politics*, 1914

Curiosity

386   Curiosity is, in great and generous minds, the first passion and the last.— Samuel Johnson, in *Rambler*, August 24, 1751

387   Every man ought to be inquisitive through every hour of his great adventure down to the day when he shall no longer cast a shadow in the sun. For if he dies without a question in his heart, what excuse is there for his continuance?— Frank Moore Colby, *The Colby Essays*, 1926

388   Curiosity is one of the lowest of the human faculties. You will have noticed in daily life that when people are inquisitive they nearly always have bad memories and are usually stupid at bottom.— E. M. Forster, *Aspects of the Novel*, 1927

389   Disinterested intellectual curiosity is the life blood of real civilization.— G.

M. Trevelyan, *English Social History*, 1942

Cynicism

390   Cynicism is intellectual dandyism without the coxcomb's feathers.— George Meredith, *The Egoist*, 1879

391   The only deadly sin I know is cynicism.— Henry Lewis Stimson, *On Active Service in Peace and War*, 1948

392   Cynicism is, after all, simply idealism gone sour.— Will Herberg, *Judaism and Modern Man*, 1951

393   The so-called sophisticated who prides himself on cynicism, is only seeking to escape his own inadequacies.— Edgar F. Magnin, *How to Lead aRicher and Fuller Life*, 1951

Death

394   Death is better, a milder fate than tyranny.— Aeschylus, *Agememnon,* ca. 458 B.C.

395   We all labor against our own cure, for death is the cure of all diseases.— Thomas Browne, *Religio Medici*, 1643

396   Even Rome cannot give us dispensation from death.— Molière, *L'Etourdi,* 1665

397   Those most like the dead are those most loath to die.— Jean de La Fontaine, *Fables*, 1668

398   It is only the dead who do not return.— Bertrand Barère de Vieuzac, speech, 1794

399   Death cancels everything but truth; and strips a man of everything but genius and virtue. It is a sort of natural canonization. It makes the meanest of us sacred — it installs the poet in his immortality, and lifts him to the skies.— William Hazlitt, The Spirit of the Age, 1825

400   Fame is the sun of the dead.— Honoré de Balzac, *Le Recherche de l'Absolu,* 1834

401   Any relic of the dead is precious, if they were valued living.— Emily Brontë, *Wuthering Heights*, 1847

402   It is better to be a fool than to be dead.— Robert Louis Stevenson, *Virginibus Puerisque,* 1881

403   To die proudly when it is no longer possible to live proudly. Death of one's own free choice, death at the proper time, with a clear head and with joyfulness, consummated in the midst of children and witnesses.— Friedrich Nietzsche, *Twilight of the Idols*, 1889

404   Death and vulgarity are the only two facts in the nineteenth century that one cannot explain away.— Oscar Wilde, *The Picture of Dorian Gray*, 1891

405   Life levels all men: death reveals the eminent.— George Bernard Shaw, *Man and Superman*, 1903

406   To die will be an awfully big adventure.— J. M. Barrie, *Peter Pan*, 1904

407   The fight between life and death is to the finish, and death ultimately is the victor.— Jack Johnson, *Jack Johnson In the Ring and Out*, 1927

408   I can imagine myself on my deathbed, spent utterly with lust to touch the next world, like a boy asking for his first kiss from a woman.— Aleister Crowley, *The Confessions of Aleister Crowley*, 1929

409 Killing cleanly and in a way which gives you esthetic pride and pleasure has always been one of the greatest enjoyments of a part of the human race.— Ernest Hemingway, *Death in the Afternoon*, 1932

410 Kill a man, and you are an assassin. Kill millions of men, and you are a conqueror. Kill everyone, and you are a god.— Jean Rostand, *Pensées d'un Biologiste*, 1939

411 I want a busy life, a just mind and a timely death.— Zora Neale Hurston, *Dust Tracks on a Road*, 1941

412 To our real, naked selves there is not a thing on earth or in heaven worth dying for.— Eric Hoffer, *The True Believer*, 1951

413 Fear of death increases in exact proportion to increase in wealth.— Ernest Hemingway, in A. E. Hotchner, *Papa Hemingway*, 1955

414 Men are convinced of your arguments, your sincerity, and the seriousness of your efforts only by your death.— Albert Camus, *The Fall*, 1956

415 Life is a great surprise. I do not see why death should not be an even greater one.— Vladimir Nabokov, *Pale Fire*, 1962

416 In the twentieth century, death terrifies men less than the absence of real life. All these dead, mechanized, specialized actions, stealing a little bit of life a thousand times a day until the mind and body are exhausted.— Raoul Vaneigem, *The Revolution of Everyday Life*, 1967

417 As for death one gets used to it, even if it's only other people's death you get used to.— Enid Bagnold, *Autobiography*, 1969

418 Since every death diminishes a little, we grieve — not so much for the death as for ourselves.— Lynn Caine, *Widow*, 1974

419 Death mattered not — It was a mere punctuation.— Nathan Huggins, *Black Odyssey*, 1977

420 Death not merely ends life, it also bestows upon it a silent completeness, snatched from the hazardous flux to which all things human are subject.— Elizabeth Arden, *The Life of the Mind*, 1978

421 For those who live neither with religious consolations about death nor with a sense of death (or of anything else) as natural, death is the obscene mystery, the ultimate affront, the thing that cannot be controlled. It can only be denied.— Susan Sontag, *Illness As Metaphor*, 1978

422 Death is not the enemy.— Norman Cousins, *The Healing Heart*, 1983

423 I am not afraid of death, but would not want to die in some obscure or pointless way.— Isabelle Eberhardt, *The Passionate Nomad*, 1988

Decisions

424 No trumpets sound when the important decisions of our life are made. Destiny is made known silently.— Agnes George de Mille, *Dance to the Piper*, 1952

425 Decision making isn't a matter of arriving at a right or wrong answer, it's a matter of selecting the most effective course of action from among less effective courses of action.— Philip Marvin, *Developing Decisions for Action*, 1971

426 You have no idea how promising the world begins to look once you have decided to have it all for yourself. And how much healthier your decisions are once they become entirely selfish.— Anita Brookner, Hotel du Lac, 1984

427   It's easy to make good decisions when there are no bad options.— Robert Half, *Robert Half on Hiring*, 1985

428   Give people enough guidance to make the decisions you want them to make. Don't tell them what to do, but encourage them to do what is best.— Jimmy Johnson, in *Parade*, August 15, 1993

Defeat

429   The ugly and the stupid have the best of it in this world. They can sit at their ease and gape at the play. If they know nothing of victory, they are at least spared the knowledge of defeat.— Oscar Wilde, *The Picture of Dorian Gray*, 1891

430   The quickest way of ending a war is to lose it.— George Orwell, *Shooting an Elephant*, 1950

431   Post-mortems on defeat are never very useful unless they say something about the future.— James Reston, in *New York Times*, July 15, 1964

Democracy

432   In democracies, nothing is more great or more brilliant than commerce.— Alexis de Tocqueville, *Democracy in America*, 1835

433   Democracy is the recurrent suspicion that more than half of the people are right more than half of the time.— E. B. White, *The Wild Flag*, 1946

434   Under democracy one party always devotes its chief energies to trying to prove that the other party is unfit to rule — and both commonly succeed, and are right.— H. L. Mencken, *Minority Report*, 1956

435   If one man offers you democracy and another offers you a bag of grain, at what stage of starvation will you prefer the grain to the vote?— Bertrand Russell, *Silhouettes in Satire*, 1958

Desire

436   The want of a thing is perplexing enough, but the possession of it is intolerable.— John Vanbrugh, *The Confederacy*, 1705

437   Ships at a distance have every man's wish on board.— Zora Neale Hurston, *Their Eyes were Watching God*, 1937

438   Pleasure is continually disappointed, reduced, deflated, in favor of strong, noble values: Truth, Death, Progress, Struggle, Joy, etc. Its victorious rival is Desire: we are always being told about Desire, never about Pleasure.— Roland Barthes, *The Pleasure of the Text*, 1975

439   Whenever we confront an unbridled desire we are surely in the presence of a tragedy-in-the-making.— Quentin Crisp, *Manners from Heaven*, 1984

Destiny

440   Fate, then, is a name for facts not yet passed under the fire of thought; for causes which are unpenetrated.— Ralph Waldo Emerson, *The Conduct of Life*, 1860

441   Destiny is an absolutely definite and inexorable ruler. Physical ability and moral determination count for nothing. It is impossible to perform the simplest act when the gods say "no." I have no idea how they bring pressure to bear on such occasions.— Aleister Crowley, The Confessions of Aleister Crowley, 1929

442   We live under continual threat of two equally fearful, but seemingly opposed, destinies: unremitting banality and inconceivable terror. It is fantasy, served out in large rations by the popular arts, which allows most people to cope.— Susan Sontag, *Against Interpretation*, 1966

Diplomacy

443   The right of conquest has no foundation other than the right of the strongest.— Jean-Jacques Rousseau, *The Social Contract*, 1762

444   Diplomacy is the police in grand costume.— Napoleon Bonaparte, *Maxims*, 1804–15

445   If you wish to avoid foreign collision, you had better abandon the ocean.— Henry Clay, speech, January 22, 1812

446   You can always get the truth from an American statesman after he has turned seventy, or given up all hope of the Presidency.— Wendell Phillips, speech, November 7, 1860

447   To act with doubleness towards a man whose own conduct was double, was so near an approach to virtue that it

deserved to be called by no meaner name than diplomacy.— George Eliot, *Felix Holt, The Radical*, 1866

448   I asked Tom if countries always apologized when they had done wrong, and he says: "Yes; the little ones does."— Mark Twain, *Tom Sawyer Abroad*, 1894

449   How is the world ruled and how do wars start? Diplomats tell lies to journalists and then believe what they read.— Karl Kraus, *Aphorisms and More Aphorisms*, 1909

450   Diplomats make it their business to conceal the facts.— Margaret Sanger, *Woman and the New Race*, 1920

451   Diplomacy is to do and say the nastiest things in the nicest way.— Isaac Goldberg, *The Reflex*, 1930

452   Sometimes it takes two or three conferences to scare up a war, but generally one will do it.— Will Rogers, in *New York Times*, July 6, 1933

453   A diplomat these days is nothing but a head-waiter who's allowed to sit down occasionally.— Peter Ustinov, *Romanoff and Juliet*, 1956

454   Diplomats are useful only in fair weather. As soon as it rains they drown in every drop.— Charles de Gaulle, in *Newsweek*, October 1, 1962

455   The great nations have always acted like gangsters, and the small nations like prostitutes.— Stanley Kubrick, in *Guardian*, June 5, 1963

456   Diplomacy is letting someone else have your way.— Lester B. Pearson, in *Vancouver Sun*, March 18, 1965

457   Why employ intelligent and highly paid ambassadors and then go and do their work for them? You don't buy a canary and sing yourself.— Sir

Alec Douglas-Home, in *New York Times,* April 21, 1969

458   All war represents a failure of diplomacy.— Tony Benn, speech, February 28, 1991

Discipline

459   Do not pursue with the terrible scourge him who deserves a slight whip.— Horace, *Satires,* ca. 35 B.C.

460   A boy who suffers not at the hands of his teacher suffers at the hands of time.— Saadi, *Fruit Garden,* 1257

461   We find nothing easier than being wise, patient, superior. We drip with the oil of forbearance and sympathy, we are absurdly just, we forgive everything. For that very reason we ought to discipline ourselves a little.— Friedrich Nietzsche, *Twilight of the Idols,* 1889

462   You cannot train a horse with shouts and expect it to obey a whisper.— Dagobert D. Runes, *Treasury of Thought,* 1966

Discretion

463   It is not well to see everything, nor to hear everything.— Seneca, *On Anger,* ca. 55

464   The art of being wise is the art of knowing what to overlook.— William James, *The Principles of Psychology,* 1890

Distrust

465   What loneliness is more lonely than distrust?— George Eliot, *Middlemarch,* 1872

466   Distrust everyone in whom the impulse to punish is powerful.— Friedrich Nietzsche, *Thus Spoke Zarathustra,* 1883–91

467   Say nothing good of yourself, you will be distrusted; say nothing bad of yourself, you will be taken at your word.— Joseph Roux, *Meditations of a Parish Priest,* 1886

468   I distrust Great Men. They produce a desert of uniformity around them and often a pool of blood too, and I always feel a little man's pleasure when they come a cropper.— E. M. Forster, *Two Cheers for Democracy,* 1951

Dogmatism

469   From the age of fifteen, dogma has been the fundamental principle of my religion: I know no other religion; I cannot enter into the idea of any other sort of religion; religion, as a mere sentiment, is to me a dream and a mockery.— John Henry Newman, *Apologia Pro Vita Sua,* 1864

470   Men possessed with an idea cannot be reasoned with.— James Anthony Froude, *Short Studies on Great Subjects,* 1867–82

471   The modern world is filled with men who hold dogmas so strongly that they do not even know they are dogmas.— Gilbert K. Chesterton, *Heretics,* 1905

472 Men still want the crutch of dogma, of beliefs fixed by authority, to relieve them of the trouble of thinking and responsibility of directing their activity by thought.— John Dewey, *Democracy and Education*, 1916

473 When people are least sure, they are often most dogmatic.— John Kenneth Galbraith, *The Great Crash, 1929*, 1955

474 When distant and unfamiliar and complex things are communicated to great masses of people, the truth suffers a considerable and often a radical distortion. The complex is made over into the simple, the hypothetical into the dogmatic.— Walter Lippmann, *The Public Philosophy*, 1955

475 The mind petrifies if a circle is drawn around it, and it can hardly be denied that dogma draws a circle round the mind.— George Moore, *Confessions of a Young Man*, 1888

Doubt

476 If you would be a real seeker after truth, it is necessary that at least once in your life you doubt, as far as possible, all things.— René Descartes, *Principles of Philosophy*, 1644

477 Doubt is not a pleasant condition, but certainty is absurd.— Voltaire, letter, November 28, 1770

478 An honest man can never surrender an honest doubt.— Walter Malone, *The Agnostic's Creed*, 1886

479 A mind that questions everything, unless strong enough to bear the weight of its ignorance, risks questioning itself

and being engulfed in doubt.— Emile Durkheim, *Suicide*, 1897

480 Doubt is the beginning, not the end, of wisdom.— George Iles, *Jottings*, 1918

481 Believe those who are seeking the truth; doubt those who have found it.— André Gide, *So Be It*, 1959

482 Doubt is to certainty as neurosis is to psychosis. The neurotic is in doubt and has fears about persons and things; the psychotic has convictions and makes claims about them. In short, the neurotic has problems, the psychotic has solutions.— Thomas Szasz, *The Second Sin*, 1973

Dreams

483 For I see now that I am asleep that I dream when I am awake.— Pedro Calderón de la Barca, *Life is a Dream*, 1635

484 I really, deeply believe that dreams do come true. Often, they might not come when you want them. They come in their own time.— Diana Ross, *Secrets of a Sparrow*, 1993

Duty

485 Where it is a duty to worship the sun it is pretty sure to be a crime to examine the laws of heat.— John Morley, *Voltaire*, 1872

486 Nobody is so constituted as to be able to live everywhere and anywhere; and he who has great duties to perform,

which lay claim to all his strength, has, in this respect, a very limited choice. — Friedrich Nietzsche, *Ecce Homo*, 1888

487 When a stupid man is doing something he is ashamed of, he always declares that it is his duty. — George Bernard Shaw, *Caesar and Cleopatra*, 1903

488 Rights that do not flow from duty well performed are not worth having. — Mahatma Gandhi, *Non-Violence in Peace and War, Volume 2*, 1949

489 The burning conviction that we have a holy duty toward others is often a way of attaching our drowning selves to a passing raft. — Eric Hoffer, *The True Believer*, 1951

490 Duty largely consists of pretending that the trivial is critical. — John Fowles, *The Magus*, 1965

491 If a poet has any obligation toward society, it is to write well. — Joseph Brodsky, *Less Than One: Selected Essays*, 1983

Economics

492 The real price of everything, what everything really costs to the man who wants to acquire it, is the toil and trouble of acquiring it. — Adam Smith, *The Wealth of Nations*, 1776

493 We estimate the wisdom of nations by seeing what they did with their surplus capital. — Ralph Waldo Emerson, *English Traits*, 1856

494 The right merchant is one who has the just average of faculties we call common sense. — Ralph Waldo Emerson, *The Conduct of Life*, 1860

495 Entrepreneurial profit is the expression of the value of what the entrepreneur contributes to production. — Joseph A. Schumpeter, *The Theory of Economic Development*, 1934

496 The instability of the economy is equaled only by the instability of economists. — John Henry Williams, in *New York Times*, June 2, 1956

497 One of the greatest pieces of economic wisdom is to know what you do not know. — John Kenneth Galbraith, in *Time*, March 3, 1961

498 If ignorance paid dividends, most Americans could make a fortune out of what they don't know about economics. — Luther Hodges, in *Wall Street Journal*, March 14, 1962

499 Production and consumption are the nipples of modern society. Thus suckled, humanity grows in strength and beauty; rising standard of living, all modern conveniences, distractions of all kinds, culture for all, the comfort of your dreams. — Raoul Vaneigem, *The Revolution of Everyday Life*, 1967

500 Most of the economics as taught is a form of brain damage. — Ernst F. Schumacher, in *The Reader*, March 25, 1977

Education

501 Education is the art of making men ethical. — Georg Wilhelm Friedrich Hegel, *The Philosophy of Right*, 1821

502 Anyone who has passed through the regular graduations of a classical education, and is not made a fool by it, may consider himself as having had a very narrow escape.— William Hazlitt, *Table-Talk*, 1821–22

503   What is the first part of politics? Education. The second? Education. And the third? Education.— Jules Michelet, *Le People*, 1846

504   Education at school continues what has been done at home: it crystallizes the optical illusion, consolidates it with book learning, theoretically legitimizes the traditional trash and trains the children to know without understanding.— Aleksandr Herzen, *My Past and Thoughts*, 1921

505   We are faced with the paradoxical fact that education has become one of the chief obstacles to intelligence and freedom of thought.— Bertrand Russell, *Skeptical Essays*, 1928

506   Teaching is not a lost art, but the regard for it is a lost tradition.— Jacques Barzun, in *Newsweek*, December 5, 1955

Egotism

507   We like so much to hear people talk of us and of our motives.— Marie de Sevigne, *Letters of Madame de Sevigne to Her Daughter and Friends*, 1811

508   The egoism which enters into our theories does not affect their sincerity; rather, the more our egoism is satisfied, the more robust is our belief.— George Eliot, *Middlemarch*, 1871

509   The worst disease which can afflict business executives in their work is not, as popularly supposed, alcoholism; it's egotism.— Harold S. Geneen, *Managing*, 1984

510   Egotism is the anesthetic that dulls

the pains of stupidity.— Frank Leahy, in *Look Magazine*, January 10, 1955

Eloquence

511   True eloquence consists in saying all that should be, not all that could be said.— François Duke de La Rochefoucauld, VI, *Maxims*, 1665

512   Eloquence is a painting of thought.— Blaise Pascal, *Pensées*, 1670

513   Eloquence may exist without a proportional degree of wisdom.— Edmund Burke, *Reflections on the Revolution in France*, 1790

Enemies

514   The truth is forced upon us very quickly, by a foe.— Aristophanes, *The Birds*, ca. 415 B.C.

515   There is no safety in regaining the favor of an enemy.— Publilius Syrus, *Moral Sayings*, 1st c. B.C.

516   Do not trust the horse, Trojans. Whatever it is, I fear the Greeks even when they bring gifts.— Virgil, *Aeneid*, 19 B.C.

517   A state which has freshly achieved liberty makes enemies and no friends.— Niccolò Machiavelli, *The Prince*, 1513

518   A wise man gets more use from his enemies than a fool from his friends.— Baltasar Gracián, *The Art of Worldly Wisdom*, 1647

519   I have only ever made one prayer to God, a very short one: "O Lord, make my enemies ridiculous." And God granted it.—Voltaire, letter, May 16, 1767

520 You can calculate the worth of a man by the number of his enemies.— Gustave Flaubert, letter, June 14, 1853

521 Let us learn to respect sincerity of conviction in our opponents.— Otto von Bismarck, speech, December 18, 1863

522 A man cannot be too careful in the choice of his enemies.— Oscar Wilde, *The Picture of Dorian Gray*, 1891

523 It takes your enemy and your friend, working together, to hurt you to the heart; the one to slander you and the other to get the news to you.— Mark Twain, *Following the Equator*, 1897

524 You shall judge of a man by his foes as well as by his friends.— Joseph Conrad, *Lord Jim*, 1900

525 Calamities are of two kinds: misfortune to ourselves, and good fortune to others.— Ambrose Bierce, *The Devil's Dictionary*, 1906

526 Instead of loving your enemy, treat your friend a little better.— Edgar Watson Howe, *Ventures in Common Sense*, 1919

527 Out of necessity one has to learn from one's enemies.— Leon Trotsky, *Literature and Revolution*,1924

528 If it has to choose who is to be crucified, the crowd will always save Barabbas.— Jean Cocteau, *Le Rallep à Ordre*, 1926

529 All our foes are mortal.— Paul Valéry, *Tel Quel*, 1943

530 Abatement in the hostility of one's enemies must never be thought to signify they have been won over. It only means that one has ceased to constitute a threat.— Quentin Crisp, *The Naked Civil Servant*, 1968

531 One of the most time-consuming things is to have an enemy.— E. B. White, in *Essays of E. B. White*, 1977

532 Don't worry about your enemies, it's your allies who will do you in.— James Abourezk, in *Playboy*, March 1979

533 I hate admitting that my enemies have a point.— Salman Rushdie, *The Satanic Verses*, 1988

Envy

534 Envy among other ingredients has a mixture of the love of justice in it. We are more angry at undeserved than at deserved good-fortune.— William Hazlitt, *Characteristics*, 1821

535 In a consumer society there are inevitably two kinds of slaves: the prisoners of addiction and the prisoners of envy.— Ivan Illich, *Tools for Conviviality*, 1973

Equality

536 What makes equality such a difficult business is that we only want it with our superiors.— Henry Becque, *Querelles littéaires*, 1890

537 There is no merit in equality, unless it be equality with the best.— John Lancaster Spalding, *Thoughts and Theories of Life and Education*, 1897

538 If a man is genuinely superior to his fellows the first thing that he believes is in the equality of man.— Gilbert K. Chesterton, *Heretics*, 1905

539   Equality is a mortuary word.— Christopher Fry, *Venus Observed*, 1950

540   We clamor for equality chiefly in matters in which we ourselves cannot hope to obtain excellence.— Eric Hoffer, *The Passionate State of Mind*, 1954

Eroticism

541   Everyone is dragged on by their favorite pleasure.— Virgil, *Eclogues*, 37 B.C.

542   A nice man is a man of nasty ideas.— Jonathan Swift, *Thoughts on Various Subjects*, 1711

543   Eros is the first, the creator, the principle from which all things proceed.— Arthur Schopenhauer, *The World as Will and Idea*, 1819

544   Christianity has done a great deed for love by making a sin of it.— Anatole France, *The Garden of Epicurus*, 1894

545   There is no unhappier creature on earth than a fetishist who yearns for a woman's shoe and has to embrace the whole woman.— Karl Kraus, *Aphorisms and More Aphorisms*, 1909

546   Well-bred English people never have imagination.— Dorothy L. Sayers, *Clouds of Witness*, 1956

childhood.— René Descartes, *Principles of Philosophy*, 1644

548   Nothing is more harmful to a new truth than an old error.— Johann Wolfgang von Goethe, *Proverbs in Prose*, 1819

549   The broadest and most prevalent error requires the most disinterested virtue to sustain it.— Henry David Thoreau, *On the Duty of Civil Disobedience*, 1849

550   Great blunders are often made, like large ropes, of a multitude of fibers.— Victor Hugo, *Les Misérables*, 1862

551   The study of error is not only in the highest degree prophylactic, but it serves as a stimulating introduction to the study of truth.— Walter Lippmann, *Public Opinion*, 1922

552   Error is certainty's constant companion. Error is the corollary of evidence. And anything said about truth may equally well be said about error: the delusion will be no greater.— Louis Aragon, *Paris Peasant*, 1926

553   Man approaches the unattainable truth through a succession of errors.— Aldous Huxley, *Do What You Will: Wordsworth in the Tropics*, 1929

554   I've done some things I wish I could erase. I invented mistakes. But the mistakes must be seen in context, and they must be weighed along with the positives.— Sammy Davis, Jr., in *Ebony*, July, 1990

Errors

547   The chief cause of human error is to be found in prejudices picked up in

Ethics

555   The world is full of judgment-days, and into every assembly that a man enters, in every action he attempts, he is gauged and stamped.— Ralph Waldo Emerson, *Essays, First Series*, 1841

556   The blind willingness to sacrifice people to truth, however, has always been the danger of an ethics abstracted from life.— Carol Gilligan, *In a Different Voice*, 1982

Exaggeration

557   An element of exaggeration clings to the popular judgment: great vices are made greater, great virtues greater also; interesting incidents are made more interesting, softer legends more soft.— Walter Bagehot, *The Waverley Novels*, 1858

558   Camp is a vision of the world in terms of style but a particular style. It is the love of the exaggerated.— Susan Sontag, *Against Interpretation and Other Essays*, 1966

Excellence

559   Excellence encourages one about life generally; it shows the spiritual wealth of the world.— George Eliot, *Daniel Deronda*, 1876

560   The sad truth is that excellence makes people nervous.— Shana Alexander, *The Feminist Eye*, 1970

Executives

561   I learned in business that you had to be very careful when you told somebody that's working for you to do something, because the chances were very high he'd do it. In government, you don't have to worry about that.— George P. Shultz, in *New York Times*, October 14, 1984

562   Executives are like joggers. If you stop a jogger, he goes on running on the spot. If you drag an executive away from his business, he goes on running on the spot, pawing the ground, talking business.— Jean Baudrillard, *Cool Memories*, 1987

563   I am still looking for the modern equivalent of those Quakers who ran successful businesses, made money because they offered honest products and treated their people decently. This business creed, sadly, seems long forgotten.— Anita Roddick, *Body and Soul*, 1991

Expansion

564   Of all follies there is none greater than wanting to make the world a better place.— Molière, *Le Misanthrope*, 1666

565   We shall not make Britain's mistake. Too wise to try to govern the world, we shall merely own it.— Ludwell Denny, *America Conquers Britain*, 1930

566   Small nations are like indecently dressed women. They tempt the evil-minded.— Julius Nyerere, in *The Reporter*, April 9, 1964

Experience

567 Bad times have a scientific value. These are occasions a good learner would not miss.— Ralph Waldo Emerson, *The Conduct of Life*, 1860

568 Not to transmit an experience is to betray it.— Elie Wiesel, in *Christian Science Monitor*, September 18, 1979

569 Experience is a good teacher, but she sends in terrific bills.— Minna Thomas Antrim, *Naked Truth and Veiled Allusions*, 1901

570 One can develop new capacities and strengths with which to meet the natural vicissitudes of living; that one may gain a sense of inner peace through greater self-acceptance, through a more realistic perspective on one's relationships and experiences.— Eda LeShan, *The Conspiracy Against Childhood*, 1907

571 Every man who has lived for fifty years has buried a whole world or even two; he has grown used to its disappearance and accustomed to the new scenery of another act.— Aleksandr Herzen, *My Past and Thoughts*, 1921

572 Experience isn't interesting till it begins to repeat itself— in fact, till it does that, it hardly is experience.— Elizabeth Bowen, *The Death of the Heart*, 1938

573 How different the new order would be if we could consult the veteran instead of the politician.— Henry Miller, *The Wisdom of the Heart*, 1941

574 I was thinking that we all learn by experience, but some of us have to go to summer school.— Peter De Vries, *The Tunnel of Love*, 1954

575 You cannot create experience. You must undergo it.— Albert Camus, *Notebooks 1935–1942*, 1962

576 It is always self-defeating to pretend to the style of a generation younger than your own; it simply erases your own experience in history.— Renata Adler, in *New York Times*, July, 1968

Facts

577 Facts are stubborn things.— Alain René Lasage, *L'Historie de Gil Blas*, 1735

578 You can only form the minds of reasoning animals upon Facts: nothing else will ever be of any service to them. Stick to Facts, sir!— Charles Dickens, *Hard Times*, 1854

579 The trouble with facts is that there are so many of them.— Samuel McChord Crothers, *The Gentle Reader*, 1903

580 Facts do not cease to exist because they are ignored.— Aldous Huxley, *Proper Studies*, 1927

581 People don't ask for facts in making up their minds. They would rather have one good, soul-satisfying emotion than a dozen facts.— Robert Keith Leavitt, *Voyages and Discourses*, 1939

582 One of the most untruthful things possible is a collection of facts, because they can be made to appear so many different ways.— Karl A. Menninger, *A Psychiatrist's World*, 1959

583 Facts are never neutral; they are impregnated with value judgments.— Peter Gay, *Style in History*, 1974

584 The greatest American superstition is belief in facts.— Herman A. Count von Keyserling, in *Kansas City Times*, January 25, 1977

Failure

585   I would prefer even to fail with honor than win by cheating.— Sophocles, *Philoctetes*, 409 B.C.

586   There is the greatest practical benefit in making a few failures early in life.— T. H. Huxley, *On Medical Education*, 1870

587   In the stress of modern life, how little room is left for that most comfortable vanity that whispers in our ears that failures are not faults!— Agnes Repplier, *Books and Men*, 1888

588   It is in our faults and failings, not in our virtues, that we touch each other, and find sympathy. It is in our follies that we are one.— Jerome K. Jerome, Idle Thoughts of an Idle Fellow, 1889

589   All human actions are equivalent and all are on principle doomed to failure.— Jean-Paul Sartre, *Being and Nothingness*, 1943

590   I don't like people who have never fallen or stumbled. Their virtue is lifeless and it isn't of much value. Life hasn't revealed its beauty to them.— Boris Pasternak, *Doctor Zhivago*, 1957

591   There can be no real freedom without the freedom to fail.— Eric Hoffer, *The Odeal of Change*, 1964

592   Why is it so painful to watch a person sink? Because there is something unnatural in it, for nature demands personal progress, evolution, and every backward step means wasted energy.— August Strindberg, *A Madman's Defense*, 1968

593   Perfectionist standards do not allow for failure.— Marion Woodman, *Addiction to Perfection: The Still Unravished Bride*, 1982

594   I touch the future. I teach.— Christa McAuliffe, Speech, August, 1985

595 I was never afraid of failure after that because, I think, coming that close to death you get kissed. With the years, the actual experience of course fades, but the flavor of it doesn't. I just had a real sense of what choice do I have but to live fully?— Debra Winger, in *Parade*, March 6, 1994

Faith

596   As a rule we believe as much as we can. We would believe everything if we could.— William James, *The Problems of Psychology*, 1890

597   Faith is often the boast of a man who is too lazy to investigate.— F. M. Knowles, *A Cheerful Year Book*, 1906

598   Faith may be defined briefly as an illogical belief in the occurrence of the improbable.— H. L. Mencken, *Prejudices, Third Series*, 1922

Fame

599   Fame and tranquility can never be bedfellows.— Michel Eyquem de Montaigne, *Essays*, 1580

600   Fame is so sweet that we love anything with which we connect it, even death.— Blaise Pascal, *Pensées*, 1670

601   The love of fame is almost another name for the love of excellence; or it is the ambition to attain the highest excellence, sanctioned by the highest authority, that of time.—William Hazlitt, *The Round Table*, 1817

602 Fame usually comes to those who are thinking about something else.—Oliver Wendell Holmes Sr., *The Autocrat of the Breakfast Table*, 1858

603 To want fame is to prefer dying scorned than forgotten.—Emile M. Cioran, *The New Gods*, 1969

Fanatics

604 There is only one step from fanaticism to barbarism.—Denis Diderot, *Essai sur le mérite de la vertu*, 1745

605 A fanatic is a man that does what he thinks the Lord would do if He knew the facts of the case.—Finley Peter Dunne, *Mr. Dooley's Opinions*, 1890

606 Man can be identified as an animal that makes dogmas.—Gilbert K. Chesterton, *Heretics*, 1905

607 Fanaticism consists in redoubling your effort when you have forgotten your aim.—George Santayana, *The Life of Reason*, 1905–06

608 Defined in psychological terms, a fanatic is a man who consciously overcompensates a secret doubt.—Aldous Huxley, *Proper Studies*, 1927

609 The fanatic is incorruptible: if he kills for an idea, he can just as well get himself killed for one; in either case, tyrant or martyr, he is a monster.—Emile M. Cioran, *A Short History of Decay*, 1949

610 In times of disorder and stress, the fanatics play a prominent role; in times

of peace, the critics. Both are shot after the revolution.—Edmund Wilson, *Memoirs of Hecate County*, 1949

611 Fervor is the weapon of choice of the impotent.—Frantz Fanon, *Black Skins, White Masks*, 1952

612 Take away hatred from some people, and you have men without faith.—Eric Hoffer, *The Passionate State of Mind*, 1954

613 It is part of the nature of fanaticism that it loses sight of the totality of evil and rushes like a bull at the red cloth instead of at the man who holds it.—Dietrich Bonhoeffer, *Ethics*, 1955

614 If there is anything more dangerous to the life of the mind than having no independent commitment to ideas, it is having an excess of commitment to some special and constricting idea.—Richard Hofstadter, *Anti-Intellectualism in American Life*, 1963

615 What is objectionable, what is dangerous about extremists is not that they are extreme, but that they are intolerant. The evil is not what they say about their cause, but what they say about their opponents.—Robert F. Kennedy, *The Pursuit of Justice*, 1964

616 A resolute minority has usually prevailed over an easygoing or wobbly majority whose prime purpose was to be left alone.—James Reston, *Sketches in the Sand*, 1967

Fathers

617 A man's desire for a son is usually nothing but the wish to duplicate himself in order that such a remarkable pattern may not be lost to the world.— Helen Rowland, *Reflections of a Bachelor Girl*, 1903

618   There are to us no ties at all just in being a father. A son is distinctly an acquired taste. It's the practice of parenthood that makes you feel that, after all, there may be something in it.— Heywood C. Broun, *Pieces of Hate*, 1922

Faults

619   People may flatter themselves just as much by thinking that their faults are always present to other people's minds.— Elizabeth Gaskell, *Wives and Daughters*, 1866

620   A man can become so accustomed to the thought of his own faults that he will begin to cherish them as charming little "personal characteristics."— Helen Rowland, *A Guide to Men*, 1922

Fear

621   Who lives in fear will never be a free man.— Horace, *Epistles*, 13 B.C.

622   True nobility is exempt from fear.— William Shakespeare, *Henry VI, Part II*, 1592

623   Extreme fear can neither fight nor fly.— William Shakespeare, *The Rape of Lucrece*, 1594

624   'Twas only fear first in the world made gods.— Ben Jonson, *Sejanus*, 1603

625   Fear is sharp-sighted and can see things under ground, and much more in the skies.— Miguel de Cervantes, *Don Quixote*, 1605–15

626   Fear could never make virtue.— Voltaire, *Philosophical Dictionary*, 1764

627   Fear is the foundation of most governments.— John Adams, *Thoughts on Government*, 1776

628   An utterly fearless man is a far more dangerous comrade than a coward.— Herman Melville, *Moby Dick*, 1851

629   A good scare is worth more to a man than good advice.— Edgar Watson Howe, *Country Town Sayings*, 1911

630   The one permanent emotion of the inferior man is fear —fear of the unknown, the complex, the inexplicable. What he wants above everything else is safety.— H. L. Mencken, *Prejudices, First Series*, 1919

631   The man who has ceased to fear has ceased to care.— F. H. Bradley, *Aphorisms*, 1930

632   Fear is a noose that binds until it strangles.— Jean Toomer, *Definitions and Aphorisms*, 1931

633   Warrior, jailer, priest — the eternal trinity which symbolizes our fear of life.— Henry Miller, *The Colossus of Maroussi*, 1941

634   Fear is the main source of superstition, and one of the main sources of cruelty.— Bertrand Russell, *Unpopular Essays*, 1950

635   You can discover what your enemy fears most by observing the means he uses to frighten you.— Eric Hoffer, *The Passionate State of Mind*, 1954

636   Nothing is more despicable than respect based on fear.— Albert Camus, *Notebooks 1935–1942*, 1962

637　We are all dangerous till our fears grow thoughtful.—John Ciardi, *This Strangest Everything*, 1966

638　The enemy [is] living in constant fear.—Norman Cousins, *The Healing Heart*, 1983

639　Fear is not a good teacher. The lessons of fear are quickly forgotten.—Mary Catherine Bateson, *A World of Ideas*, 1989

Females

640　Fickle and changeable always is woman.—Virgil, *Aeneid*, 1st c. B.C.

641　O tiger's heart wrapped in a woman's hide!—William Shakespeare, *Henry VI, Part III*, 1591

642　Women are from their very Infancy debarr'd those advantages [of education] with the want of which they are afterwards reproached, and nursed up in those vices with which will hereafter be upbraided them.—Mary Astell, *A Serious Proposal to the Ladies for the Advancement of their True and Greatest Interest*, 1694

643　There are many examples of women that have excelled in learning, and even in war, but this is no reason we should bring 'em all up to Latin and Greek or else military discipline, instead of needle-work and housewifry.—Bernard Mandeville, *The Fable of the Bees*, 1714

644　For what is done or learned by one class of women becomes, by virtue of their common womanhood, the property of all women.—Emily Blackwell, *Medicine as a Profession for Women*, 1860

645　A woman finds the natural lay of the land almost unconsciously; and not feeling it incumbent on her to be guide and philosopher to any successor, she takes little pains to mark the route by which she is making her ascent.—Antoinette Brown Blackwell, *The Sexes Throughout Nature*, 1875

646　You may try but you can never imagine what it is to have a man's form of genius in you, and to suffer the slavery of being a girl.—George Eliot, *Daniel Deronda*, 1876

647　If a woman possesses manly virtues one should run away from her; and if she does not possess them she runs away from herself.—Friedrich Nietzsche, *Twilight of the Idols*, 1889

648　A woman can be anything that the man who loves her would have her be.—J. M. Barrie, *Tommy and Grizel*, 1900

649　Man proposes, woman forecloses.—Minna Thomas Antrim, *Naked Truth and Veiled Allusions*, 1901

650　Women and elephants never forget an injury.—Saki, *Reginald*, 1904

651　If men knew how women pass the time when they are alone, they'd never marry.—O. Henry, *The Four Million*, 1906

652　We have medicines to make women speak; we have none to make them keep silence.—Anatole France, *The Man Who Married a Dumb Wife*, 1912

653　What breadth, what beauty and power of human nature and development there must be in a woman to get over all the palisades, all the fences, within which she is held captive!—Aleksandr Herzen, *My Past and Thoughts*, 1921

654   Woman is a being dominated by the creative urge and no understanding of her as an individual can be gained unless the significance and effects of that great fact can be grasped.— Beatrice Hinkle, *The Psychology of the Artist*, 1923

655   Women are wiser than men because they know less and understand more.— James Stephens, *The Crock of Gold*, 1930

656   In their quest for rights [women] have naturally placed emphasis on their wrongs, rather than their achievements and possessions, and have retold history as a story of their long Martyrdom.— Mary Ritter Beard, *Understanding Women*, 1931

657   An intelligent woman is a woman with whom one can be as stupid as one wants.— Paul Valéry, *Mauvaises pensées et autres*, 1941

658   All observations point to the fact that the intellectual woman is masculinized; in her, warm, intuitive knowledge has yielded to cold unproductive thinking.— Helene Deutsch, *The Psychology of Women*, 1944–45

659   A woman is handicapped by her sex, and handicaps society, either by slavishly copying the pattern of man's advance in the professions, or by refusing to compete with man at all.— Betty Friedan, *The Feminine Mystique*, 1963

660   Many women do not recognize themselves as discriminated against; no better proof could be found of the totality of their conditioning.— Kate Millett, *Sexual Politics*, 1969

661   Sadly, man recognizes that the ideal, submissive woman he has created for himself is somehow not quite what he wanted.— Eva Figes, *Patriarchal Attitudes*, 1970

662   Because of our social circumstances, male and female are really two cultures and their life experiences are utterly different.— Kate Millett, *Sexual Politics*, 1970

663   Women's Liberation calls it enslavement but the real truth about the sexual revolution is that it has made of sex an almost chaotically limitless and therefore unmanageable realm in the life of women.— Midge Decter, *The New Chastity and Other Arguments Against Women's Liberation*, 1972

664   Growing up female in America. What a liability! You grew up with your ears full of cosmetic ads, love songs, advice columns, whoreoscopes, Hollywood gossip, and moral dilemmas on the level of TV soap operas.— Erica Jong, *Fear of Flying*, 1973

665   Women's battle for financial equality has barely been joined, much less won. Society still traditionally assigns to woman the role of money-handler rather than money-maker.— Paula Nelson, *The Joy of Money*, 1975

666   Theories by women about women have only recently begun to appear in print. Theories by men about women are abundant.— Patricia Meyer Spacks, *The Female Imagination*, 1975

667   Once women begin to question the inevitability of their subordination and to reject the conventions formerly associated with it, they can no longer retreat to the safety of those conventions.— Christopher Lasch, *The Culture of Narcissism*, 1979

668   While men represent powerful activity as assertion and aggression, women in contrast portray acts of nurturance as acts of strength.— Carol Gilligan, *In a Different Voice*, 1982

669   He travels fastest who travels alone, and that goes double for she. Real feminism is spinsterhood.— Florence King, *Reflections in a Jaundiced Eye*, 1989

Flattery

670   Flattery corrupts both the receiver and the giver.— Edmund Burke, *Reflections on the Revolution in France*, 1790

671   Between flattery and admiration there often flows a river of contempt.— Minna Thomas Antrim, *Naked Truth and Veiled Allusions*, 1901

Flirting

672   A smile is the chosen vehicle for all ambiguities.— Herman Melville, *Pierre*, 1852

673   The amount of women in London who flirt with their own husbands is perfectly scandalous. It looks so bad. It is simply washing one's clean linen in public.— Oscar Wilde, *The Importance of Being Earnest*, 1895

674   She gave me a smile I could feel in my hip pocket.— Raymond Chandler, *Farewell My Lovely*, 1940

Food

675   Strange to see how a good dinner and feasting reconciles everybody.— Samuel Pepys, *Diary*, November 9, 1665

676   'Tis a superstition to insist on a special diet. All is made at last of the same chemical atoms.— Ralph Waldo Emerson, *The Conduct of Life*, 1860

677   In America we eat, collectively, with a glum urge for food to fill us. We are ignorant of flavor. We are as a nation taste-blind.— M. F. K. Fisher, *Serve it Forth*, 1937

678   People ask me: "Why do you write about food, and eating, and drinking? Why don't you write about the struggle for power and security, and about love, the way the others do?" The easiest answer is to say that, like most other humans, I am hungry.— M. F. K. Fisher, *The Gastronomical Me*, 1943

Fools

679   Once harm has been done, even a fool understands it.— Homer, *The Iliad*, ca. 700 B.C.

680   Better a witty fool than a foolish wit.— William Shakespeare, *Twelfth Night*, 1601

681   A learned fool is a greater fool than an ignorant fool.— Molière, *The Learned Woman*, 1672

682   The haste of a fool is the slowest thing in the world.— Thomas Shadwell, *A True Widow*, 1679

683   Fools and intelligent people are equally harmless. It is half-fools and the half-intelligent who are the most dangerous.— Johann Wolfgang von Goethe, *Proverbs in Prose*, 1819

684   Strong and sharp as our wit may be, it is not as strong as the memory of fools, nor so keen as their resentment.— Charles Caleb Colton, *Lacon*, 1820–22

685   Let a fool be made serviceable according to his folly.— Joseph Conrad, *Under Western Eyes*, 1911

686   The best servants of the people, like the best valets, must whisper unpleasant truths in the master's ear. It is the court fool, not the foolish courtier, whom the king can least afford to lose.— Walter Lippmann, *A Preface to Politics*, 1914

687   By rights, satire is a lonely and introspective occupation, for nobody can describe a fool to the life without much patient self-inspection.— Frank Moore Colby, *The Colby Essays*, 1926

688   Scratch a king and find a fool!— Dorothy Parker, *Salome's Dancing-Lesson*, 1931

Force

689   Force without reason falls of its own weight.— Horace, *Odes*, 23 B.C.

690   Force and fraud are in war the two cardinal virtues.— Thomas Hobbes, *Leviathan*, 1651

691   Who overcomes / by force hath overcome but half his foe.— John Milton, *Paradise Lost*, 1667

692   Our patience will achieve more than our force.— Edmund Burke, *Reflections on the Revolution in France*, 1790

693   I am not aware that any community has a right to force another to be civilized.— John Stuart Mill, *On Liberty*, 1859

694   Civilization is nothing more than the effort to reduce the use of force to the last resort.— José Ortega y Gasset, *The Revolt of the Masses*, 1930

695   Whatever needs to be maintained through force is doomed.— Henry Miller, *The Wisdom of the Heart*, 1941

Foreign Policy

696   War is not the continuation of policy. It is the breakdown of policy.— Hans von Seeckt, *Thoughts of a Soldier*, 1929

697   Foreign policy is really domestic policy with its hat on.— Hubert H. Humphrey, speech, June 29, 1966

698   The first requirement of a statesman is that he be dull.— Dean Acheson, in *Observer*, June 21, 1970

699   We cannot play innocents abroad in a world that is not innocent.— Ronald Reagan, speech, February 6, 1985

700   Ultimately, the danger is not that military spending no longer is the adjunct of foreign policy, but that foreign policy becomes the adjunct of military spending.— Norman Cousins, *Pathology of Power*, 1987

701   Watching foreign affairs is sometimes like watching a magician; the eye is drawn to the hand performing the dramatic flourishes, leaving the other hand — the one doing the important job — unnoticed.— David K. Shipler, in *New York Times*, March 15, 1987

702   The statesman must weigh the rewards of success against the penalties of failure. And he is permitted only one guess.— Henry Kissinger, in *Newsweek*, October 22, 1990

703   In foreign policy you have to wait twenty-five years to see how it comes out.— James Reston, in *International Herald Tribune*, November 18, 1991

Freedom

704 Man is free the moment he wants to be.— Voltaire, *Brutus*, 1748

705 The poor man is never free; he serves in every country.— Voltaire, *Les Guèbres*, 1769

706 Man in general, if reduced to himself, is too wicked to be free.— Joseph de Maistre, *Four Chapters on Russia*, 1859

707 Liberation is not deliverance.— Victor Hugo, *Les Misérables*, 1862

708 The only thing about liberty that I love is the fight for it; I care nothing about the possession of it.— Henrik Ibsen, letter, February 17, 1871

709 The deadliest form of democracy is not autocracy but liberty frenzied.— Otto Kahn, speech, January 14, 1918

710 There is nothing with which it is so dangerous to take liberties as liberty itself.— André Breton, *Surrealism and Painting*, 1928

711 Freedom is the freedom to say that two plus two makes four. If that is granted, all else follows.— George Orwell, *1984*, 1949

712 Men are created different; they lose their social freedom and their individual autonomy in seeking to become like each other.— David Riesman, *The Lonely Crowd*, 1950

713 Unless a man has the talents to make something of himself, freedom is an irksome burden.— Eric Hoffer, *The True Believer*, 1951

714 It has been well said that a hungry man is more interested in four sandwiches than four freedoms.— Henry Cabot Lodge Jr., in *New York Times*, March 29, 1955

715 Freedom is a hard-bought thing.— Paul Robeson, *Here I Stand*, 1958

716 Liberty does not always have clean hands.— André Malraux, speech, November 12, 1966

717 There's something contagious about demanding freedom.— Robin Morgan, *Sisterhood is Powerful*, 1970

718 Human freedom involves our capacity to pause, to choose the one response toward which we wish to throw our weight.— Rollo May, *The Courage to Create*, 1975

719 We who officially value freedom of speech above life itself seem to have nothing to talk about but the weather.— Barbara Ehrenreich, *The Worst Years of Our Lives*, 1985

Friendship

720 Old friendships are like meats served up repeatedly, cold, comfortless, and distasteful. The stomach turns against them.— William Hazlitt, *The Plain Speaker*, 1826

721 The holy passion of friendship is of so sweet and steady and loyal and enduring a nature that it will last through a whole lifetime, if not asked to lend money.— Mark Twain, *Pudd'nhead Wilson*, 1894

722 The path of social advancement is, and must be, strewn with broken friendships.— H. G. Wells, *Kipps*, 1905

Future

723   If nations always moved from one set of furnished rooms to another — and always into a better set — things might be easier, but the trouble is that there is no one to prepare the new rooms. The future is worse than the ocean — there is nothing there.— Aleksandr Herzen, *From the Other Shore*, 1849

724   If you do not think about the future, you cannot have one.— John Galsworthy, *Swan Song*, 1928

Genius

725   When a true genius appears in the world, you may know him by this sign, that the dunces are all in confederacy against him.— Jonathan Swift, *Thoughts on Various Subjects*, 1711

726   There are people who possess not so much genius as a certain talent for perceiving the desires of the century, or even of the decade, before it has done so itself.— G. C. Lichtenberg, *Aphorisms*, 1765–99

727   While Genius was thus wasting his strength in eccentric flights, I saw a person of a very different appearance, named Application.— Anna Letitia Barbauld, *The Hill of Science*, 1773

728   Genius is its own end, and draws its means and the style of its architecture from within.— Ralph Waldo Emerson, *The Method of Nature*, 1841

729   Genius is the ability to see things invisible, to manipulate things intangible, to paint things that have no features.— Joseph Joubert, Pensées, 1842

730   It is not because the touch of genius has roused genius to production, but because the admiration of genius has made talent ambitious, that the harvest is still so abundant.— Margaret Fuller, *Art, Literature and the Drama*, 1858

731   Conceit spoils the finest genius. There is not much danger that real talent or goodness will be overlooked long; even if it is, the consciousness of possessing and using it well should satisfy one.— Louisa May Alcott, *Little Women*, 1868

732   Genius, in truth, means little more than the faculty of perceiving in an unhabitual way.— William James, *Principles of Psychology*, 1890

733   The public is wonderfully tolerant. It forgives everything except genius.— Oscar Wilde, *Intentions: The Critic as Artist*, 1891

734   Men of genius are not quick judges of character. Deep thinking and high imagining blunt that trivial instinct by which you and I size people up.— Max Beerbohm, *And Even Now*, 1920

735   We know that the nature of genius is to provide idiots with ideas twenty years later.— Louis Aragon, *Treatise on Style*, 1928

736   Idleness [is] either enforced or voluntary.— Agatha Christie, *The Moving Finger*, 1941

737   One is not born a genius. One becomes a genius.— Simone de Beauvoir, *The Second Sex*, 1949

738   The function of genius is not to give new answers, but to pose new questions which time and mediocrity can solve.— H. R. Trevor-Roper, *Men and Events*, 1958

739 Genius, like truth, has a shabby and neglected mien.— Edward Dahlberg, *Alms for Oblivion*, 1964

740 Popular in our time, unpopular in his. So runs the stereotype of rejected genius.— Robert Hughes, in *Time*, March 11, 1985

Glory

741 Oh how quickly the glory of the world passes away!— Thomas à Kempis, *Imitation of Christ*, ca. 1420

742 You may my glories and my state depose, / But not my griefs; still I am king of those.— William Shakespeare, *Richard II*, 1595

743 Popularity? It is glory's small change.— Victor Hugo, *Ruy Blas*, 1838

744 Glory is only given to those who have always dreamed of it.— Charles de Gaulle, *Vers l'armée de métier*, 1934

745 Glory is largely a theatrical concept. There is no striving for glory without a vivid awareness of an audience.— Eric Hoffer, *The True Believer*, 1951

Good and Evil

746 Often an entire city has suffered because of an evil man.— Hesiod, *Works and Days*, ca. 700 B.C.

747 I would far rather be ignorant than knowledgeable of evils.— Aeschylus, *The Suppliants*, 5th c. B.C.

748 Evil men by their own nature cannot ever prosper.— Euripedes, *Ion*, ca. 417 B.C.

749 He who is bent on doing evil can never want occasion.— Publilius Syrus, *Moral Sayings*, 1st c. B.C.

750 Ignorance of good and evil is the most upsetting fact of human life.— Cicero, *De Finibus*, ca. 45 B.C.

751 The evil that men do lives after them, / The good is oft interred with their bones.— William Shakespeare, *Julius Caesar*, 1599

752 Virtue is bold, and goodness never fearful.— William Shakespeare, *Measure for Measure*, 1604

753 As the saying is, *homo solus aut deus, aut daemon*: a man alone is either a saint or a devil.— Robert Burton, *The Anatomy of Melancholy*, 1621

754 Good and evil are names that signify our appetites and aversions.— Thomas Hobbes, *Leviathan*, 1651

755 There is hardly a man clever enough to recognize the full extent of the evil he does.— François Duke de La Rochefoucauld, VI, *Maxims*, 1665

756 Men never do evil so completely and cheerfully as when they do it from religious conviction.— Blaise Pascal, *Pensées*, 1670

757 Our greatest evils flow from ourselves.— Jean-Jacques Rousseau, *Émile*, 1762

758 No man chooses evil because it is evil; he only mistakes it for happiness, the good he seeks.— Mary Wollstonecraft, *A Vindication of the Rights of Men*, 1790

759 If it were possible to make an accurate calculation of the evils which police regulations occasion, and of those which they prevent, the number of the former would, in all cases, exceed that of the latter.— Karl Wilhelm, Baron von Humboldt, *Limits of State Action*, 1792

760   Every political good carried to the extreme must be productive of evil.— Mary Wollstonecraft, *The French Revolution*, 1794

761   The greater part of what my neighbors call good I believe in my soul to be bad, and if I repent of anything, it is very likely to be my good behavior.— Henry David Thoreau, Walden, 1854

762   All history treats almost exclusively of wicked men who, in the course of time, have come to be looked upon as good men. All progress is the result of successful crime.— Friedrich Nietzsche, *The Dawn*, 1861

763   As long as war is regarded as wicked, it will always have its fascination. When it is looked upon as vulgar, it will cease to be popular.— Oscar Wilde, *The Critic as Artist,* 1891

764   It is the evil that lies in ourselves that is ever least tolerant of the evil that dwells within others.— Maurice Maeterlinck, *Wisdom and Destiny*, 1898

765   The belief in a supernatural source of evil is not necessary; men alone are quite capable of every wickedness.— Joseph Conrad, *Under Western Eyes*, 1911

766   Nature, in her indifference, makes no distinction between good and evil.— Anatole France, *Crainquebille,* 1916

767   Only among people who think no evil can Evil monstrously flourish.— Logan Pearsall Smith, *Afterthoughts,* 1931

768   There is no explanation for evil. It must be looked upon as a necessary part of the order of the universe. To ignore it is childish; to bewail it senseless.— William Somerset Maugham, *The Summing Up,* 1938

769   Must I do all the evil I can before I learn to shun it? Is it not enough to know the evil to shun it? If not, we should be sincere enough to admit that we love evil too well to give it up.— Mahatma Gandhi, *Non-Violence in Peace and War, Volume 2,* 1949

770   When you choose the lesser of two evils, always remember that it is still an evil.— Max Lerner, *Actions and Passions,* 1949

771   Much of the most important evils that mankind have to consider are those which they inflict upon each other through stupidity or malevolence or both.— Bertrand Russell, *Unpopular Essays,* 1950

772   It is by its promise of a sense of power that evil often attracts the weak.— Eric Hoffer, *The Passionate State of Mind,* 1954

773   Evil alone has oil for every wheel.— Edna St. Vincent Millay, *Mine the Harvest,* 1954

774   The face of "evil" is always the face of total need.— William S. Burroughs, *The Naked Lunch,* 1959

775   The sad truth is that most evil is done by people who never make up their minds to be either good or evil.— Hannah Arendt, in *New Yorker,* December 5, 1977

Gossip

776   No gossip ever dies away entirely, if many people voice it: it too is a kind of divinity.— Hesiod, *Works and Days,* ca. 700 B.C.

777   If you hear that someone is speaking ill of you, instead of trying to defend yourself you should say: "He obviously does not know me very well, since there are so many other faults he could have mentioned.—Epictetus, *Enchiridion*, 2nd c.

778 We are charmed even when they abuse us.—Marie de Sevigne, *Letters of Madame de Sevigne to Her Daughter and Friends*, 1811

779 Gossip is a sort of smoke that comes from the dirty tobacco-pipes of those who diffuse it: it proves nothing but the bad taste of the smoker.—George Eliot, *Daniel Deronda*, 1876

780 There is only one thing in the world worse than being talked about, and that is not being talked about.—Oscar Wilde, *The Picture of Dorian Gray*, 1891

781 No one gossips about other people's secret virtues.—Bertrand Russell, *On Education*, 1926

782 While gossip among women is universally ridiculed as low and trivial, gossip among men, especially if it is about women, is called theory, or idea, or fact.—Andrea Dworkin, *Right-Wing Women*, 1978

Government

783 It is very easy to accuse a government of imperfection, for all mortal things are full of it.—Michel Eyquem de Montaigne, *Essays*, 1580

784 The pleasure of governing must certainly be exquisite, if we may judge from the vast numbers who are eager to be concerned with it.—Voltaire, *Philosophical Dictionary*, 1764

785 Society is produced by our wants and government by our wickedness.—Thomas Paine, *Common Sense*, 1776

786 A government of statesmen or of clerks? Humbug or Humdrum?—Benjamin Disraeli, *Coningsby*, 1844

787 If government knew how, I should like to see it check, not multiply, the population. When it reaches its true law of action, every man that is born will be hailed as essential.—Ralph Waldo Emerson, *The Conduct of Life*, 1860

788 The chief element in the art of statesmanship under modern conditions is the ability to elucidate the confused and clamorous interests which converge upon the seat of government.—Walter Lippmann, *A Preface to Morals*, 1929

789 The Senate is the only show in the world where the cash customers have to sit in the balcony.—Gracie Allen, *How to Become President*, 1940

790 To the believer [Marxism] presents, first, a system of ultimate ends that embody the meaning of life and are absolute standards by which to judge events and actions.—Joseph A. Schumpeter, *Capitalism, Socialism and Democracy*, 1942

791 It is a function of government to invent philosophies to explain the demands of its own convenience.—Murray Kempton, *America Comes of Middle Age*, 1963

792 To govern is always to choose among disadvantages.—Charles de Gaulle, in *New York Times*, November 14, 1965

793 Anything that the private sector can do, the government can do it worse.—Dixy Lee Ray, in *Mother Jones*, May, 1977

794   Giving money and power to government is like giving whiskey and car keys to teenage boys.— P. J. O'Rourke, *Parliament of Whores,* 1991

Gratitude

---

795   Whoever has lived long enough to find out what life is, knows how deep a debt of gratitude we owe to Adam, the first great benefactor of our race. He brought death into the world.— Mark Twain, *Pudd'nhead Wilson,* 1894

796   The debt of gratitude we owe our mother and father goes forward, not backward. What we owe our parents is the bill presented to us by our children.— Nancy Friday, *My Mother/ My Self,* 1977

Greatness

---

797   The bravest sight in the world is to see a great man struggling against adversity.— Seneca, *De Providentia,* 1st c.

798   No great thing is created suddenly.— Epictetus, *Discourses,* 2nd c.

799   Greatness knows itself.— William Shakespeare, *Henry IV, Part I,* 1597

800   Desire of greatness is a godlike sin.— John Dryden, *Absalom and Achitophel,* 1681

801   No man was ever great by imitation.— Samuel Johnson, *Rasselas,* 1759

802   A great man does enough for us when he refrains from doing us harm.— Pierre de Beaumarchais, *The Barber of Seville,* 1775

803   Great men, like great cities, have many crooked arts, and dark alleys in their hearts.— Charles Caleb Colton, *Lacon,* 1820–22

804   No man is truly great who is great only in his lifetime. The test of greatness is the page of history.— William Hazlitt, *Table Talk,* 1821–22

805   No sadder proof can be given by a man of his own littleness than disbelief in great men.— Thomas Carlyle, *Heroes and Hero Worship,* 1840

806   A great man's failures to understand define him.— André Gide, *Pretexts,* 1903

807   There are big men, men of intellect, intellectual men, men of talent and men of action; but the great man is difficult to find, and it needs— apart from discernment — a certain greatness to find him.— Margot Asquith, *The Autobiography of Margot Asquith,* 1920

808   Great men are but life-sized. Most of them, indeed, are rather short.— Max Beerbohm, *And Even Now,* 1920

809   Let us never forget that the greatest man is never more than an animal disguised as a god.— Francis Picabia, in *La Vie Moderne,* February 25, 1923

810   The privilege of the great is to see catastrophes from the terrace.— Hyppolyte-Jean Giraudoux, *Tiger at the Gates,* 1935

811   Whom the gods wish to destroy they first call promising.— Cyril Connolly, *Enemies of Promise,* 1938

812   All great deeds and all great thoughts have a ridiculous beginning.— Albert Camus, *The Myth of Sisyphus,* 1942

813   Great men with great truths have seldom had much support from their associates.— Philip Wylie, *Generation of Vipers,* 1942

814 A great man's greatest good luck is to die at the right time.— Eric Hoffer, *The Passionate State of Mind,* 1954

815 As machines become more and more efficient and perfect, so it will become clear that imperfection is the greatness of man.— Ernst Fischer, *The Necessity of Art,* 1959

816 Few great men could pass Personnel.— Paul Goodman, *Growing Up Absurd,* 1960

817 Nothing so comforts the military mind as the maxim of a great but dead general. — Barbara Tuchman, *The Guns of August,* 1962

818 I have found that great people do have in common an immense belief in themselves and in their mission. They also have great determination as well as an ability to work hard. At the crucial moment of decision, they draw on their accumulated wisdom.— Yousuf Karsh, in *Parade,* December 3, 1978

Grief

819 See how time makes all grief decay.— Adelaide A. Proctor, *Life in Death,* 1869

820 Grief can take care of itself, but to get the full value of a joy you must have somebody to divide it with.— Mark Twain, *Following the Equator,* 1897

Happiness

821 Only when a man's life comes to its end in prosperity can one call that man happy.— Aeschylus, *Agamemnon,* 5th c. B.C.

822 Even in the common affairs of life, in love, friendship, and marriage how little security have we when we trust our happiness in the hand of others.— William Hazlitt, *Table Talk,* 1822

823 We are never happy; we can only remember that we were so once.— Alexander Smith, *Dreamthorp,* 1863

824 It is only when we are very happy that we can bear to gaze merrily upon the vast and limitless expanse of water, rolling on and on with such persistent, irritating monotony, to the accompaniment of our thoughts, whether grave or gay.— Baroness Emmuska Orczy, *The Scarlet Pimpernel,* 1905

825 There is something curiously boring about somebody else's happiness.— Aldous Huxley, *Limbo,* 1920

826 The world of the happy is quite different from that of the unhappy.— Ludwig Wittgenstein, *Tractatus Logico-Philosophicus,* 1922

Heroism

827 To have no heroes is to have no aspiration, to live on the momentum of the past, to be thrown back upon routine, sensuality, and the narrow self.— Charles Horton Cooley, *Human Nature and the Social Order,* 1902

828   Heroes are created by popular demand, sometimes out of the scantiest materials, or none at all.— Gerald White Johnson, *American Heroes and Hero-Worship*, 1943

829   Show me a hero and I will write you a tragedy.— F. Scott Fitzgerald, *The Crack-Up*, 1945

830   History selects its heroes and its villains, and few of us resist participation either at the parade or at the guillotine.— William F. Buckley, Jr., *The Jeweler's Eye*, 1968

831   What is a society without a heroic dimension?— Jean Baudrillard, *America*, 1986

832   The fame of heroes owes little to the extent of their conquests and all to the success of the tributes paid to them. – Jean Genet, *Prisoner of Love*, 1986

History

833   History can be well written only in a free country.— Voltaire, letter, May 27, 1737

834   Only through history does a nation become completely conscious of itself. Accordingly, history is to be regarded as the national conscience of the human race.— Arthur Schopenhauer, *The World as Will and Idea*, 1819

835   Custom is despot of mankind.— Aleksandr Pushkin, *Eugene Onegin*, 1823

836   History is after all nothing but a pack of tricks which we play upon the dead.— Voltaire, in J. Morley, *Voltaire*, 1828

837   The historian's first duties are sacrilege and the locking of false gods. They are his indispensable instruments for establishing the truth.— Jules Michelet, *Historie de France*, 1833–67

838   All true histories contain instruction; though, in some, the treasure may be hard to find, and when found, so trivial in quantity that the dry, shriveled kernel scarcely compensates for the trouble of cracking the nut.— Anne Brontë, *Agnes Grey*, 1847

839   History is a gallery of pictures in which there are few originals and many copies.— Alexis de Tocqueville, *The Old Regime and the French Revolution*, 1856

840   The talent of historians lies in their creating a true ensemble out of facts which are but half true.— Joseph-Ernest Renan, *La Vie de Jésus*, 1863

841   The best history is but like the art of Rembrandt; it casts a vivid light on certain selected causes, on those which were best and greatest; it leaves all the rest in shadow and unseen.— Walter Bagehot, *Physics and Politics*, 1872

842   Only strong personalities can endure history, the weak ones are extinguished by it.— Friedrich Nietzsche, *Thoughts out of Season*, 1874

843   All the historical books which contain no lies are extremely tedious.— Anatole France, *The Crime of Sylvestre Bonnard*, 1881

844   History, that excitable and lying old lady.— Guy de Maupassant, *On the Water*, 1888

845   The one duty we owe to history is to rewrite it.— Oscar Wilde, *The Critic as Artist*, 1891

846   The very ink in which history is written is merely fluid prejudice.— Mark Twain, *Following the Equator*, 1897

847   The historian is a prophet in reverse.— Friedrich von Schlegel, *Athenaeum*, 1798–1800

848   We learn from history that we learn nothing from history.— George Bernard Shaw, *Man and Superman*, 1903

849   The historian, essentially, wants more documents than he can really use; the dramatist only wants more liberties than he can really take.— Henry James, *The Aspern Papers*, 1909

850   It is not the historian's business to be complimentary; it is his business to lay bare the facts of the case, as he understands them dispassionately, impartially and without ulterior motives. — Lytton Strachey, *Eminent Victorians*, 1918

851   History is the study of other people's mistakes.— Philip Guedalla, *Supers and Supermen*, 1920

852   Human history becomes more and more a race between education and catastrophe.— H. G. Wells, *The Outline of History*, 1920

853   Events in the past may be roughly divided into those which probably never happened and those which do not matter. This is what makes the trade of historian so attractive.— William Ralph Inge, *Assessments and Anticipations*, 1929

854   History is not what you thought. It is what you can remember. All other history defeats itself.— W. C. Sellar, *1066 and All That*, 1930

855   History is principally the inaccurate narration of events which ought not to have happened.— Ernest Albert Hooten, *Twilight of Man*, 1939

856   To study history means submitting to chaos and nevertheless retaining faith in order and meaning. It is a very serious task, young man, and possibly a tragic one.— Hermann Hesse, *The Glass Bead Game*, 1943

857   History does not long entrust the care of freedom to the weak or the timid.— Dwight D. Eisenhower, Inaugural address, January 20, 1953

858The past is a foreign country; they do things differently there.— L. P. Hartley, *The Go-Between*, 1953

859   In the tumult of men and events, solitude was my temptation; now it is my friend. What other satisfaction can be sought once you have confronted History?— Charles de Gaulle, *War Memoirs*, 1959

860   History is the transformation of tumultuous conquerors into silent footnotes.— Paul Eldridge, *Maxims for a Modern Man*, 1965

861   The only thing new in the world is the history you don't know.— Harry S Truman, in M. Miller, *Plain Speaking: An Oral Biography of Harry S Truman*, 1974

862   The past is the only dead thing that smells sweet.— Cyril Connolly, in D. Pryce-Jones, *Journal and Memoir*, 1983

863   We are like ignorant shepherds living on a site where great civilizations once flourished. The shepherds play with the fragments that pop up to the surface, having no notion of the beautiful structures of which they were once a part.— Allan Bloom, *The Closing of the American Mind*, 1987

864   If past history was all there was to the game, the richest people would be librarians.— Warren Buffett, in *Washington Post*, April 17, 1988

865   Does history repeat itself, the first time as tragedy, the second time as farce? No, that's too grand, too considered a

process. History just burps, and we taste again that raw-onion sandwich it swallowed centuries ago.— Julian Barnes, *A History of the World in 101/2 Chapters*, 1989

866   We live in a world where amnesia is the most wished-for state. When did history become a bad word?— John Guare, in *International Herald Tribune*, June 13, 1990

Honesty

867   Found a Society of Honest Men, and all the thieves will join it.— Alain, *Propos d'un Normand*, 1906–14

868   Honest men are the fools and the saints, and you and I are neither.— Taylor Caldwell, *Dynasty of Death*, 1938

Honor

869   Dishonor will not trouble me, once I am dead.— Euripedes, *Alcestis*, 438 B.C.

870   When neither their property nor their honor is touched, the majority of men live content.— Niccolò Machiavelli, *The Prince*, 1513

871   Honor, / How much we fight with weakness to preserve thee.— John Ford, *The Broken Heart*, 1633

872   Honor, without money, is just a disease.— Jean-Baptiste Racine, *Les Plaindeurs*, 1668

873   The louder he talked of his honor, the faster we counted our spoons.—

Ralph Waldo Emerson, *The Conduct of Life*, 1860

Hope

874   He that liveth in hope danceth without music.— George Herbert, *Outlandish Proverbs*, 1940

875   When hopes and dreams are loose in the streets, it is well for the timid to lock doors, shutter windows and lie low until the wrath has passed.— Eric Hoffer, *The True Believer*, 1951

Humility

876   What is most needed for learning is a humble mind.— Confucius, *The Book of History*, ca. 500 B.C.

877   Humility is a virtue all preach, none practice, and yet everybody is content to hear. The master thinks it good doctrine for his servant, the laity for the clergy, and the clergy for the laity.— John Selden, *Table Talk*, 1686

Humor

878   A sense of humor judges one's actions and the actions of others from a wider reference and finds them incongruous. It dampens enthusiasm; it mocks hope; it pardons shortcomings; it consoles failure. It recommends moderation.— Thornton Wilder, *The Eighth Day*, 1967

879   Humor comes from self-confidence. There's an aggressive element to wit.— Rita Mae Brown, *Starting From Scratch*, 1988

880   Wit penetrates; humor envelops. Wit is a function of verbal intelligence; humor is imagination operating on good nature.— Peggy Noonan, *What I Saw at the Revolution*, 1990

Husbands

881   The lame man makes the best husband.— Athenaeus, *Deipnosophistai*, ca. 200

882   He is dreadfully married. He's the most married man I ever saw in my life.— Artemus Ward, *Artemus Ward's Lecture*, 1869

883   Marrying a man is like buying something you've been admiring for a long time in a shop window. You may love it when you get it home, but it doesn't always go with everything else in the house.— Jean Kerr, *The Snake Has All the Lines*, 1960

Hypocrisy

884   No habit or quality is more easily acquired than hypocrisy, nor any thing sooner learned than to deny the sentiments of our hearts but the seeds of every passion are innate to us, and nobody comes into the world without them.— Bernard Mandeville, *The Fable of the Bees*, 1714

885   In all ages, hypocrites, called priests, have put crowns upon the heads of thieves, called kings.— Robert G. Ingersoll, *Prose-Poems and Selections*, 1884

886   If it were not for the intellectual snobs who pay— in solid cash— the arts would perish with their starving practitioners. Let us thank heaven for hypocrisy.— Aldous Huxley, *Jesting Pilate*, 1926

887   All I can say is, if you cannot ride two horses, you have no right in the circus.— James Maxton, in *Daily Herald*, January 12, 1931

Idealism

888   Don't use that foreign word, "ideals." We have that excellent native word "lies."— Henrik Ibsen, *The Wild Duck*, 1884

889   An ideal is a port toward which we resolve to steer.— Felix Adler, *Life and Destiny*, 1903

890   All idealism is falsehood in the face of necessity. Friedrich Nietzsche, *Ecce Homo, Part II*, 1908

891   In our ideals we unwittingly reveal our vices.— Jean Rostand, *Julien on une conscience*, 1928

892   When they come downstairs from their Ivory Towers, Idealists are apt to walk straight into the gutter.— Logan Pearsall Smith, *Afterthoughts*, 1931

893   The road from political idealism to political realism us strewn with corpses of our dead selves.— André Malraux, in *Saturday Review*, December 9, 1961

Ideas

894   The best ideas are common property.— Seneca, *Epistles*, 1st c.

895   Uniform ideas originating among entire peoples unknown to each other must have a common ground of truth.— Giambattista Vico, *The New Science*, 1744

896   Nothing is so perfectly amusing as a total change of ideas.— Laurence Sterne, *Tristram Shandy*, 1760–67

897   Ideas too are a life and a world.— G. C. Lichtenberg, *Aphorisms*, 1765 — 99

898   I've dreamt in my life dreams that have stayed with me ever after, and changed my ideas: they've gone through and through me, like wine through water, and altered the color of my mind.— Emily Brontë, *Wuthering Heights*, 1847

899   Harold, like the rest of us, had many impressions which saved him the trouble of distinct ideas.— George Eliot, *Felix Holt, The Radical*, 1866

900   One of the greatest pains to human nature is the pain of a new idea.— Walter Bagehot, *Physics and Politics*, 1869

901   If we had a keen vision and feeling it would be like hearing the grass grow and the squirrel's heart beat, and we should die of the roar which lies on the other side of silence. As it is, the quickest of us walk about well wadded with stupidity.— George Eliot, *Middlemarch*, 1872

902   A fixed idea ends in madness or heroism.— Victor Hugo, *Quatre-vingt-treize*, 1879

903   The value of an idea has nothing whatsoever to do with the sincerity of the man who expresses it.— Oscar Wilde, *The Picture of Dorian Gray*, 1891

904   Ideas rose in clouds; I felt them collide until pairs interlocked, so to speak, making a stable combination.— Henri Poincaré, *Mathematical Creation*, 1908

905   To die for an idea is to place a pretty high price upon conjectures.— Anatole France, *Le Révolte des Anges*, 1914

906   A powerful idea communicates some of its strength to him who challenges it.— Marcel Proust, *Remembrance of Things Past*, 1918

907   To die for an idea; it is unquestionably noble. But how much nobler it would be if men died for ideas that were true!— H. L. Mencken, *Prejudices, First Series*, 1919

908   A "new thinker," when studied closely, is merely a man who does not know what other people have thought.— Frank Moore Colby, *The Margin of Hesitation*, 1921

909   Life has taught me to think, but thinking has not taught me how to live.— Aleksandr Herzen, *My Past and Thoughts*, 1921

910   The censor can decapitate ideas which but for him might have lived forever.— Heywood C. Broun, *Pieces of Hate*, 1922

911   Ideas are fatal to caste.— E. M. Forster, *A Passage to India*, 1924

912   Nothing is more dangerous than an idea, when a man has only one idea.— Alain, *Propos sue la religion*, 1938

913   There is no adequate defense, except stupidity, against the impact of a new idea.— Percy W. Bridgman, *The Intelligent Individual and Society*, 1938

914 People find ideas a bore because they do not distinguish between live ones and stuffed ones on a shelf.— Ezra Pound, *Guide to Kulchur*, 1938

915 These people who are always briskly doing something and as busy as waltzing mice, they have little, sharp, staccato ideas, such as: "I see where I can make an annual cut of $3.47 in my meat budget." But they have no slow, big ideas.— Brenda Ueland, *If You Want to Write*, 1938

916 It is better to entertain an idea than to take it home to live with you for the rest of your life.— Randall Jarrell, *Pictures from an Institution*, 1954

917 Ideas are refined and multiplied in the commerce of minds. In their splendor, images effect a very simple communion of souls.— Gaston Bachelard, *The Poetics of Reverie*, 1960

918 Ideas improve. The meaning of words participates in the improvement. Plagiarism is necessary. Progress implies it. It embraces an author's phrase, makes use of his expressions, erases a false idea, and replaces it with the right idea.— Guy Debord, *The Society of the Spectacle*, 1967

919 Lying in bed just before going to sleep is the worst time for organized thinking; it is the best time for free thinking. Ideas drift like clouds in an undecided breeze, taking first this direction and then that.— E. L. Konigsburg, *The Mixed-Up Files of Mrs. Basil E. Frankweiler*, 1967

920 To shoot a man because one disagrees with his interpretation of Darwin or Hegel is a sinister tribute to the supremacy of ideas in human affairs— but

a tribute nevertheless.— George Steiner, *Language and Silence*, 1967

921 I have always fought for ideas— until I learned that it isn't ideas but grief, struggle, and flashes of vision which enlighten.— Margaret Anderson, *The Strange Necessity*, 1969

922 Ideas are powerful things, requiring not a studious contemplation but an action, even if it is only an inner action. Their acquisition obligates each man in some way to change his life, even if it is only his inner life. They demand to be stood for.— Midge Decter, *The Liberated Woman and Other Americans*, 1971

923 He arrived at ideas the slow way, never skating over the clear, hard ice of logic, nor soaring on the slipstreams of imagination, but slogging, plodding along on the heavy ground of existence.— Ursula Le Guin, *The Lathe of Heaven*, 1971

924 Ideas move rapidly when their time comes.— Carolyn Heilbrun, *Toward a Recognition of Androgyny*, 1973

925 If you do not express your own original ideas, if you do not listen to your own being, you will have betrayed yourself. Also, you will have betrayed your community in failing to make your contribution.— Rollo May, 1975

926 Great people talk about ideas, average people talk about things, and small people talk about wine.— Fran Lebowitz, *Social Studies*, 1977

927 There are no new ideas still waiting in the wings to save us as women, as human. There are only old and forgotten ones, new combinations, extrapolations and recognitions from within ourselves— along with the renewed courage to try them out.— Audre Lorde, *Poetry Is Not a Luxury*, 1977

928 A sensation must have fallen very low to deign to turn into an idea.— Emile M. Cioran, *Anathemas and Admirations*, 1986

929 The value of an idea lies in the using of it.— Thomas Edison, in *Government Executive*, 1987

930 I don't believe in miracles because it's been a long time since we've had any.— Joseph Heller, *A World of Ideas*, 1989

931 We all live every day in virtual environments, defined by our ideas.— Michael Crichton, *Disclosure*, 1994

Identity

932 What is called an acute knowledge of human nature is mostly nothing but the observer's own weaknesses reflected back from others.— G. C. Lichtenberg, *Aphorisms*, 1765 — 99

933 A strong sense of identity gives man an idea he can do no wrong; too little accomplishes the same.— Djuna Barnes, *Nightwood*, 1937

934 Identity is a bag and a gag. Yet it exists for me with all the force of a fatal disease. Obviously I am here, a mind and a body. To say there's no proof my body exists would be arty and specious and if my mind is more ephemeral, less provable .— Judith Rossner, *Nine Months in the Life of an Old Maid*, 1969

Idleness

935 Idleness is an appendix to nobility.— Robert Burton, *Anatomy of Melancholy*, 1621

936 Idleness, like kisses, to be sweet must be stolen.— Jerome K. Jerome, *Idle Thoughts of an Idle Fellow*, 1889

937 Let us be grateful to Adam, our benefactor. He cut us out of the "blessing" of idleness and won for us the "curse" of labor.— Mark Twain, Following the Equator, 1897

938 The soul is made for action, and cannot rest till it be employed. Idleness is its rust. Unless it will up and think and taste and see, all is in vain.— Thomas Traherne, *Centuries*, 1908

939 It is in our idleness, in our dreams, that the submerged truth sometimes comes to the top.— Virginia Woolf, *A Room of One's Own*, 1929

940 There is nothing worse than an idle hour, with no occupation offering. People who have many such hours are simply animals waiting docilely for death. We all come to that state soon or late. It is the curse of senility.— H. L. Mencken, Minority Report, 1956

941 Idle people are often bored and bored people, unless they sleep a lot, are cruel. It is not accident that boredom and cruelty are great preoccupations in our time.— Renata Adler, *Speedboat*, 1976

Ignorance

942 There is no sin but ignorance.— Christopher Marlowe, *The Jew of Malta*, 1589

943 I never met a man so ignorant that I could not learn something from him.— Galileo Galilei, *Dialogues concerning Two New Sciences*, 1638

944   Ignorance is a voluntary misfortune.— Nicholas Ling, *Politeaphuia*, 1669

945   I do not believe in the collective wisdom of individual ignorance.— Thomas Carlyle, The Age of Reason, 1794

946   There is nothing more frightful than ignorance in action.— Johann Wolfgang von Goethe, *Proverbs in Prose*, 1819

947   To be conscious that you are ignorant is a great step to knowledge.— Benjamin Disraeli, *Sybil*, 1845

948   It is fortunate that each generation does not comprehend its own ignorance. We are thus enabled to call our ancestors barbarous.— Charles Dudley Warner, *Backlog Studies*, 1873

949   Ignorance gives one a large range of probabilities.— George Eliot, *Daniel Deronda*, 1876

950   Ignorance of the past does not guarantee freedom from its imperfections.— Reinhold Niebuhr, *Leaves from the Notebook of a Tamed Cynic*, 1930

951   I can stand what I know. It's what I don't know that frightens me.— Frances Newton, *Light, Like the Sun*, 1937

952   In expanding the field of knowledge we but increase the horizon of ignorance.— Henry Miller, *The Wisdom of the Heart*, 1941

953   Ignorance is not bliss— it is oblivion.— Philip Wylie, *Generation of Vipers*, 1942

954   Ignorance is an evil weed, which dictators may cultivate among their dupes, but which no democracy can afford among its citizens.— W. H. Beveridge, *Full Employment in a Full Society*, 1944

955   Nothing in the world is more dangerous than sincere ignorance and conscientious stupidity.— Martin Luther King, Jr., *Strength to Love*, 1963

956   Only the ignorant know everything.— Dagobert D. Runes, *Treasury of Thought*, 1966

957   It is certain, in any case, that ignorance, allied with power, is the most ferocious enemy justice can have.— James Baldwin, *The Price of The Ticket*, 1972

958   He always said she was smart, but their conversations were a mined field in which at any moment she might make the wrong verbal move and find her ignorance exploding in her face.— Judith Rossner, *Looking for Mr. Goodbar*, 1975

Illusion

959   For what we call illusions are often, in truth, a wider vision of past and present realities— a willing movement of a man's soul with the larger sweep of the world's forces— a movement towards a more assured end than the chances of a single life.— George Eliot, *Felix Holt, The Radical*, 1866

960   Illusion is an anodyne, bred by the gap between wish and reality.— Herman Wouk, *War and Remembrance*, 1985

Imagination

961   It is often said that men are ruled by their imaginations; but it would be truer to say they are governed by the weakness of their imaginations.— Walter Bagehot, *The English Constitution*, 1867

962   To know is nothing at all; to imagine is everything.— Anatole France, *The Crime of Sylvestre Bonnard*, 1881

963   Reality seems valueless by comparison with the dreams of fevered imaginations; reality is therefore abandoned.— Emile Durkheim, *Suicide*, 1897

964   Only in men's imagination does every truth find an effective and undeniable existence. Imagination, not invention, is the supreme master of art as of life.— Joseph Conrad, *A Personal Record*, 1912

965   Nature uses human imagination to lift her work of creation to even higher levels.— Luigi Pirandello, *Six Characters in Search of an Author*, 1921

966   Fear of error which everything recalls to me at every moment of the flight of my ideas, this mania for control, makes men prefer reason's imagination to the imagination of the senses. And yet it is always the imagination alone which is at work.— Louis Aragon, *Paris Peasant*, 1926

967   Every great advance in science has issued from a new audacity of imagination.— John Dewey, *The Quest for Certainty*, 1929

968   There is no connection between the political ideas of our educated class and the deep places of the imagination.— Lionel Trilling, *The Liberal Imagination*, 1950

969   People without imagination are beginning to tire of the importance attached to comfort, to culture, to leisure, to all that destroys imagination.— Raoul Vaneigem, *The Revolution of Everyday Life*, 1967

970   Imagination is the outreaching of mind, the bombardment of the conscious mind with ideas, impulses, images and every sort of psychic phenomena welling up from the preconscious. It is the capacity to "dream dreams and see visions."— Rollo May, *The Courage to Create*, 1975

971   Inspiring visions rarely (I'm tempted to say never) include numbers.— Tom Peters, *Thriving on Chaos*, 1987

972   The power of imagination created the illusion that my vision went much farther than the naked eye could actually see.— Nelson Mandela, *Higher Than Hope*, 1991

Individuality

973   Individualism is rather like innocence; there must be something unconscious about it.— Louis Kronenberger, *Company Manners*, 1954

974   A child develops individuality long before he develops taste. I have seen my kid straggle into the kitchen in the morning with outfits that need only one accessory — an empty bottle of gin.— Erma Bombeck, *If Life is a Bowl of Cherries, What Am I Doing in the Pits*, 1971

975   It takes great courage to break with one's past history and stand alone.— Marion Woodman, *Addiction to Perfection: The Still Unravished Bride*, 1982

Infatuation

976   Those who love fashion their own dreams.— Virgil, *Eclogues*, 37 B.C.

977   Many a man in love with a dimple makes the mistake of marrying the whole girl.— Stephen Leacock, *Literary Lapses*, 1910

Information

978   Information's pretty thin stuff, unless mixed with experience.— Clarence Day, *The Crow's Nest*, 1921

979   Despite the continuing expansion or even explosion of information, there will forever be limits beyond which the devices of science cannot lead a man.— June Singer, *Boundaries of the Soul*, 1972

980   Were one merely to seek information, one should inquire of the man who hates, but if one wishes to know what truly is, one better ask the one who loves.— Hermann Broch, *The Spell*, 1976

Injustice

981   The strictest justice is sometimes the greatest injustice.— Terence, *Heuaton Timorumenos*, 163 B.C.

982   The danger of success is that it makes us forget the world's dreadful injustice.— Jules Renard, *Journal*, 1908

983   Philanthropy is commendable, but it must not cause the philanthropist to overlook the circumstances of economic injustice which make philanthropy necessary.— Martin Luther King, Jr., *Strength to Love*, 1963

Intellect and Intellectuals

984   The most intellectual of men are moved quite as much by the circumstances which they are used to as by their own will. The active voluntary part of a man is very small, and if it were not economized by a sleepy kind of habit, its results would be null.— Walter Bagehot, *The English Constitution*, 1867

985   Only those who know the supremacy of the intellectual life can understand the grief of one who falls from that serene activity into the absorbing soul-wasting struggle with worldly annoyances.— George Eliot, Middlemarch, 1872

986   The mind is like a richly woven tapestry in which the colors are distilled from the experiences of the senses, and the design drawn from the convolutions of the intellect.— Carson McCullers, *Reflections on a Golden Eye*, 1941

987   Men are not narrow in their intellectual interests by nature; it takes special and vigorous training to accomplish that end.— Jacob Viner, *Scholarship in Graduate Training*, 1953

988   One of the functions of intelligence is to take account of the dangers that come from trusting solely to the intelligence.— Lewis Mumford, *The Transformation of Man*, 1956

989   The sign of an intelligent people is their ability to control emotions by the application of reason.— Marya Mannes, *More in Anger*, 1958

990   Intellectual sodomy, which comes from the refusal to be simple about plain matters, is as gross and abundant today

as sexual perversion and they are nowise different from one another.— Edward Dahlberg, *Alms for Oblivion*, 1964

991   It is easier to fake intellect than virginity.— Alexander King, *Rich Man, Poor Man, Freud and Fruit*, 1965

992   It's easy to forget what intelligence consists of: luck and speculation. Here and there a windfall, here and there a scoop.— John LeCarre, *The Looking-Glass War*, 1965

993   Intellect distinguishes between the possible and the impossible; reason distinguishes between the sensible and senseless. Even the possible can be senseless.— Max Born, *My Life and My Views*, 1968

994   Intellectuals are too sentimental for me.— Margaret Anderson, *The Strange Necessity*, 1969

995   I've always felt that a person's intelligence is directly reflected by the number of conflicting points of view he can entertain simultaneously on the same topic.— Lisa Alther, *Kinflicks*, 1977

996   Intelligence is really a kind of taste: taste in ideas.— Susan Sontag, *On Photography*, 1977

997   To accuse another of having weak kidneys, lungs, or heart, is not a crime; on the contrary, saying he has a weak brain is a crime.— Primo Levi, *Other People's Trades*, 1985

998   There's always something suspect about an intellectual on the winning side.— Václav Havel, *Disturbing the Peace*, 1986

999   Is an intelligent human being likely to be much more than a large-scale manufacturer of misunderstanding?— Philip Roth, *The Counterlife*, 1986

Intentions

1000   If I knew for a certainty that a man was coming to my house with the conscious design of doing me good, I should run for my life.— Henry David Thoreau, *Walden*, 1854

1001   It is always with the best intentions that the worst work is done.— Oscar Wilde, *Intentions*, 1891

Jealousy

1002   Anger and jealousy can no more bear to lose sight of their objects than love.— George Eliot, *The Mill on the Floss*, 1860

1003   The "Green-Eyed Monster" causes much woe, but the absence of this ugly serpent argues the presence of a corpse whose name is Eros.— Minna Thomas Antrim, *Naked Truth and Veiled Allusions*, 1901

1004   Jealousy is no more than feeling alone against smiling enemies.— Elizabeth Bowen, *The House in Paris*, 1936

1005   To jealousy, nothing is more frightful than laughter.— Françoise Sagan, *La Chamade*, 1965

1006   Jealousy is all the fun you think they had.— Erica Jong, *Fear of Flying*, 1973

1007   Jealousy, he thought, was as physical as fear; the same dryness of the mouth, the thudding heart, the restlessness which destroyed appetite and peace.— P. D. James, *Death of an Expert Witness*, 1977

Journalism

1008 Journalism is a giant catapult set in motion by pygmy hatreds.— Honore de Balzac, *Droll Stories*, 1837

1009 Journalism is popular, but it is popular mainly as fiction. Life is one world, and life seen in the newspapers another.— Gilbert K. Chesterton, *All Things Considered*, 1908

1010 Literature is the art of writing something that will be read twice; journalism what will be grasped at once.— Cyril Connolly, *Enemies of Promise*, 1938

1011 Journalism — an ability to meet the challenge of filling the space.— Rebecca West, in *The New York Herald Tribune*, April 22, 1956

1012 Journalism is in fact history on the run. — Thomas Griffith, *The Waist-High Culture*, 1959

1013 I have read the newspapers avidly. It is my one form of continuous fiction.— Aneurin Bevan, in *The Times*, March 29, 1960

1014 In America, journalism is apt to be regarded as an extension of history: in Britain, as an extension of conversation.— Anthony Sampson, *The Anatomy of Britain*, 1962

1015 The bosses of our mass media, press, radio, film and television, succeed in their aim of taking our minds off disaster. Thus, the distraction they offer demands the antidote of maximum concentration on disaster.— Ernst Fischer, *Art Against Ideology*, 1966

1016 The media transforms the great silence of things into its opposite. Formerly constituting a secret, the real now talks constantly. News reports, information, statistics, and surveys are everywhere.— Michel de Certeau, *The Practice of Everyday Life*, 1974

1017 Journalism constructs momentarily arrested equilibriums and gives disorder an implied order. That is already two steps from reality.— Thomas Griffith, *How True: A Skeptic's Guide to Believing the News*, 1974

1018 It was when "reporters" became "journalists" and when "objectivity" gave way to "searching for the truth," that an aura of distrust and fear arose around the New Journalist.— Georgie Anne Geyer, "Whatever Happened to Lois Lane!," in *Los Angeles Times*, February 4, 1979

1019 Everything is being compressed into tiny tablets. You take a little pill of news every day 23 minutes and that's supposed to be enough.— Walter Cronkite, in *Newsweek*, December 5, 1983

1020 The news is staged, anticipated, reported, analyzed until all interest is wrung from it and abandoned for some new novelty.— Thomas Griffith, in *Time*, December 30, 1985

1021 I see journalists as the manual workers, the laborers of the word. Journalism can only be literature when it is passionate.— Marguerite Duras, *Practicalities*, 1987

1022 The greatest felony in the news business today is to be behind, or to miss a big story. So speed and quantity substitute for thoroughness and quality, for accuracy and context.— Carl Bernstein, in *Guardian*, June 3, 1992

1023 News organizations and some journalists have transformed from their traditional role as watchdogs of power into institutions of power themselves with an ability, indeed, a susceptibility, to abuse that power.— Joan Konner, "The Only Constant is Change," in *Columbia Journalism Review*, January/February, 1993

Judgment

1024   The acknowledgment of ignorance is one of the surest proofs of judgment that I can find.— Michel Eyquem de Montaigne, *Essays*, 1580

1025   Everyone blames his memory; no one blames his judgment.— François Duke de La Rochefoucauld, VI, *Maxims*, 1665

1026   It is the property of fools, to be always judging.— Thomas Fuller, *Gnomologia*, 1732

1027   The number of those who undergo the fatigue of judging for themselves is very small indeed.— Richard Brinsley Sheridan, *The Critic*, 1779

1028   Feeling without judgment is a washy draught indeed; but judgment untempered by feeling is too bitter and husky a morsel for human deglutition.— Charlotte Brontë, *Jane Eyre*, 1847

1029   Nothing is beautiful, only man: on this piece of naïveté rests all aesthetics, it is the first truth of aesthetics. Let us immediately add its second: nothing is ugly but degenerate man — the domain of aesthetic judgment is therewith defined.— Friedrich Nietzsche, *Twilight of the Idols*, 1889

1030   It is a capital mistake to theorize before you have all the evidence. It biases the judgment.— Arthur Conan Doyle, *The Adventures of Sherlock Holmes*, 1891

1031   Organization can never be a substitute for initiative and for judgment.— Louis D. Brandeis, *Business — A Profession*, 1914

1032   Whoever is winning at the moment will always seem to be invincible.— George Orwell, *Shooting an Elephant*, 1950

1033   I have noted that persons with bad judgment are more insistent that we do what they think best.— Lionel Abel, *Important Nonsense*, 1986

1034   A negative judgment gives you more satisfaction than praise, provided it smacks of jealousy.— Jean Baudrillard, *Cool Memories*, 1987

Justice

1035   All virtue is summed up in dealing justly.— Aristotle, *Nicomachean Ethics*, ca. 325 B.C.

1036   The Law speaks too softly to be heard amid the din of arms.— Gaius Marius, statement, ca. 92 B.C.

1037   If the world were just, there would be no need of valor.— Agesilaus, in Plutarch, *Lives*, ca. 1st-2nd c.

1038   Do not expect justice where might is right.— Phaedrus, *Fables*, 1st c.

1039   Men are not hanged for stealing horses, but that horses may not be stolen.— George Savile, *Political, Moral, and Miscellaneous Thoughts and Reflections*, 1750

1040   National injustice is the surest road to national downfall.— William E. Gladstone, speech, 1878

1041   Injustice is relatively easy to bear; what stings is justice.— H. L. Mencken, *Prejudices, Third Series*, 1922

1042   It is easier to fight for principles than to live up to them.— Alfred Adler, *Problems of Neurosis*, 1929

1043   In a free society the state does not administer the affairs of men. It administers justice among men who conduct their own affairs.— Walter Lippmann, *The Good Society*, 1937

1044   Behind the complicated details of the world stand the simplicities: God is good, the grown-up man or woman knows the answer to every question, there is such a thing as truth, and justice is as measured and faultless as a clock.— Graham Henry Greene, *The Ministry of Fear*, 1943

1045   It is better to have a war for justice than peace in injustice.— Charles Péguy, *Basic Verities*, 1943

1046   How fond men are of justice when it comes to judging the crimes of former generations.— Armand Salacrou, *Boulevard Durand*, 1961

1047   Impartiality is not neutrality— it is partiality for justice.— Stanisław J. Lec, *Unkempt Thoughts*, 1962

1048   The acts of people are baffling unless we realize that their wits are disordered. Man is driven to justice by his lunacy.— Edward Dahlberg, *The Carnal Myth*, 1968

Knowledge

1049   This is the bitterest pain among men, to have much knowledge but no power.— Herodotus, *The History*, ca. 450 B.C.

1050   There are three principal means of acquiring knowledge: observation of nature, reflection, and experimentation. Observation collects facts; reflection combines them; experimentation verifies the result of that combination.— Denis Diderot, *On the Interpretation of Nature*, 1753

1051   The desire of knowledge, like the thirst of riches, increases ever with the acquisition of it.— Laurence Sterne, *Tristam Shandy*, 1760

1052   Knowledge is proud that he has learned so much / Wisdom is humble that he knows no more.— William Cowper, *The Task*, 1785

1053   The utmost extent of man's knowledge, is to know that he knows nothing.— Joseph Addison, *Interesting Anecdotes, Memoirs, Allegories, Essays, and Poetical Fragments*, 1794

1054   We do not need to be shoemakers to know if our shoes fit, and just as little have we any need to be professionals to acquire knowledge of matters of universal interest.— Georg Wilhelm Friedrich Hegel, *The Philosophy of Right*, 1821

1055   As the biggest library if it is in disorder is not as useful as a small but well-arranged one, so you may accumulate a vast amount of knowledge but it will be of far less value than a much smaller amount if you have not thought it over for yourself.— Arthur Schopenhauer, *Parerga and Paralipomena*, 1851

1056   Of a truth, Knowledge is power, but it is a power reined by scruple, having a conscience of what must be and what may be.— George Eliot, *Daniel Deronda*, 1876

1057   The strongest knowledge (that of the total unfreedom of the human will) is nonetheless the poorest in successes:

for it always has the strongest opponent, human vanity.— Friedrich Nietzsche, *Assorted Opinions and Maxims*, 1879

1058   Depend upon it there comes a time when for every addition of knowledge you forget something that you knew before. It is of the highest importance, therefore, not to have useless facts elbowing out the useful ones.— Arthur Conan Doyle, *A Study in Scarlet*, 1887

1059   Our treasure lies in the beehive of our knowledge. We are perpetually on the way thither, being by nature winged insects and honey gatherers of the mind.— Friedrich Nietzsche, *The Genealogy of Morals*, 1887

1060   The man of knowledge must be able not only to love his enemies but also to hate his friends.— Friedrich Nietzsche, *Ecce Homo*, 1888

1061   Only the shallow know themselves.— Oscar Wilde, *Phrases and Philosophies for the Use of the Young*, 1894

1062   Knowledge is happiness, because to have knowledge — broad, deep knowledge — is to know true ends from false, and lofty things from low.— Helen Keller, *The Story of My Life*, 1903

1063   Knowledge does not keep any better than fish.— Alfred North Whitehead, *The Aims of Education*, 1929

1064   There can be no knowledge without emotion. We may be aware of a truth, yet until we have felt its force, it is not ours. To the cognition of the brain must be added the experience of the soul.— Arnold Bennett, *The Journals of Arnold Bennett*, 1932

1065   Sin, guilt, neurosis— they are one and the same, the fruit of the tree of knowledge.— Henry Miller, *The Wisdom of the Heart*, 1941

1066   The larger the island of knowledge, the longer the shore line of wonder.— Ralph W. Sockman, *Now to Live!*, 1946

1067   There is no knowledge without a new problem.— Leo Baeck, *Judaism and Science*, 1949

1068   Through the mythology of Einstein, the world blissfully regained the image of knowledge reduced to a formula.— Roland Barthes, Mythologies, 1957

1069   Everything has been said yet few have taken advantage of it. Since all our knowledge is essentially banal, it can only be of value to minds that are not.— Raoul Vaneigem, *The Revolution of Everyday Life*, 1967

1070   I have always suspected that too much knowledge is a dangerous thing. It is a boon to people who don't have deep feelings; their pleasure comes from what they know.— Margaret Anderson, *The Strange Necessity*, 1969

1071   Knowledge is not a loose-leaf notebook of facts.— Jacob Bronowski, *The Ascent of Man*, 1973

1072   The passionate controversies of one era are viewed as sterile preoccupations by another, for knowledge alters what we seek as well as what we find.— Freda Adler, *Sisters in Crime*, 1975

1073   Some knowledge and some song and some beauty must be kept for those days before the world again plunges into darkness.— Marion Zimmer Bradley, *The Mists of Avalon*, 1982

1074   The greatest obstacle to discovery is not ignorance — it is the illusion of knowledge.— Daniel J. Boorstein, in *Washington Post*, January 29, 1984

1075 A novel that does not uncover a hitherto unknown segment of existence is immoral. Knowledge is the novel's only morality.— Milan Kundera, in *New York Review of Books,* July 19, 1984

1076 We do not want our world to perish. But in our quest for knowledge, century by century, we have placed all our trust in a cold, impartial intellect which only brings us nearer to destruction.— Dora Russell, *Challenge to the Cold War,* 1985

1077 Knowledge is the most democratic source of power.— Alvin Toffler, *Powershift: Knowledge, Wealth, and Violence at the Edge of the 21st Century,* 1990

Language

1078 I strive to be brief, and I become obscure.— Horace, *Ars Poetica,* 1st c. B.C.

1079 A plurality of words does not necessarily represent a plurality of things.— Joseph Albo, *Book of Principles,* 1428

1080 They have been at a great feast of languages, and stolen the scraps.— William Shakespeare, *Love's Labor's Lost,* 1594

1081 Words can be treasonable as well as deeds.— Baruch Spinoza, *Tractatus Theologicus-Politicus,* 1670

1082 Language is the expression of ideas, and if the people of one country cannot preserve an identity of ideas they cannot retain an identity of language.— Noah Webster, *American Dictionary of the English Language,* 1828

1083 All words are pegs to hang ideas on.— Henry Ward Beecher, *Proverbs from Plymouth Pulpit,* 1887

1084 It is a sad truth, but we have lost the faculty of giving lovely names to things. Names are everything.— Oscar Wilde, *The Picture of Dorian Gray,* 1891

1085 Nowadays to be intelligible is to be found out.— Oscar Wilde, *Lady Windermere's Fan,* 1892

1086 A good catchword can obscure analysis for fifty years.— Johan Huizinga, *The Waning of the Middle Ages,* 1924

1087 Words form the thread on which we string our experiences.— Aldous Huxley, *The Olive Tree,* 1937

1088 Well-chosen phrases are a great help in the smuggling of offensive ideas.— Vladimir Jabotinsky, *The War and the Jew,* 1942

1089 When an age is in throes of profound transition, the first thing to disintegrate is language.— Rollo May, *Power and Innocence,* 1972

1090 One does not inhabit a country; one inhabits a language. That is our country, our fatherland and no other.— Emile M. Cioran, *Anathemas and Admirations,* 1986

1091 Language, as symbol, determines much of the nature and quality of our experience.— Sonia Johnson, *The Ship That Sailed into the Living Room,* 1991

Laughter

1092 Comedy naturally wears itself out — destroys the very food on which it lives; and by constantly and successfully exposing the follies and weaknesses of mankind to ridicule, in the end leaves itself nothing worth laughing at.— William Hazlitt, *The Round Table*, 1817

1093   Anyone who takes himself too seriously always runs the risk of looking ridiculous; anyone who can consistently laugh at himself does not.— Václav Havel, *Disturbing the Peace*, 1986

Law and Lawyers

1094   Where the laws are not supreme, there demagogues spring up.— Aristotle, *Politics*, 4th c. B.C.

1095   Laws are silent in time of war.— Cicero, *Pro Milone*, 1st c. B.C.

1096   The Law is but words and paper without the hands of swords of men.— James Harrington, *The Commonwealth of Oceana*, 1656

1097   Laws and customs may be creative of vice; and should be therefore perpetually under process of observation and correction: but laws and customs cannot be creative of virtue: they may encourage and help to preserve it; but they cannot originate it.— Harriet Martineau, *Society in America*, 1837

1098   If there were no bad people, there would be no good lawyers.— Charles Dickens, *The Old Curiosity Shop*, 1841

1099   The lawyer's truth is not Truth, but consistency or a consistent expediency.— Henry David Thoreau, *On the Duty of Civil Disobedience*, 1849

1100   The law will never make men free, it is men that have to make the law free.— Henry David Thoreau, *Slavery in Massachusetts*, 1854

1101   The law, in its majestic equality, forbids the rich as well as the poor to sleep under bridges, to beg in the streets, and to steal bread.— Anatole France, *Le Lys rouge*, 1894

1102   To succeed in the other trades, capacity must be shown; in the law, concealment of it will do.— Mark Twain, *Following the Equator*, 1897

1103   A country survives its legislation. That truth should not comfort the conservative nor depress the radical. For it means that public policy can enlarge its scope and increase its audacity, can try big experiments without trembling too much.— Walter Lippmann, *A Preface to Politics*, 1914

1104   In point of substantial merit — the law school belongs in the modern university no more than a school of fencing and dancing.— Thorstein Veblen, *The Higher Learning in America*, 1918

1105   People are getting smarter nowadays; they are letting lawyers, instead of their conscience, be their guide.— Will Rogers, *The Illiterate Digest*, 1924

1106   It is the right of our people to organize to oppose any law and any part of the Constitution with which they are not in sympathy.— Alfred E. Smith, speech, December 2 1927

1107   We all know here that the law is the most powerful of schools for the imagination. No poet ever interpreted nature as freely as a lawyer interprets the truth.— Hyppolyte-Jean Giraudoux, *Tiger at the Gates*, 1935

1108   An unjust law is itself a species of violence.— Mahatma Gandhi, *Non-Violence in Peace and War*, Volume 2, 1949

1109   Life and death do not wait for legal action.— Daphne Du Maurier, *My Cousin Rachel*, 1952

1110   A lawyer with his briefcase can steal more than a hundred men with guns.— Mario Puzo, *The Godfather*, 1969

1111   In the strange heat all litigation brings to bear on things, the very process of litigation fosters the most profound misunderstandings in the world.— Renata Adler, *Reckless Disregard*, 1986

Leadership

1112   Woe to the land that's governed by a child!— William Shakespeare, *Richard III*, 1591

1113   A leader is a dealer in hope.— Napoleon Bonaparte, *Maxims*, 1804–15

1114   A statesman should be possessed of good sense, a primary political quality; and it's fortunate possessor needs a second quality — the courage to show that he has it.   Louis-Adolphe Thiers, speech, May 6, 1834

1115   A great statesman is he who knows when to depart from traditions, as well as when to adhere to them.— John Stuart Mill, *Representative Government*, 1861

1116   The real leader has no need to lead — he is content to point the way.— Henry Miller, *The Wisdom of the Heart*, 1941

1117   Unlucky the country that needs a hero.— Bertolt Brecht, *Leben das Galilei*, 1943

1118   Charlatanism of some degree is indispensable to effective leadership.— Eric Hoffer, *The True Believer*, 1951

1119   People, like sheep, tend to follow a leader — occasionally in the right direction.— Alexander Chase, *Perspectives*, 1966

1120   You can't lead a cavalry charge if you think you look funny on a horse.— John Peers, *1001 Logical Laws*, 1979

1121   In this era of world leadership, the metal detector is the altar and the mini-cam may be god.— Hugh Sidey, in *Time*, June 17, 1984

1122   A leader must have the courage to act against an expert's advice.— James Callaghan, in *The Harvard Business Review*, November 1, 1986

1123   The trick of statesmanship is to turn the inevitable to one's own advantage.— Christopher Layne, in *Atlantic Monthly*, June, 1989

Learning

1124   O! this learning, what a thing it is.— William Shakespeare, *The Taming of the Shrew*, 1596

1125   There is no great concurrence between learning and wisdom.— Francis Bacon, *The Advancement of Learning*, 1605

1126   A little learning is a dangerous thing.— Alexander Pope, *An Essay on Criticism*, 1711

1127   A great deal of learning can be packed into an empty head.— Karl Kraus, *Aphorisms and More Aphorisms*, 1909

1128   There are three ingredients in the good life: learning, earning and yearning.— Christopher Morley, *Parnassus on Wheels*, 1917

1129   Learning carries within itself certain dangers.— Leon Trotsky, *Literature and Revolution*, 1924

1130   Perhaps I am doomed to retrace my steps under the illusion that I am exploring, doomed to try and learn what I should simply recognize, learning a mere fraction of what I have forgotten.— André Breton, *Nadja*, 1928

Leisure

1131   The idea that leisure is of value in itself is only conditionally true. The average man simply spends his leisure as a dog spends it. His recreations are all puerile, and the time supposed to benefit him really only stupefies him.— H. L. Mencken, Minority Report, 1956

1132   We are closer to the ants than to butterflies. Very few people can endure much leisure.— Gerald Brenan, *Thoughts in a Dry Season*, 1979

Lies

1133   A liar should have a good memory.— Quintilian, *Institutio Oratorio*, 1st c. A.D.

1134   The most dangerous untruths are truths slightly distorted.— G. C. Lichtenberg, *Aphorisms*, 1765

1135   Convictions are more dangerous to truth than lies.— Friedrich Nietzsche, *All Too Human*, 1878

1136   The cruelest lies are often told in silence.— Robert Louis Stevenson, *Virginibus Puerisque*, 1881

1137   Some people are under the impression that all that is required to make a good fisherman is the ability to tell lies easily and without blushing; but this is a mistake.— Jerome K. Jerome, *Three Men in a Boat*, 1889

1138   Telling lies is a fault in a boy, an art in a lover, an accomplishment in a bachelor, and second-nature in a married man.— Helen Rowland, *A Guide to Men*, 1922

1139   Lies, injustice, and hypocrisy are a part of every ordinary community. Most people achieve a sort of protective immunity, a kind of callousness, toward them. If they didn't, they couldn't endure.— Nella Larsen, *Quicksand*, 1928

1140   It is only in lies, wholeheartedly and bravely told, that human nature attains through words and speech the forbearance, the nobility, the romance, the idealism, that it falls so short of in fact and in deeds.— Clare Boothe Luce, in *Vanity Fair*, October, 1930

1141   Falsity cannot keep an idea from being beautiful; there are certain errors of such ingenuity that one could regret their not ranking among the achievements of the human.— Jean Rostand, *Pensées d'un Biologiste*, 1939

1142   In human relations kindness and lies are worth a thousand truths.— Graham Henry Greene, *The Heart of the Matter*, 1948

1143   Gradually I came to realize that people will more readily swallow lies than truth, as if the taste of lies was homey, appetizing: a habit.— Martha Gellhorn, *The Face of War*, 1959

Life

1144   Men of age object too much, consult too long, adventure too little, repent too soon, and seldom drive business home to the full period, but content themselves with a mediocrity of success.— Francis Bacon, *Essays*, 1597–1625

1145 We are the creatures of imagination, passion, and self-will, more than of reason or even of self-interest. Even in the common transactions and daily intercourse of life, we are governed by whim, caprice, prejudice, or accident.— William Hazlitt, *On the Predominant Principles and Excitements in the Human Mind*, in *Examine*, February 26, 1815

1146 Life is given to us on the definite understanding that we boldly defend it to the last.— Charles Dickens, *The Chimes*, 1844

1147 Life is infinitely stranger than anything which the mind of man could invent. We would not dare to conceive the things which are really merely commonplaces of existence.— Arthur Conan Doyle, *The Adventures of Sherlock Holmes*, 1891

1148 It often happens that the real tragedies of life occur in such an inartistic manner that they hurt us by their crude violence, their absolute incoherence, their absurd want of meaning, their entire lack of style.— Oscar Wilde, *The Picture of Dorian Gray*, 1891

1149 The drama of life begins with a wail and ends with a sigh.— Minna Thomas Antrim, *Naked Truth and Veiled Allusions*, 1901

1150 There is no cure for birth and death save to enjoy the interval.— George Santayana, *Soliloquies in England*, 1922

1151 Viewed narrowly, all life is universal hunger and the expression of energy associated with it.— Mary Ritter Beard, *Understanding Women*, 1931

1152 Life, the permission to know death.— Djuna Barnes, *Nightwood*, 1937

1153 If you look at life one way, there is always cause for alarm.— Elizabeth Bowen, *The Death of the Heart*, 1939

1154 Anyone informed that the universe is expanding and contracting in pulsations of eighty billion years has a right to ask, "What's in it for me?"— Peter De Vries, *Glory of the Hummingbird*, 1939

1155 Life is either a daring adventure or nothing. To keep our faces toward change and behave like free spirits in the presence of fate is strength undefeatable.— Helen Keller, *Let Us Have Faith*, 1940

1156 Life seems to be an experience in ascending and descending. You think you're beginning to live for a single aim —for discovery of cosmic truths— when all you're really doing is to move from place to place as if devoted primarily to real estate.— Margaret Anderson, *The Fiery Mountain*, 1951

1157 Man cannot live without some knowledge of the purpose of life. If he can find no purpose in life he creates one in the inevitability of death.— Chester Himes, *Beyond the Angry Black*, 1966

1158 The first half of life is spent mainly in finding out who we are through seeing ourselves in our interaction with others.— June Singer, *Boundaries of the Soul*, 1972

1159 I like living. I have sometimes been wildly, despairingly, acutely miserable, racked with sorrow, but through it all I still know quite certainly that just to be alive is a grand thing.— Agatha Christie, *An Autobiography*, 1977

1160 Life is a tragedy full of joy.—

Bernard Malamud, in *New York Times*, January 29, 1979

1161   It is a tribute to the peculiar horror of contemporary life that it makes the worst features of earlier times—the stupefaction of the masses, the obsessed and driven lives of the bourgeoisie—seem attractive by comparison.— Christopher Lasch, *The Culture of Narcissism*, 1979

1162   Life improves slowly and goes wrong fast, and only catastrophe is clearly visible.— Edward Teller, The Pursuit of Simplicity, 1980

1163   If I had my whole life to live over again, I don't think I'd have the strength.— Flip Wilson, in *Reader's Digest*, November, 1982

1164   The aims of life are the best defense against death.— Primo Levi, *The Drowned and the Saved*, 1988

1165   It began in mystery, and it will end in mystery, but what a savage and beautiful country lies in between.— Diane Ackerman, *A Natural History of the Senses*, 1990

1166   I have made a lot of mistakes. But I've worked hard. I have no fear of death. More important, I don't fear life.— Steven Seagal, in *Parade*, April 17, 1994

Literature

1167   I hate vulgar realism in literature. The man who could call a spade a spade should be compelled to use one. It is the only thing he is fit for.— Oscar Wilde, *The Picture of Dorian Gray*, 1891

1168   To provoke dreams of terror in the slumber of prosperity has become the moral duty of literature.— Ernst Fischer, *Art Against Ideology*, 1966

1169   Hack fiction exploits curiosity without really satisfying it or making connections between it and anything else in the world.— Vincent Canby, in *New York Times*, February 3, 1980

Logic

1170   The fatal errors of life are not due to man's being unreasonable. An unreasonable moment may be one's finest. They are due to a man's being logical.— Oscar Wilde, *De Profundis*, 1905

1171   The principles of logic and metaphysics and true simply because we never allow them to be anything else.— A. J. Ayer, *Language, Truth and Logic*, 1936

Loneliness

1172   God created man and, finding him not sufficiently alone, gave him a companion to make him feel his solitude more keenly.— Paul Valéry, *Tel Quel*, 1943

1173   The dread of loneliness is greater than the fear of bondage, so we get married.— Cyril Connolly, *The Unquiet Grave*, 1945

1174   Now I realize the price [of achievement] was small.— Gordon Parks, in *Life*, May 31, 1963

1175   Loneliness is never more cruel than when it is felt in close propinquity with someone who has ceased to communicate.— Germaine Greer, *The Female Eunuch*, 1970

1176 I've also seen that great men are often lonely. This is understandable, because they have built such high standards for themselves that they often feel alone. But that same loneliness is part of their ability to create.— Yousuf Karsh, in *Parade*, December 3, 1978

1177 But she knew that she had encountered one of the more devastating kinds of loneliness in existence: that of being in close contact with someone to whom she was a nonperson, and who thereby rendered her invisible and of no consequence.— Dorothy Gilman, *Mrs. Pollifax and the Whirling Dervish*, 1990

1178 Being alone and liking it is, for a woman, an act of treachery, an infidelity far more threatening than adultery.— Molly Haskell, *Love and Other infectious Diseases*, 1990

Love

1179 A man in love and out of cash is in a sorry plight.— Plautus, *Curculio*, ca. 200 B.C.

1180 Love is a kind of anxious fear.— Ovid, *Heroides*, ca. 10 B.C.

1181 Love sought is good, but given unsought is better.— William Shakespeare, *Twelfth Night*, 1601

1182 There is something inexpressibly charming in falling in love and, surely, the whole pleasure lies in the fact that love isn't lasting.— Molière, *Don Juan*, 1665

1183 Love is a talkative passion.— Thomas Wilson, *Sacra Privata*, ca. 1755

1184 One cannot love a reserved person. — Jane Austen, *Emma*, 1816

1185 I do not think that what is called Love at first sight is so great an absurdity as it is sometimes imagined to be. We generally make up our minds beforehand to the sort of person we should like, grave or gay, black, brown, or fair.— William Hazlitt, *Table Talk*, 1822

1186 Grudge no expense — yield to no opposition —forget fatigue — till, by the strength of prayer and sacrifice, the spirit of love shall have overcome.— Maria Weston Chapman, in *Liberator*, August 13, 1836

1187 Twenty years of romance makes a woman look like a ruin; but twenty years of marriage makes her something like a public building.— Oscar Wilde, *A Woman of No Importance*, 1893

1188 To be loved is to be fortunate, but to be hated is to achieve distinction.— Minna Thomas Antrim, *Naked Truth and Veiled Allusions*, 1901

1189 It's all right to tell a wife the brutal truth, but you've got to go sort of east with your lady-love.— Zoë Akins, *Daddy's Gone A-Hunting*, 1921

1190 Falling in love consists merely in uncorking the imagination and bottling the common-sense.— Helen Rowland, *A Guide to Men*, 1922

1191 The love we give away is the only love we keep.— Elbert Hubbard, *Note Book*, 1927

1192 Men and women are not free to love decently until they have analyzed themselves completely and swept away every mystery from sex; and this means the acquisition of a profound philosophical theory based on wide reading of anthropology.— Aleister Crowley, *The Confessions of Aleister Crowley*, 1929

1193 To love without criticism is to be betrayed.— Djuna Barnes, *Nightwood*, 1937

1194   There is no fury like a woman searching for a new lover.— Cyril Connolly, *The Unquiet Grave*, 1945

1195   Most people experience love without noticing there is anything remarkable about it.— Boris Pasternak, *Doctor Zhivago*, 1958

1196   You need someone to love you while you're looking for someone to love.— Shalegh Delaney, *A Taste of Honey*, 1959

1197   To cease to be loved is for the child practically synonymous with ceasing to live.— Karl A. Menninger, *A Psychiatrist's World*, 1959

1198   Human love is often but the encounter of two weaknesses.— François Mauriac, *Cain, Where Is Your Brother*, 1962

1199   People who talk about revolution and class struggle without referring explicitly to everyday life, without understanding what is subversive about love and what is positive in the refusal of constraints, such people have a corpse in their mouth.— Raoul Vaneigem, *The Revolution of Everyday Life*, 1967

1200   The tragedy is not the love that doesn't last. The tragedy is the love that lasts.— Shirley Hazzard, *The Transit of Venus*, 1968

1201   Love is the only effective counter to death.— Maureen Duffy, *Wounds*, 1969

1202   I must learn to love the fool in me the one who feels too much, talks too much, takes too many chances, wins sometimes and loses often, lacks self-control, loves and hates, hurts and gets hurt, promises and breaks promises, laughs and cries.— Theodore Isaac Rubin, *Love Me, Love My Fool*, 1976

1203   Falling in love is not an extension of one's limits or boundaries; it is a partial and temporary collapse of them.— M. Scott Peck, *The Road Less Traveled*, 1978

1204   Perhaps loving something is the only starting place there is for making your life your own.— Alice Koller, *An Unknown Woman*, 1982

1205   Love is an exploding cigar which we willingly smoke.— Lynda Barry, *Big Ideas*, 1983

1206   Love is just a system for getting someone to call you darling after sex.— Julian Barnes, *Talking It Over*, 1991

Majority

1207   A majority is always the best repartee.— Benjamin Disraeli, *Tancred*, 1847

1208   When were the good and the brave ever in a majority?— Henry David Thoreau, *A Plea for Captain John Brown*, 1859

1209   Success, recognition, and conformity are the bywords of the modern world where everyone seems to crave the anesthetizing security of being identified with the majority.— Martin Luther King, Jr., *Strength to Love*, 1963

1210   All politics are based on the indifference of the majority.— James Reston, in *New York Times*, June 12, 1968

Males

1211   Were there no women, men might live like gods.— Thomas Dekker, *The Honest Whore*, 1630

1212 It is too great an insult to our sex to insist that the extent of our intelligence is an opinion of a petticoat.— Moliére, *The Learned Ladies*, 1672

1213 A man is always afraid of a woman who loves him too well.— John Gay, *The Beggar's Opera*, 1728

1214 I like men who have a future and women who have a past.— Oscar Wilde, *The Picture of Dorian Gray*, 1891

1215 When a woman is very, very bad, she is awful, but when a man is correspondingly good, he is weird.— Minna Thomas Antrim, *Naked Truth and Veiled Allusions*, 1901

1216 Every man over forty is a scoundrel.— George Bernard Shaw, *Man and Superman*, 1903

1217 You want the unvarnished and ungarnished truth, and I'm no hand for that. I'm a lawyer.— Mary Roberts, *The Man in Lower Ten*, 1909

1218 Every man wants a woman to appeal to his better side, his nobler instincts and his higher nature—and another woman to help him forget them.— Helen Rowland, *A Guide to Men*, 1922

1219 A man would never get the notion of writing a book on the peculiar situation of the human male.— Simone de Beauvoir, *The Second Sex*, 1953

1220 Before they're plumbers or writers or taxi drivers or unemployed or journalists, men are men. Whether heterosexual or homosexual. The only difference is that some of them remind you of it as soon as you meet them, and others wait for a little while.— Marguerite Duras, *Practicalities*, 1987

Marriage

1221 There is nothing nobler or more admirable than when two people who see eye to eye keep house as man and wife, confounding their enemies and delighting their friends.— Homer, *The Odyssey*, ca. 700 B.C.

1222 He who would marry is on the road to repentance.— Philemon, *Fragment*, ca. 310 B.C.

1223 'Twas a happy marriage betwixt a blind wife and a deaf husband.— Michel Eyquem de Montaigne, *Essays*, 1580–95

1224 Many a good hanging prevents a bad marriage.— William Shakespeare, *Twelfth Night*, 1601

1225 I will marry a silly girl so that I will not be made a fool of.— Molière, *The School for Wives*, 1662

1226 I think marriage is shocking. How can one dream of lying next to a man?— Molière, *The Learned Ladies*, 1672

1227 Marriage has many pains, but celibacy has no pleasures.— Samuel Johnson, *Rasselas*, 1759

1228 It is a truth universally acknowledged that a single man in possession of a good fortune must be in want of a wife.— Jane Austen, *Pride and Prejudice*, 1813

1229 To marry is to halve your rights and double your duties.— Arthur Schopenhauer, *The World as Will and Idea*, 1819

1230 It destroys one's nerves to be amicable every day to the same human being.— Benjamin Disraeli, *The Young Duke*, 1831

1231 Ven you're a married man, Samivel, you'll understand a good many things you don't understand now; but vether it's worth while, goin' through so much, to learn so little, as the charity-boy said ven he got to the end of the alphabet, is a matter o' taste. — Charles Dickens, *The Pickwick Papers*, 1836–37

1232 Remember, it's as easy to marry a rich woman as a poor woman. — William Makepeace Thackeray, *The History of Pendennis*, 1849

1233 People don't have fortunes left them in that style nowadays; men have to work and women to marry for money. It's a dreadfully unjust world. — Louisa May Alcott, *Little Women*, 1868

1234 When a woman marries again it is because she detested her first husband. When a man marries again it is because he adored his first wife. Women try their luck; men risk theirs. — Oscar Wilde, *The Picture of Dorian Gray*, 1891

1235 Marrying an old bachelor is like buying second-hand furniture. — Helen Rowland, *Reflections of a Bachelor Girl*, 1903

1236 Marriage is popular because it combines the maximum of temptation with the maximum of opportunity. — George Bernard Shaw, *Man and Superman*, 1903

1237 Variability is one of the virtues of a woman. It avoids the crude requirement of polygamy. So long as you have one good wife you are sure to have a spiritual harem. — Gilbert K. Chesterton, *Alarms and Discursions*, 1910

1238 Marriage is a good deal like the circus: there is not as much in it as is represented in the advertising. — Edgar Watson Howe, *Country Town Sayings*, 1911

1239 Marriage is based on the theory that when a man discovers a particular brand of beer exactly to his taste he should at once throw up his job and go to work in the brewery. — George Jean Nathan, *The Theatre, the Drama, the Girls*, 1921

1240 Before marriage, a man will go home and lie awake all night thinking about something you said; after marriage, he'll go to sleep before you finish saying it. — Helen Rowland, *A Guide to Men*, 1922

1241 The trouble with wedlock is, there's not enough wed and too much lock. — Christopher Morley, *Kitty Foyle*, 1939

1242 Marriage is a very good thing, but I think it's a mistake to make a habit of it. — William Somerset Maugham, *The Mixture as Before*, 1940

1243 The curse which lies upon marriage is that too often the individuals are joined in their weakness rather than in their strength — each asking from the other instead of finding pleasure in giving. — Simone de Beauvoir, *The Second Sex*, 1949

1244 No matter how happily a woman may be married, it always pleases her to discover that there is a nice man who wishes that she were not. — H. L. Mencken, *A Mencken Chrestomathy*, 1949

1245 Were marriage no more than a convenient screen for sexuality, some less cumbersome and costly protection must have been found by this time to replace it. One concludes therefore that people do not marry to cohabit; they cohabit to marry. — Virgilia Peterson, *A Matter of Life and Death*, 1961

1246 Chains do not hold a marriage together. It is threads, hundreds of tiny threads which sew people together through the years. That is what makes a marriage last — more than passion or even sex! — Simone Signoret, in *Daily Mail*, July 4, 1978

Masses

1247   For the crowd, the incredible has sometimes more power and is more credible than the truth. — Menander, *Fragment 622*, 3rd c. B.C.

1248   The Masses are cowardly, fickle, and ever ready to be deceived. — Niccolò Machiavelli, *The Prince*, 1513

1249   The multitude is always in the wrong. — Wentworth Dillon, *Essay in Translated Verse*, 1684

1250   The populace drag down the gods to their own level. — Ralph Waldo Emerson, *Journals*, 1858

1251   All that is necessary to raise imbecility into what the mob regards as profundity is to lift it off the floor, and put it on a platform. — George Jean Nathan, in *American Mercury*, September, 1929

Math

1252   A man of a strong affinity for facts is thoroughly persuaded of the truths of arithmetic. — Ralph Waldo Emerson, *The Conduct of Life*, 1860

1253   Mathematics may be defined as the subject in which we never know what we are talking about, nor whether what we are saying is true. — Bertrand Russell, *Mysticism and Logic*, 1917

1254   Mathematics is the language of size. — Lancelot Hogben, *Mathematics for the Million: How to Master the Magic of Numbers*, 1936

1255   Geometry is the art of correct reasoning on incorrect figures. — George Polya, *How to Solve It: A New Aspect of Mathematical Method*, 1945

Maturity

1256   Grown-ups never understand anything for themselves, and it is tiresome for children to be always and forever explaining things to them. — Antoine-Marie-Roger de Saint-Exupéry, *The Little Prince*, 1943

1257   To mature is in part to realize that while complete intimacy and omniscience and power cannot be had, self-transcendence, growth, and closeness to others are nevertheless within one's reach. — Sissela Bok, *Secrets*, 1983

1258   Radio wasn't outside our lives. It coincided with and helped to shape our childhood and adolescence. As we slogged toward maturity, it also grew up and turned into television, leaving behind, like dead skin, transistorized talk-radio and nonstop music. — Vincent Canby, in *New York Times*, January 30, 1987

Mediocrity

1259   Mediocrity obtains more with application than superiority without it.— Baltasar Gracián, *The Art of Worldly Wisdom*, 1647

1260   Mediocre minds usually dismiss anything which reaches beyond their own understanding.— François Duke de La Rochefoucauld, VI, *Maxims*, 1665

1261   If every man worked at that for which nature fitted him, the cows would be well tended.— Jean Pierre Claris de Florian, *La Vacher de la Garde-chasse*, 1792

1262   The general tendency of things throughout the world is to render mediocrity the ascendant power among mankind.— John Stuart Mill, *On Liberty*, 1859

1263   Mediocre men often have the most acquired knowledge.— Claude Bernard, *Introduction to the Study of Experimental Medicine*, 1865

1264   In the republic of mediocrity genius is dangerous.— Robert G. Ingersoll, *Liberty in Literature*, 1890

1265   Mediocrity knows nothing higher than itself, but talent instantly recognizes genius.— Arthur Conan Doyle, *The Valley of Fear*, 1914

1266   There's no such hell on earth as that of a man who knows himself doomed to mediocrity in the work he loves.— Philip Barry, *You and I*, 1922

1267   Only a mediocre person is always at his best.— William Somerset Maugham, in *Forbes Magazine*, August 1, 1977

Memory

1268   A man's real possession is his memory. In nothing else is he rich, in

nothing else is he poor.— Alexander Smith, *Dreamthorp*, 1863

1269   The proper memory for a politician is one that knows what to remember and what to forget.— John Morley, *Recollections*, 1917

1270   Our memories are card-indexes consulted, and then put back in disorder by authorities whom we do not control.— Cyril Connolly, *The Unquiet Grave*, 1945

1271   I can understand that memory must be selective, else it would choke on the glut of experience. What I cannot understand is why it selects what it does.— Virgilia Peterson, *A Matter of Life and Death*, 1961

Military

1272   The superior man is easy to serve and difficult to please.— Confucius, *Analects*, ca. 480 B.C.

1273   It is much safer to obey than to govern.— Thomas à Kempis, *Imitation of Christ*, ca. 1420

1274   Ambition, / The soldier's virtue.— William Shakespeare, *Antony and Cleopatra*, 1606–07

1275   There is no merit without rank, but there is no rank without some merit.— François Duke de La Rochefoucauld, VI, *Maxims*, 1665

1276   A handful of soldiers is always better than a mouthful of arguments.— G. C. Lichtenberg, *Aphorisms*, 1765–99

1277   What millions died that Caesar might be great!— Thomas Campbell, *Pleasures of Hope*, 1799

1278 The people are always in the wrong when they are faced by the armed forces.— Napoleon Bonaparte, letter, October 2, 1810

1279 The army is a nation within the nation; it is a vice of our time.— Alfred-Victor, Comte de Vigny, *Servitude et grandeur militaires*, 1835

1280 Hero-worship is strongest where there is least regard for human freedom.— Herbert Spencer, *Social Statics*, 1851

1281 It is an interesting question how far men would retain their relative rank if they were divested of their clothes.— Henry David Thoreau, *Walden*, 1854

1282 A man in armor is his armor's slave.— Robert Browning, *Herakles*, 1871

1283 The man who obeys is nearly always better than the man who commands.— Joseph-Ernest Renan, *Dialogues et fragments philosophiques*, 1876

1284 When the military man approaches, the world locks up its spoons and packs off its womankind.— George Bernard Shaw, *Man and Superman*, 1903

1285 To delight in war is a merit in the soldier, a dangerous quality in the captain, and a positive crime in the statesman.— George Santayana, *The Life of Reason*, 1905–06

1286 It's the orders you disobey that make you famous.— Douglas MacArthur, in *Time*, September 11, 1978

1287 A man's name, title, and rank are artificial and impermanent; they do nothing to reveal what he really is, even to himself.— Hyppolyte-Jean Giraudoux, *Siegfried*, 1928

1288 The most important quality in a leader is that of being acknowledged as such. All leaders whose fitness is questioned are clearly lacking in force.— André Maurois, *The Art of Living*, 1939

1289 The military caste did not originate as a party of patriots, but as a party of bandits.— H. L. Mencken, *Minority Report*, 1956

1290 The worst calamity after a stupid general is an intelligent general.— Charles de Gaulle, *The Words of the General*, 1962

1291 Men love war because it allows them to look serious. Because it is the one thing that stops women laughing at them.— John Fowles, *The Magus*, 1965

Mind

1292 Only the mind cannot be sent into exile.— Ovid, *Expistulae ex Ponto*, ca. 5 A.D.

1293 It is not enough to have a good mind; the main thing is to use it well.— René Descartes, *Discourse on the Method*, 1637

1294 The mind of a man is like a clock that is always running down and requires to be as constantly wound up.— William Hazlitt, *Sketches and Essays*, 1839

Minority

1295 The minority is always right.— Henrik Ibsen, *An Enemy of the People*, 1882

1296 It is hell to belong to a suppressed minority.— Claude McKay, *A Long Way from Home*, 1937

Modesty

1297 Although modesty is natural to man, it is not natural to children. Modesty only begins with the knowledge of evil.— Jean-Jacques Rousseau, *Emile*, 1762

1298 Modesty is the lowest of the virtues, and is a real confession of the deficiency it indicates. He who undervalues himself is justly undervalued by others.— William Hazlitt, *Table Talk*, 1822

1299 I have often wished I had time to cultivate modesty. But I am too busy thinking about myself.— Edith Sitwell, in *Observer*, April 30, 1950

Money

1300 Dollars! All their cares, hopes, joys, affections, virtues, and associations seemed to be melted down into dollars. Whatever the chance contributions that fell into the slow cauldron of their talk, they made the gruel thick and slab with dollars.— Charles Dickens, *Martin Chuzzlewit*, 1844

1301 The rich man is always sold to the institution which makes him rich. Absolutely speaking, the more money, the less virtue.— Henry David Thoreau, *On the Duty of Civil Disobedience*, 1849

1302 The universal regard for money is the one hopeful fact in our civilization. Money is the most important thing in the world. It represents health, strength, honor, generosity and beauty. Not the least of its virtues is that it destroys base people.— George Bernard Shaw, *Major Barbara*, 1905

1303 The seven deadly sins: Food, clothing, firing, rent, taxes, respectability and children. Nothing can lift those seven millstones from Man's neck but money; and the spirit cannot soar until the millstones are lifted.— George Bernard Shaw, *Major Barbara*, 1905

1304 Most men love money and security more, and creation and construction less, as they get older.— John Maynard Keynes, *Essays in Persuasion*, 1931

1305 God is on the side of those with plenty of money and large armies.— Jean Anouilh, *L'Alouette*, 1953

1306 Until and unless you discover that money is the root of all good, you ask for your own destruction.— Ayn Rand, *Atlas Shrugged*, 1957

1307 Americans want action for their money. They are fascinated by its self-reproducing qualities if it's put to work.— Paula Nelson, *The Joy of Money*, 1975

1308 Money never remains just coins and pieces of paper. Money can be translated into the beauty of living, a support in misfortune, an education, or future security. It also can be translated into a source of bitterness.— Sylvia Porter, *Sylvia Porter's Money Book*, 1975

Morale

1309 Nothing in life is so exhilarating as to be shot at without result.— Winston S. Churchill, *The Malakand Field Force*, 1898

1310 The sound of the drum drives out thought; for that very reason it is the most military of instruments.— Joseph Joubert, *Pensées*, 1842

1311   It is essential to persuade the soldier that those he is being urged to massacre are bandits who do not deserve to live; before killing other good, decent fellows like himself, his gun would fall from his hands.— André Gide, *Journals*, February 10, 1943

1312   What counts is not necessarily the size of the dog in the fight — it's the size of the fight in the dog.— Dwight D. Eisenhower, speech, January 31, 1958

Morality

1313   As the strong man exults in his physical ability, delighting in such exercises as call his muscles into action, so glories the analyst in that moral activity which disentangles.— Edgar Allan Poe, *The Murders in the Rue Morgue*, 1841

1314   Our whole life is startlingly moral.— Henry David Thoreau, *Walden*, 1854

1315   In morals, truth is but little prized when it is a mere sentiment, and only attains its full value when realized in the world as fact.— Joseph-Ernest Renan, *The Life of Jesus*, 1863

1316   The true meaning of religion is thus not simply morality, but morality touched by emotion.— Matthew Arnold, *Literature and Dogma*, 1873

1317   Morality is the best of all devices for leading mankind by the nose.— Friedrich Nietzsche, *The Anti-Christ*, 1888

1318   Moral indignation is jealousy with a halo.— H. G. Wells, *The Wife of Sir Isaac Harmon*, 1914

1319   One becomes moral as soon as one is unhappy.— Marcel Proust, *A l'ombre des jeunes filles en fleurs*, 1918

1320   The defense of morals is the battle-cry which best rallies stupidity against change.— Alfred North Whitehead, *Adventures of Ideas*, 1933

1321   Morality cannot be legislated but behavior can be regulated. Judicial decrees may not change the heart, but they can restrain the heartless.— Martin Luther King, Jr., *Strength to Love*, 1963

1322   You can't be right against everybody.— Simone de Beauvoir, *Les Belles Images*, 1966

1323   Morality comes with the sad wisdom of age, when the sense of curiosity has withered.— Graham Henry Greene, *A Sort of Life*, 1971

1324   If one would discern the centers of dominance in any society, one need only look to its definitions of "virtue" and "vice" or "legal" and "criminal," for in the strength to set standards resides the strength to maintain control.— Freda Adler, *Sisters in Crime*, 1975

1325   There is nothing in nature that can't be taken as a sign of both morality and invigoration.— Gretel Ehrlich, *The Solace of Open Spaces*, 1985

Narcissism

1326   He who is enamored of himself will at least have the advantage of being inconvenienced by few rivals.— G. C. Lichtenberg, *Aphorisms*, 1764–99

1327   Self-love seems so often unrequited.— Anthony Powell, *The Acceptance World*, 1955

1328 No person loving or admiring himself is alone.— Theodor Reik, *Of Love and Lust*, 1957

Nationalism

1329 In individuals insanity is rare, but in groups, parties, nations and epochs it is the rule.— Friedrich Nietzsche, *Beyond Good and Evil*, 1886

1330 A nation is a historical group of men of recognizable cohesion, held together by a common enemy.— Theodor Herzl, *The Jewish State*, 1896

1331 The nationalist has a broad hatred and a narrow love. He cannot stifle a predilection for dead cities.— André Gide, *Journals*, 1918

1332 Nationalism is an infantile disease. It is the measles of mankind.— Albert Einstein, letter, 1921

1333 Patriotism is a lively sense of responsibility. Nationalism is a silly cock crowing on its own dunghill.— Richard Aldington, *The Colonel's Daughter*, 1931

1334 Nationalism is our form of incest, is our idolatry, is our insanity. "Patriotism" is its cult.— Erich Fromm, *The Sane Society*, 1955

1335 All nations have present, or past, or future reasons for thinking themselves incomparable.— Paul Valéry, *Selected Writings*, 1964

1336 A nation' s strength ultimately consists in what it can do on its own, and not in what it can borrow from others.— Indira Gandhi, in *Christian Science Monitor*, March 25, 1985

1337 A country losing touch with its own history is like an old man losing his glasses, a distressing sight, at once vulnerable, unsure, and easily disoriented.— George Walden, in *Times*, December 20, 1986

Nature

1338 So much of truth, only under an ancient obsolete vesture, but the spirit of it still true, do I find in the Paganism of old nations. Nature is still divine, the revelation of the workings of God; the Hero is still worshipable.— Thomas Carlyle, *On Heroes and Hero-Worship*, 1841

1339 We can never have enough of nature. We must be refreshed by the sight of inexhaustible vigor, vast and titanic features, the sea-coast with its wrecks, the wilderness with its living and its decaying trees, the thunder-cloud, and the rain.— Henry David Thoreau, *Walden*, 1854

1340 Nature is just enough; but men and women must comprehend and accept her suggestions.— Antoinette Brown Blackwell, *The Sexes Throughout Nature*, 1875

1341 More and more as we come closer and closer in touch with nature and its teachings are we able to see the Divine and are therefore fitted to interpret correctly the various languages spoken by all forms of nature about us.— George Washington Carver, *How to Search for Truth*, 1930

1342 Copy nature and you infringe on the work of our Lord. Interpret nature and you are an artist.— Jacques Lipchitz, in *New York Times*, April 28, 1964

Necessity

1343 Necessity makes an honest man a knave.— Daniel Defoe, *The Serious Reflections of Robinson Crusoe*, 1720

1344 Necessity does the work of courage.— George Eliot, *Romola*, 1863

1345 Man cannot be free if he does not know that he is subject to necessity, because his freedom is always won in his never wholly successful attempts to liberate himself from necessity.— Hannah Arendt, *The Human Condition*, 1958

1346 For a young child everything that happens is a necessity.— John Berger, *A Fortunate Man*, 1967

1347 A society that has made "nostalgia" a marketable commodity on the cultural exchange quickly repudiates the suggestion that life in the past was in any important way better than life today.— Christopher Lasch, *The Culture of Narcissism*, 1979

Nonviolence

1348 Nonviolence is a powerful and just weapon which cuts without wounding and ennobles the man who wields it. It is a sword that heals.— Martin Luther King, Jr., *Why We Can't Wait*, 1964

1349 Pain is real when you get other people to believe in it. If no one believes in it but you, your pain is madness or hysteria.— Naomi Wolf, *The Beauty Myth*, 1990

Obedience

1350 Whoever obeys the gods, to him they particularly listen.— Homer, *The Iliad*, ca. 700 B.C.

1351 He who has never learned to obey cannot be a good commander.— Aristotle, *Politics*, 4th c. B.C.

1352 Every human being has, like Socrates, an attendant spirit; and wise are they who obey its signals. If it does not always tell us what to do, it always cautions us what not to do.— Lydia M. Child, *Philothea: A Romance*, 1836

Opinion

1353 Opinion is darker than knowledge and brighter than ignorance.— Plato, *The Republic*, ca. 370 B.C.

1354 Opinion in good men is but knowledge in the making.— John Milton, *Areopagitica*, 1644

1355 Men who borrow their opinions can never repay their debts.— Edward F. Halifax, *Miscellaneous Thoughts and Reflections*, 1750

1356 We accumulate our opinions at an age when our understanding is at its weakest.— G. C. Lichtenberg, *Aphorisms*, 1765–99

1357 The man who never alters his opinion is like standing water, and breeds reptiles of the mind.— William Blake, *The Marriage of Heaven and Hell*, 1790

1358 The recipe for perpetual ignorance is: be satisfied with your opinions and content with your knowledge.— Elbert Hubbard, *The Philistine*, 1897

1359   The private citizen, beset by partisan appeals for the loan of his Public Opinion, will soon see, perhaps, that these appeals are not a compliment to his intelligence, but an imposition on his good nature and an insult to his sense of evidence.— Walter Lippmann, *Public Opinion*, 1922

1360   All empty souls tend to extreme opinion.— William Butler Yeats, *Dramatis Personae*, 1936

1361   The dissenting opinions of one generation become the prevailing interpretation of the next.— Burton J. Hendrik, *Bulwarks of the Republic*, 1937

1362   Opinion is that exercise of the human will which helps us to make a decision without information.— John Erskine, *The Complete Life*, 1943

1363   I am convinced that the best service a retired general can perform is to turn in his tongue along with his suit, and to mothball his opinions.— Omar Bradley, in *New York Times*, May 17, 1959

1364   Between friends differences in taste or opinion are irritating in direct proportion to their triviality.— W. H. Auden, *The Dyer's Hand*, 1962

1365   Novelists are perhaps the last people in the world to be entrusted with opinions. The nature of a novel is that it has no opinions, only the dialectic of contrary views, some of which, all of which, may be untenable and even silly.— Anthony Burgess, *You've Had Your Time*, 1990

Optimism

1366   The place where optimism most flourishes is the lunatic asylum.— Havelock Ellis, *The Dance of Life*, 1923

1367   The optimist proclaims that we live in the best of all possible worlds; the pessimist fears this is true.— James B. Cabell, *The Silver Stallion*, 1926

Parents

1368   [Do we become parents] in order to be insulted and looked down upon in our old age?— Joseph A. Schumpeter, *Capitalism, Socialism and Democracy*, 1942

1369   The truth is that parents are not really interested in justice. They just want quiet.— Bill Cosby, *On Meting Out Discipline*, 1986

Passion

1370   Perish the man who can love lightly.— Sextus Propertius, *Elegies*, ca. 26 B.C.

1371   Man is only truly great when he acts from the passions.— Benjamin Disraeli, *Conningsby*, 1844

1372   You can no more bridle passions with logic than you can justify them in the law courts. Passions are facts and not dogmas.— Aleksandr Herzen, *My Past and Thoughts*, 1921

1373   Often, the thing we pursue most passionately is but a substitute for the one thing we really want and cannot have.— Eric Hoffer, *The Passionate State of Mind*, 1954

Past

1374   Why doesn't the past decently bury itself, instead of sitting waiting to be admired by the present? – D. H. Lawrence, *St. Mawr*, 1925

1375   The beauty of the past belongs to the past.— Margaret Bourke-White, in *Christian Science Monitor*, December 5, 1986

Patience

1376   Beware the fury of a patient man.— John Dryden, *Absalom and Achitophel*, 1681

1377   Patience is a necessary ingredient of genius.— Benjamin Disraeli, *Contarini Fleming*, 1832

1378   Of all the virtues the virtue of patience is most foreign to youth.— John Jay Chapman, *Memories and Milestones*, 1915

Patriotism

1379   Lovely and honorable it is to die for one's country.— Horace, *Odes*, 1st c. B.C.

1380   Who serves his country well has no need of ancestors.— Voltaire, *Mérope*, 1743

1381   Patriotism is the last refuse of a scoundrel.— Samuel Johnson, letter, April 7, 1775

1382   Love of our country is another of those specious illusions, which have been invented by impostors in order to render the multitude the blind instruments of their crooked designs.— William Godwin, *An Enquiry concerning the Principles of Political Justice*, 1793

1383   Patriotism is in political life what faith is in religion.— John E. E. Dalberg, in *The Home and Foreign Review*, July, 1862

1384   In time of war the loudest patriots are the greatest profiteers.— August Bebel, speech, November, 1870

1385   Conceit, arrogance, and egotism are the essentials of patriotism.— Emma Goldman, *Anarchism*, 1917

1386   Patriotism is often an arbitrary veneration of real estate above principles.— George Jean Nathan, *Testament of a Critic*, 1931

1387   Patriotism is a pernicious, psychopathic form of idiocy.— George Bernard Shaw, in *L'Esprit Français*, 1932

1388   Talking of patriotism, what humbug it is; it is a word which always commemorates a robbery.   Mark Twain, *Notebook*, 1935

1389   Whenever you hear a man speak of his love for his country it is a sign that he expects to be paid for it.— H. L. Mencken, *A Mencken Chrestomathy*, 1949

Peace

1390   Peace is an armistice in a war that is continuously going on.— Thucydides,

History of the Peloponnesian War, 431–413 B.C.

1391   War makes rattling good history; but Peace is poor reading.— Thomas Hardy, *The Dynasts*, 1904–08

1392   Peace: A monotonous interval between fights.— Elbert Hubbard, *The Roycroft Dictionary and Book of Epigrams*, 1923

1393   Nobody ever forgets where he buried the hatchet.— Frank McKinney Hubbard, in *Indianapolis News*, January 4, 1925

1394   Peace is that state in which fear of any kind is unknown.— John Buchan, *Pilgrim's Way*, 1940

1395   God and the politicians willing, the United States can declare peace upon the world, and win it.— Ely Culbertson, *Must We Fight Russia?* 1946

1396   Peace is when time doesn't matter as it passes by.— Maria Schell, in *Time*, March 3, 1958

1397   We must learn which ceremonies may be breached occasionally at our convenience and which ones may never be if we are to live pleasantly with our fellow man.— Amy Vanderbilt, *New Complete Book of Etiquette*, 1963

1398   Once a great wrong has been done, it never dies. People speak the words of peace, but their hearts do not forgive. Generations perform ceremonies of reconciliation but there is no end.— Paule Marshall, *The Chosen Place, The Timeless People*, 1969

1399   I see little hope for a peaceful world until men are excluded from the realm of foreign policy altogether and all decisions concerning international relations are reserved for women,

preferably married ones.— W. H. Auden, *A Certain World*, 1970

People

1400   What is the city but the people?— William Shakespeare, *Coriolanus*, 1608

1401   Among democratic nations, each new generation is a new people.— Alexis de Tocqueville, *Democracy in America*, 1835

1402   You can fool too many of the people too much of the time.— James Thurber, *Fables for Our Time*, 1940

Perfection

1403   It's a delightful thing to think of perfection; but it's vastly more amusing to talk of errors and absurdities.— Fanny Burney, *Camilla*, 1796

1404   No one ever approaches perfection except by stealth, and unknown to themselves.— William Hazlitt, *Sketches and Essays*, 1839

1405   You cannot get white flour out of a coal sack, nor perfection out of human nature.— Charles Haddon Spurgeon, *John Ploughman's Talks*, 1869

1406   The indefatigable pursuit of an unattainable perfection — even though nothing more than the pounding of an old piano— is what alone gives a meaning to our life on this unavailing star.— Logan Pearsall Smith, *Afterthoughts*, 1931

1407   Perfection has one grave defect: It

is apt to be dull.— William Somerset Maugham, *The Summing Up*, 1938

1408 [Perfection does not] allow for life, and certainly not death.— Marion Woodman, *Addiction to Perfection: The Still Unravished Bride*, 1982

Philosophy

1409 For there never was yet philosopher / That could endure the toothache patiently.— William Shakespeare, *Much Ado About Nothing*, 1598–99

1410 To be a philosopher is not merely to have subtle thoughts, nor even to found a school, but so to love wisdom as to live according to its dictates a life of simplicity, independence, magnanimity, and trust.— Henry David Thoreau, *Walden*, 1854

1411 The philosophy of one century is the common sense of the next.— Henry Ward Beecher, *Life Thoughts*, 1858

1412 The philosopher believes that the value of his philosophy lies in the whole, in the building: posterity discovers it in the bricks with which he built and which are then often used again for better building.— Friedrich Nietzsche, *Assorted Opinions and Maxims*, 1879

1413 I do not know what the spirit of a philosopher could more wish to be than a good dancer. For the dance is his ideal, also his fine art, finally also the only kind of piety he knows, his "divine service."— Friedrich Nietzsche, *The Gay Science*, 1887

1414 The guiding motto is the life of every natural philosopher should be,

"Seek simplicity and distrust it."— Alfred North Whitehead, *The Concept of Nature*, 1920

1415 The greatest horrors in the history of mankind are not due to the ambition of the Napoleons or the vengeance of the Agamemnons, but to the doctrinaire philosophers.— Aleister Crowley, *The Confessions of Aleister Crowley*, 1929

1416 Perhaps it is of more value to infuriate philosophers than to go along with them.— Wallace Stevens, *Opus Posthumous*, 1959

1417 Perhaps it is the fate of philosophers to be misunderstood.— Edward C. Moore, *William James*, 1965

1418 There are more truths in twenty-four hours of a man's life than in all the philosophies.— Raoul Vaneigem, *The Revolution of Everyday Life*, 1967

Pleasure

1419 The human mind always runs downhill from toil to pleasure.— Terence, *Andria*, 166 B.C.

1420 And painful pleasure turns to pleasing pain.— Edmund Spenser, *The Fairie Queene*, 1590

1421 I shouldn't be surprised if the greatest rule of all weren't to give pleasure.— Molière, *The School for Wives*, 1662

1422 The body sins once, and has done with its sin, for action is a mode of purification. Nothing remains then but the recollection of a pleasure, or the luxury of a regret.— Oscar Wilde, *The Picture of Dorian Gray*, 1891

1423 A fool bolts pleasure, then complains of moral indigestion. — Minna Thomas Antrim, *Naked Truth and Veiled Allusions*, 1901

Poetry

1424 Poetry lifts the veil from the hidden beauty of the world, and makes familiar objects be as if they were not familiar. — Percy Bysshe Shelley, A Defense of Poetry, 1821

1425 He who draws noble delights from the sentiments of poetry is a true poet, though he has never written a line in all his life. — George Sand, *The Haunted Pool*, 1851

1426 Poets are the only people to whom love is not only a crucial, but an indispensable experience, which entitles them to mistake it for a universal one. — Hannah Arendt, *The Human Condition*, 1958

1427 Poetry is no more a narcotic than a stimulant; it is a universal bittersweet mixture for all possible household emergencies and its action varies accordingly as it is taken in a wineglass or a tablespoon, inhaled, gargled or rubbed on the chest. — Robert Graves, in *New York Times*, October 9, 1960

1428 Nine-tenths of English poetic literature is the result either of vulgar careerism or of a poet trying to keep his hand in. Most poets are dead by their late twenties. — Robert Graves, in *Observer*, November 11, 1962

1429 No poet or novelist wishes he were the only one who ever lived, but most of them wish they were the only one alive, and quite a number fondly believe their wish has been granted. — W. H. Auden, *The Dyer's Hand*, 1963

1430 I cannot accept the doctrine that in poetry there is a "suspension of belief." A poet must never make a statement simply because it sounds poetically exciting; he must also believe it to be true. — W. H. Auden, *A Certain World*, 1970

1431 Society has no obligation toward the poet. — Joseph Brodsky, *Less Than One: Selected Essays*, 1983

1432 What is a poem but a hazardous attempt at self-understanding? It is the deepest part of autobiography. — Robert Penn Warren, in *New York Times*, May 12, 1985

Politics

1433 Under every stone lurks a politician. — Aristophanes, *Thesmophoriazusae*, 410 B.C.

1434 It is as hard and severe a thing to be a true politician as to be truly moral. — Francis Bacon, *The Advancement of Learning*, 1605

1435 No man can be a politician, except he be first a historian or a traveler; for except he can see what must be, or what may be, he is no politician. — James Harrington, *The Commonwealth of Oceana*, 1656

1436 Politics and the pulpit are terms that have little agreement. — Edmund Burke, *Reflections on the Revolution in France*, 1790

1437 In politics nothing is contemptible. — Benjamin Disraeli, *Vivian Grey*, 1826

1438 In politics experiments mean revolutions.— Benjamin Disraeli, *Popanilla*, 1827

1439 Those who would treat politics and morality apart will never understand the one or the other.— John Morley, *Rousseau*, 1876

1440 No wonder that, when a political career is so precarious, men of worth and capacity hesitate to embrace it. They cannot afford to be thrown out of their life's course by a mere accident.— James Bryce, *The American Commonwealth*, 1888

1441 He knows nothing and he thinks he knows everything. That points clearly to a political career.— George Bernard Shaw, *Major Barbara*, 1905

1442 The politician is an acrobat. He keeps his balance by saying the opposite of what he does.— Maurice Barrès, *Mes cahiers*, 1923

1443 Political principles resemble military tactics; they are usually designed for a war which is over.— R. H. Tawney, *Equality*, 1931

1444 Everything begins in mysticism and ends in politics.— Charles Péguy, *Basic Verities*, 1943

1445 Politics is the art of preventing people from taking part in affairs which properly concern them.— Paul Valéry, *Tel Quel*, 1943

1446 Power politics is the diplomatic name for the law of the jungle.— Ely Culbertson, *Must We Fight Russia?*, 1946

1447 In government offices which are sensitive to the vehemence and passion of mass sentiment public men have no sure tenure. They are in effect perpetual office seekers, always on trial for their political lives.— Walter Lippmann, *The Public Philosophy*, 1955

1448 It is now known that men enter local politics solely as a result of being unhappily married.— C. Northcote Parkinson, *Parkinson's Law*, 1958

1449 I have never found, in a long experience of politics, that criticism is ever inhibited by ignorance.— Harold Macmillan, in *Wall Street Journal*, August 13, 1963

1450 Men are to a great extent products of their institutional environment.— M. Judd Harmon, *Political Thought*, 1964

1451 The belief that politics can be scientific must inevitably produce tyrannies. Politics cannot be a science, because in politics theory and practice cannot be separated, and the sciences depend upon their separation.— W. H. Auden, *A Certain World*, 1970

1452 The politician being interviewed clearly takes a great deal of trouble to imagine an ending to his sentence: and if he stopped short? His entire policy would be jeopardized!— Roland Barthes, *The Pleasure of the Text*, 1975

1453 To "know your place" is a good idea in politics. That is not to say "stay in your place" or "hang on to your place," because ambition or boredom may dictate upward or downward mobility, but a sense of place — a feel for one's own position.— William Safire, *Before The Fall*, 1975

1454 If we insist that public life be reserved for those whose personal history is pristine, we are not going to get paragons of virtue running our affairs. We will get the very rich, who contract out the messy things in life.— Charles Krauthammer, in *Time*, September 10, 1984

1455   The legions of reporters who cover politics don't want to quit the clash and thunder of electoral combat for the dry duty of analyzing the federal budget. As a consequence, we have created the perpetual presidential campaign.— Hugh Sidey, in *Time*, November 5, 1984

1456   Beware the politically obsessed. They are often bright and interesting, but they have something missing in their natures; there is a hole, an empty place, and they use politics to fill it up. It leaves them somehow misshapen.— Peggy Noonan, *What I Saw at the Revolution*, 1990

Possession

1457   Possession, it is true, crowns exertion with rest.— Karl Wilhelm, Baron von Humboldt, *Limits of State Action*, 1792

1458   Some men are born to own, and can animate all their possessions. Others cannot: their owning is not graceful; seems to be a compromise of their character: they seem to steal their own dividends.— Ralph Waldo Emerson, *The Conduct of Life*, 1860

1459   He greatly valued his possessions, chiefly because they were his, and derived genuine pleasure from contemplating a painting, a statuette, a rare lace curtain — no matter what — after he had bought it and placed it among his household gods.— Kate Chopin, *The Awakening*, 1899

Poverty

1460   We all live in a state of ambitious poverty.— Juvenal, *Satires*, ca. 110

1461   O world! How apt the poor are to be proud.— William Shakespeare, *Twelfth Night*, 1601

1462   Give me the poverty that enjoys true wealth.— Henry David Thoreau, *Walden*, 1854

1463   We do not need to minimize the poverty of the ghetto or the suffering inflicted by whites on blacks in order to see that the increasingly dangerous and unpredictable conditions of middle-class life have given rise to similar strategies for survival.— Christopher Lasch, *The Culture of Narcissism*, 1979

Power

1464   The desire for power in excess caused angels to fall; the desire for knowledge in excess caused man to fall; but in charity is no excess, neither can man or angels come in danger by it.— Francis Bacon, *Essays*, 1597–1625

1465   It is a strange desire to seek power and to lose liberty.— Francis Bacon, *Essays*, 1597–1625

1466   Who is all-powerful should fear everything.— Pierre Corneille, *Cinna*, 1640

1467   The sole advantage of power is that you can do more good.— Baltasar Gracián, *The Art of Worldly Wisdom*, 1647

1468   In all supremacy of power, there is inherent a prerogative to pardon.—

Benjamin Whichcote, *Moral and Religious Aphorisms,* 1703

1469   He that fails in his endeavors after wealth or power will not long retain either honesty or courage.— Samuel Johnson, in *Adventurer,* October 16, 1753

1470   No man is wise enough nor good enough to be trusted with unlimited power.— Charles Caleb Colton, *Lacon,* 1820–22

1471   Power makes you attractive; it even makes women love old men.— Joseph Joubert, *Pensées,* 1842

1472   The depository of power is always unpopular.— Benjamin Disraeli, *Coningsby,* 1844

1473   People demand freedom only when they have no power.— Friedrich Nietzsche, *The Will to Power,* 1888

1474   The need to exert power, when thwarted in the open fields of life, is the more likely to assert itself in trifles.— Charles Horton Cooley, *Human Nature and the Social Order,* 1902

1475   The possession of unlimited power will make a despot of almost any man. There is a possible Nero in the gentlest human creature that walks.— Thomas B. Aldrich, *Pankapog Papers,* 1903

1476   You cannot have power for good without having power for evil too. Even mother's milk nourishes murderers as well as heroes.— George Bernard Shaw, *Major Barbara,* 1905

1477   Power takes as ingratitude the writhing of its victims.— Rabindranath Tagore, *Stray Birds,* 1916

1478   The least one can say of power is that a vocation for it is suspicious.— Jean Rostand, *Pensées d'un Biologiste,* 1939

1479   It is not power itself, but the legitimation of the lust for power, which corrupts absolutely.— R. H. S. Crossman, in *New Statesman,* April 21, 1951

1480   Those in possession of absolute power can not only prophesy and make their prophecies come true, but they can also lie and make their lies come true.— Eric Hoffer, *The Passionate State of Mind,* 1954

1481   Power is the great regulator of the relations among states.— René Albrecht-Carrié, *A Diplomatic History of Europe Since the Congress of Vienna,* 1958

1482   People who have power respond simply. They have no minds but their own.— Ivy Compton-Burnett, *The Mighty and Their Fall,* 1961

1483   Concentrated power is not rendered harmless by the good intentions of those who create it.— Milton Friedman, *Capitalism and Freedom,* 1962

1484   Power always protects the good of some at the expense of all others.— Thomas Merton, *Faith and Violence,* 1968

1485   Power is not only what you have but what the enemy thinks you have.— Saul Alinsky, *Rules for Radicals,* 1971

1486   Power comes not from the barrel of a gun, but from one's awareness of his or her own cultural strength and the unlimited capacity to empathize with, feel for, care, and love one's brothers and sisters.— Addison Gayle, Jr., *The Black Aesthetic,* 1971

1487   Power without responsibility is the prerogative of the harlot throughout the ages.— Rudyard Kipling, *Kipling Journal,* December, 1971

1488   When power feels itself totally justified and approved it immediately destroys whatever freedom we have left; and that is fascism.— Luis Buñuel, in *New York Times Magazine,* March 11, 1973

1489   The new source of power is not money in the hands of a few but information in the hands of many.— John Naisbitt, *Megatrends,* 1984

1490   In the United States, though power corrupts, the expectation of power paralyzes.— John Kenneth Galbraith, *A View from the Stands,* 1986

1491   The exercise of power is determined by thousands of interactions between the world of the powerful and that of the powerless, all the more so because these worlds are never divided by a sharp line: everyone has a small part of himself in both.— Václav Havel, *Disturbing the Peace,* 1986

1492   For some men the power to destroy life becomes the equivalent to the female power to create life.— Myriam Miedzian, *Boys Will Be Boys,* 1991

1493   Power tires only those who do not have it.— Giulio Andreotti, in *Independent on Sunday,* April 5, 1992

Prayer

1494   Oh, I wish that God had not given me what I prayed for! It was not so good as I thought.— Johanna Spyri, *Heidi,* 1885

1495   Prayer is not asking. It is a longing of the soul. It is daily admission of one's weakness. It is better in prayer to have a heart without words than words without a heart.— Mahatma Gandhi, in *Young India,* January 23, 1930

1496   I believe in prayer. It's the best way we have to draw strength from heaven.— Josephine Baker, *Josephine,* 1977

Prejudice

1497   The color of the skin is in no way connected with strength of the mind or intellectual powers.— Benjamin Banneker, *Banneker's Almanac,* 1796

1498   Prejudice is the child of ignorance.— William Hazlitt, *Sketches and Essays,* 1839

1499   One may no more live in the world without picking up the moral prejudices of the world than one will be able to go to hell without perspiring.— H. L. Mencken, *Prejudices, Second Series,* 1920

1500   Prejudice is a raft unto which the shipwrecked mind clambers and paddles to safety.— Ben Hecht, *A Guide to the Bedevilled,* 1944

Progress

1501   I cannot help fearing that men may reach a point where they look on every new theory as a danger, every innovation as a toilsome trouble, every social advance as a first step toward revolution, and that they may absolutely refuse to move at all.— Alexis de Tocqueville, *Democracy in America,* 1840

1502   Economic progress, in capitalist society, means turmoil.— Joseph A. Schumpeter, *Capitalism, Socialism and Democracy,* 1942

1503   Martyrs are needed to create incidents. Incidents are needed to create revolutions. Revolutions are needed to create progress. — Chester Himes, *The Crisis*, 1943

1504   Is it progress if a cannibal uses knife and fork? — Stanisław Lec, *Unkempt Thoughts*, 1962

1505   Progress is the attraction that moves humanity. — Marcus, *Garvey and Garveyism*, 1963

1506   Enthusiastic partisans of the idea of progress are in danger of failing to recognize the immense riches accumulated by the human race. By underrating the achievements of the past, they devalue all those which still remain to be accomplished. — Claude Lévi-Strauss, *Tristes Tropiques*, 1955

1507   The machine has had a pernicious effect upon virtue, pity and love, and young men used to machines which induce inertia, and fear, are near impotents. — Edward Dahlberg, *Alms for Oblivion*, 1964

1508   Why do progress and beauty have to be so opposed? — Anne Morrow Lindbergh, *Hour of Glory, Hour of Lead*, 1973

1509   Progress is man's ability to complicate simplicity. — Thor Heyerdahl, *Fatu-Hiva*, 1974

Promises

1510   One must have a good memory to be able to keep the promises one makes. — Friedrich Nietzsche, *Human, All Too Human*, 1878

1511   I like to deliver more than I promise instead of the other way around.

Which is just one of my many trade secrets. — Dorothy Uhnak, *The Investigation*, 1977

Propaganda

1512   Men willingly believe what they wish. — Julius Caesar, *De Bello Gallico*, 1st c. B.C.

1513   What I tell you three times is true. — Lewis Carroll, *The Hunting of the Snark*, 1876

1514   A belief is not true because it is useful. — Henri Frédéric Amiel, *Amiel's Journal*, 1883

1515   The truth is rarely pure, and never simple. — Oscar Wilde, *The Importance of Being Earnest*, 1895

1516   When war is declared, truth is the first casualty. — Arthur Ponsonly, *Falsehood in Wartime*, 1928

1517   It is very dangerous to write the truth in war, and the truth is also very dangerous to come by. — Ernest Hemingway, speech, June 4, 1937

1518   The propagandist's purpose is to make one set of people forget that certain other sets of people are human. — Aldous Huxley, *The Olive Tree*, 1937

1519   Propaganda is a soft weapon; hold it in your hands too long, and it will move about like a snake, and strike the other way. — Jean Anouilh, *The Lark*, 1955

1520   An unexciting truth may be eclipsed by a thrilling lie. — Aldous Huxley, *Brave New World Revisited*, 1958

1521   Propaganda has a bad name, but its root meaning is simply to disseminate through a medium, and all writing therefore is propaganda for something. It's a seeding of the self in the consciousness of others.— Elizabeth A. Drew, *Poetry: A Modern Guide to Its Understanding and Enjoyment*, 1959

1522   Propaganda is that branch of the art of lying which consists in nearly deceiving your friends without quite deceiving your enemies.— F. M. Cornford, in *New Statesman*, September 15, 1978

1523   In wartime, truth is so precious that she should always be attended by a bodyguard of lies.— Winston S. Churchill, in *Time*, December 24, 1984

Public Opinion

1524   The opinion of the strongest is always the best.— Jean de La Fontaine, *Fables*, 1668

1525   Journalists have constructed for themselves a little wooden chapel, which they also call the Temple of Fame.— G. C. Lichtenberg, *Aphorisms*, 1765–99

1526   I am very fond of truth, but not at all of martyrdom.— Voltaire, letter February, 1776

1527   It is the besetting vice of democracies to substitute public opinion for law. This is the usual form in which the masses of men exhibit their tyranny.— James Fenimore Cooper, *The American Democrat*, 1838

1528   Public opinion is a weak tyrant compared with our own private opinion.— Henry David Thoreau, *Walden*, 1854

1529   Public opinion is stronger than the legislature, and nearly as strong as the Ten Commandments.— Charles Dudley Warner, *My Summer in a Garden*, 1870

1530   There is nothing that makes more cowards and feeble men than public opinion.— Henry Ward Beecher, *Proverbs from Plymouth Pulpit*, 1887

1531   What we call public opinion is generally public sentiment.— Benjamin Disraeli, speech, August 3, 1880

1532   The history of the world is the record of the weakness, frailty and death of public opinion.— Samuel Butler, *Note-Books*, 1912

1533   Its name is Public Opinion. It is held in reverence. It settles everything. Some think it is the voice of God.— Mark Twain, *Europe and Elsewhere*, 1925

1534   One should respect public opinion in so far as is necessary to avoid starvation and to keep out of prison, but anything that goes beyond this is voluntary submission to an unnecessary tyranny.— Bertrand Russell, *The Conquest of Happiness*, 1930

1535   It is tremendously to the people's interests that they should understand the causes of war — but it is very hard to get them interested in the subject.— Kenneth Burke, *Permanence and Change*, 1935

Punishment

1536   The reality of a future punishment is so clearly impressed on the human mind that even Satan is constrained to own that there is a hell.— Lemuel B. Haynes, *Universal Salvation — A Very Ancient Doctrine.* 1795

1537   All in all, punishment hardens and renders people more insensible; it concentrates; it increases the feeling of estrangement; it strengthens the power of resistance.— Friedrich Nietzsche, *The Genealogy of Morals*, 1887

1538   It's punishment to be compelled to do what one doesn't wish.— Alice Dunbar-Nelson, *Give Us Each Day*, 1984

Questions

1539   A wise man's question contains half the answer.— Solomon Ibn Gabirol, ca. 1050

1540   I will be a fool in question, hoping to be wiser by your answer.— William Shakespeare, *All's Well That Ends Well*, 1602

1541   Questions are never indiscreet. Answers sometimes are. —Oscar Wilde, *An Ideal Husband*, 1895

1542   We never stop investigating. We are never satisfied that we know enough to get by. Every question we answer leads on to another question. This has become the greatest survival trick of our species.— Desmond Morris, *The Naked Ape*, 1967

1543   The real questions refuse to be placated. They are the questions asked most frequently and answered most inadequately, the ones that reveal their true natures slowly, reluctantly, most often against your will.— Ingrid Bengis, *Combat in the Erogenous Zone*, 1973

1544   That, is the essence of science: ask an impertinent question, and you are on the way to the pertinent answer.— Jacob Bronowski, *The Ascent of Man*, 1973

Radicals

1545   The radical invents the views. When he has worn them out the conservative adopts them.— Mark Twain, *Notebook*, 1935

1546   A young man who is not a radical about something is a pretty poor risk for education.— Jacques Barzun, *The Teacher in America*, 1944

Reading

1547   To read well, that is, to read true books in a true spirit, is a noble exercise, and one that will task the reader more than any other exercise which the customs of the day esteem. It requires a training such as the athletes underwent.— Henry David Thoreau, *Walden*, 1854

1548   Early in the morning, at break of day, in all the freshness and dawn of one's strength, to read a book—I call that vicious!— Friedrich Nietzsche, *Ecce Homo*, 1908

1549   People say that life is the thing, but I prefer reading.— Logan Pearsall Smith, *Afterthoughts*, 1931

1550   What I like best is a book that's at least funny once in a while. What really knocks me out is a book that, when you're all done reading it, you wish the author that wrote it was a terrific friend of yours and you could call him up on the phone.— J. D. Salinger, *The Catcher in the Rye*, 1951

1551   Blockbusting fiction is bought as furniture. Unread, it maintains its value.

Read, it looks like money wasted. Cunningly, Americans know that books contain a person, and they want the person, not the book.— Anthony Burgess, *You've Had Your Time*, 1990

1552   There are worse crimes than burning books. One of them is not reading them.— Joseph Brodsky, in *Independent on Sunday*, May 19, 1991

Reason

1553   Reason cannot be forced into belief.— Hasdai Crescas, *Or Adonai*, 1410

1554   Let reason by thy schoolmistress.— Walter Ralegh, *Instructions to His Son*, 1616

1555   Time makes more converts than reason.— Thomas Paine, *Common Sense*, 1776

1556   A mind all logic is like a knife all blade. It makes the hand bleed that uses it.— Rabindranath Tagore, *Stray Birds*, 1916

1557   There are strange flowers of reason to match each error of the senses.— Louis Aragon, *Paris Peasant*, 1926

1558   Reason is man's instrument for arriving at the truth, intelligence is man's instrument for manipulating the world more successfully; the former is essentially human, the latter belongs to the animal part of man.— Erich Fromm, *The Sane Society*, 1955

Reform

1559   There is nothing more difficult to take in hand, more perilous to conduct, or more uncertain in its success, than to take the lead in the introduction of a new order of things.— Niccolò Machiavelli, *The Prince*, 1513

1560   To innovate is not to reform.— Edmund Burke, *A Letter to a Noble Lord*, 1796

1561   An invasion of armies can be resisted; an invasion of ideas cannot be resisted.— Victor Hugo, *Historie d'un crime*, 1877

1562   All reformers are bachelors.— George Moore, *The Bending of the Bough*, 1900

1563   Every man is a reformer until reform tramps on his toes.— Edgar Watson Howe, *Country Town Sayings*, 1911

1564   Unless the reformer can invent something which substitutes attractive virtues for attractive vices, he will fail.— Walter Lippmann, *A Preface to Politics*, 1913

1565   All Reformers, however strict their social conscience, live in houses just as big as they can pay for.— Logan Pearsall Smith, *Afterthoughts*, 1931

Religion

1566   Almost every sect of Christianity is a perversion of its essence, to accommodate it to the prejudices of the world.— William Hazlitt, *The Round Table*, 1817

1567   After coming into contact with a religious man I always feel I must wash my hands. — Friedrich Nietzsche, *Ecce Homo*, 1888

1568   The difference between a saint and a hypocrite is that one lies for his religion, the other by it. — Minna Thomas Antrim, *Naked Truth and Veiled Allusions*, 1902

1569   Never was Catholicism, never were the ideas of chivalry, impressed on men so deeply, so multifariously, as the bourgeois ideas. — Aleksandr Herzen, *My Past and Thoughts*, 1921

1570   The supreme satisfaction is to be able to despise one's neighbor and this fact goes far to account for religious intolerance. It is evidently consoling to reflect that the people next door are headed for hell. — Aleister Crowley, *The Confessions of Aleister Crowley*, 1929

1571   The church must be reminded that it is not the master or the servant of the state, but rather the conscience of the state. It must be the guide and the critic of the state, and never its tool. — Martin Luther King, Jr., *Strength to Love*, 1963

1572   There is no greater distance than that between a man in prayer and God. — Ivan Illich, *Celebration of Awareness*, 1969

1573   The great achievement of the Catholic Church lay in harmonizing, civilizing the deepest impulses of ordinary, ignorant people. — Kenneth MacKenzie Clark, *Civilization*, 1970

1574   In our patriarchal world, we are all taught — whether we like to think we are or not — that God, being male, values maleness much more than he values femaleness, that in order to propitiate God, women must propitiate men. —

Sonia Johnson, *From Housewife to Heretic*, 1981

1575   For god is nothing other than the eternally creative source of our relational power, our common strength, a god whose movement is to empower, bringing us into our own together, a god whose name in history is love. — Carter Heyward, *Our Passion for Justice*, 1984

1576   Without an understanding of myth or religion, without an understanding of the relationship between destruction and creation, death and rebirth, the individual suffers the mysteries of life as meaningless mayhem alone. — Marion Woodman, *The Pregnant Virgin*, 1985

Revenge

1577   A man that studieth revenge keeps his own wounds green, which otherwise would heal and do well. — Francis Bacon, *Essays*, 1597–1625

1578   Living well is the best revenge. — George Herbert, *Jacula Prudentum*, 1651

Revolution

1579   Never contend with a man who has nothing to lose. — Baltasar Gracián, *The Art of Worldly Wisdom*, 1647

1580   Assassination is the quickest way. — Molière, *Le Sicilien*, 1668

1581   When the people contend for their liberty they seldom get anything by their victory but new masters. — George Savile, *Political, Moral and Miscellaneous Thoughts and Reflections*, 1750

1582   By a revolution in the state, the fawning sycophant of yesterday is converted into the austere critic of the present hour.— Edmund Burke, *Reflections on the Revolution in France,* 1790

1583   If we glance at the most important revolutions in history, we see at once that the greatest number of these originated in the periodical revolutions of the human mind.— Karl Wilhelm, Baron von Humboldt, *Limits of State Action,* 1792

1584   In revolutions there are only two sorts of men, those who cause them and those who profit by them.— Napoleon Bonaparte, *Maxims,* 1804–15

1585   The Revolution is like Saturn — it eats its own children.— Georg Büchner, *Danton's Death,* 1835

1586   Only those who have nothing to lose ever revolt.— Alexis de Tocqueville, *Democracy in America,* 1835

1587   Without revolution no new history can begin.— Moses Hess, *The Philosophy of the Act,* 1843

1588   Who stops the revolution half way? The bourgeoisie.— Victor Hugo, *Les Misérables,* 1862

1589   Assassination is the extreme form of censorship.— George Bernard Shaw, *The Showing Up of Blanco Posnet,* 1911

1590   All great truths begin as blasphemies.— George Bernard Shaw, *Annajanska,* 1919

1591   The doctrine of the Kingdom of Heaven, which was the main teaching of Jesus, is certainly one of the most revolutionary doctrines that ever stirred and changed human thought.— H. G. Wells, *Outline of History,* 1920

1592   The oppressed are always morally in the right.— Robert Briffault, *Rational Evolution,* 1930

1593   A revolution only lasts fifteen years, a period which coincides with the effectiveness of a generation.— José Ortega y Gasset, *The Revolt of the Masses,* 1930

1594   Revolution is a transfer of property from class to class.— Leon Samson, *The New Humanism,* 1930

1595   The urge to save humanity is almost always only a false-face for the urge to rule it.— H. L. Mencken, *Minority Report,* 1956

1596   In revolutionary times the rich are always the people who are most afraid.— Gerald White Johnson, *American Freedom and the Press,* 1958

1597   Revolutions are brought about by men, by men who think as men of action and act as men of thought.— Kwame Nkrumah, *Consciencism,* 1964

1598   Only a moral revolution — not a social or a political revolution — only a moral revolution would lead man back to his lost truth.— Simone de Beauvoir, *Les Belles Images,* 1966

1599   The most radical revolutionary will become a conservative the day after the revolution.— Hannah Arendt, in *New Yorker,* September 12, 1970

1600   The more revolutions occur, the less things change.— Georgie Anne Geyer, *The New Latins,* 1970

1601   Revolution is the festival of the oppressed.— Germaine Greer, *The Female Eunuch,* 1970

Romance

1602 Romance, like alcohol, should be enjoyed but must not be allowed to become necessary.— Edgar Z. Friedenberg, *The Vanishing Adolescent*, 1959

1603 In real love you want the other person's good. In romantic love you want the other person.— Margaret Anderson, *The Fiery Fountains*, 1969

1604 The requirements of romantic love are difficult to satisfy in the trunk of a Dodge Dart.— Lisa Alther, *Kinflicks*, 1976

Rulers

1605 In the kingdom of the blind the one-eyed man is king.— Desiderius Erasmus, *Adagia*, 1500

1606 Uneasy lies the head that wears a crown. William Shakespeare, *Henry IV, Part II*, 1597

1607 It is never possible to rule innocently.— Louis de Saint-Just, speech, November 13, 1792

1608 A prince who gets a reputation for good nature in the first year of his reign, is laughed at in the second.— Napoleon Bonaparte, letter, April 4, 1807

1609 All kings is mostly rapscallions.— Mark Twain, *Huckleberry Finn*, 1884

1610 A man may build himself a throne of bayonets, but he cannot sit on it.— William Ralph Inge, *Philosophy of Plotinus*, 1923

Sadness

1611 Proud people breed sad sorrows for themselves.— Emily Brontë, *Wuthering Heights*, 1847

1612 Renunciation remains sorrow, though a sorrow borne willingly.— George Eliot, *The Mill on the Floss*, 1860

1613 Words are less needful to sorrow than to joy.— Helen Hunt Jackson, *Ramona*, 1884

1614 Man could not live if he were entirely impervious to sadness. Many sorrows can be endured only by being embraced, and the pleasure taken in them naturally has a somewhat melancholy character.— Emile Durkheim, *Suicide*, 1897

1615 We who live in prison, and in whose lives there is no event but sorrow, have to measure time by throbs of pain, and the record of bitter moments.— Oscar Wilde, *De Profundis*, 1905

1616 No society has been able to abolish human sadness, no political system can deliver us from the pain of living, from our fear of death, our thirst for the absolute. It is the human condition that directs the social condition, not vice versa.— Eugène Ionesco, in *Observer*, June 29, 1958

Scholarship

1617 It is the vice of the scholar to suppose that there is no knowledge in the world but that of books.— William Hazlitt, *Literary Remains*, 1836

1618   A scholar is a man with this inconvenience, that, when you ask him his opinion of any matter, he must go home and look up his manuscripts to know. — Ralph Waldo Emerson, *Journals*, 1855

1619   The scholar digs his ivory cellar in the ruins of the past and lets the present sicken as it will. — Archibald MacLeish, *The Irresponsibles*, 1940

Science

1620   Science is the knowledge of consequences, and dependence of one fact upon another. — Thomas Hobbes, *Leviathan*, 1651

1621   Science is the great antidote of the poison of enthusiasm and superstition. — Adam Smith, *The Wealth of Nations*, 1776

1622   The work of science is to substitute facts for appearances, and demonstrations for impressions. — John Ruskin, *The Stones of Venice*, 1851

1623   Science increases our power in proportion as it lowers our pride. — Claude Bernard, *Introduction to the Study of Experimental Medicine*, 1865

1624   Traditional scientific method has always been at the very best, 20–20 hindsight. It's good for seeing where you've been. — Robert Pirsig, *Zen and the Art of Motorcycle Maintenance*, 1874

1625   All sciences are now under the obligation to prepare the ground for the future task of the philosopher, which is to solve the problem of value, to determine the true hierarchy of values. — Friedrich Nietzsche, *The Genealogy of Morals*, 1887

1626   Science, like life, feeds on its own decay. New facts burst old rules; then newly divined conceptions bind old and new together into a reconciling law. — William James, *The Will to Believe*, 1897

1627   True science investigates and brings to human perception such truths and such knowledge as the people of a given time and society consider most important. Art transmits these truths from the region of perception. — Leo Tolstoy, *What Is Art?*, 1898

1628   Science is nothing but developed perception, interpreted intent, common sense rounded out and minutely articulated. — George Santayana, *The Life of Reason*, 1905–06

1629   The ordinary scientific man is strictly a sentimentalist. He is a sentimentalist in this essential sense, that he is soaked and swept away by mere associations. — Gilbert K. Chesterton, *Orthodoxy*, 1908

1630   Science is always simple and profound. It is only half truths that are dangerous. — George Bernard Shaw, *The Doctor's Dilemma*, 1911

1631   True science teaches, above all, to doubt, and to be ignorant. — Miguel de Unamuno, *The Tragic Sense of Life*, 1912

1632   Science is a cemetery of dead ideas. — Miguel de Unamuno, *The Tragic Sense of Life*, 1913

1633   Science, which cuts its way through the muddy pond of daily life without mingling with it, casts its wealth to right and left, but the puny boatmen do not know how to fish for it. — Aleksandr Herzen, *My Past and Thoughts*, 1921

1634   Science is knowledge arranged

and classified according to truth, facts, and the general laws of nature.— Luther Burbank, in *San Francisco Bulletin*, January 22, 1926

1635 When we say "science" we can either mean any manipulation of the inventive and organizing power of the human intellect: or we can mean such an extremely different thing as the religion of science, the vulgarized derivative from this pure activity.— Wyndham Lewis, *The Art of Being Ruled*, 1926

1636 It sometimes strikes me that the whole of science is a piece of impudence; that nature can afford to ignore our impertinent interference.— Aleister Crowley, *The Confessions of Aleister Crowley*, 1929

1637 Science, in the very act of solving problems, creates more of them.— Abraham Flexner, *Universities*, 1930

1638 Science should leave off making pronouncements: the river of knowledge has too often turned back on itself. James Jeans, *The Mysterious Universe*, 1931

1639 Science is the attempt to make the chaotic diversity of our sense-experience correspond to a logically uniform system of thought.— Albert Einstein, *Out of My Later Years*, 1950

1640 Both the man of science and the man of action live always at the edge of mystery, surrounded by it.— J. Robert Oppenheimer, address, December 26, 1954

1641 Science moves with the spirit of an adventure.— James D. Watson, *The Double Helix*, 1968

1642 What is a scientist after all? It is a curious man looking through a keyhole, the keyhole of nature, trying

to know what's going on.— Jacques Cousteau, in *Christian Science Monitor*, July 21, 1971

1643 The best scientist is open to experience and begins with the idea that anything is possible.— Ray Bradbury, in *Los Angeles Times*, August 9, 1976

1644 There comes a time when every scientist, even God, has to write off an experiment.— P. D. James, *Devices and Desires*, 1989

Secrets

1645 If you wish to preserve your secret, wrap it up in frankness.— Alexander Smith, *Dreamthorp*, 1863

1646 Confession is always weakness. The grave soul keeps its own secrets, and takes its own punishment in silence.— Dorothy Dix, *Dorothy Dix, Her Book*, 1926

1647 We are all, in a sense, experts on secrecy. From earliest childhood we feel its mystery and attraction. We know both the power it confers and the burden it imposes. We learn how it can delight, give breathing space and protect.— Sissela Bok, *Secrets*, 1983

Security

1648 Security is an insipid thing.— William Congreve, *Love for Love*, 1695

1649 He that has gone so far as to cut the claws of the lion, will not feel himself quite secure until he has also drawn his teeth.— Charles Caleb Colton, *Lacon*, 1820–22

1650 Only in growth, reform, and change, paradoxically enough, is true security to be found.— Anne Morrow Lindbergh, *The Wave of the Future*, 1940

1651 Most people want security in this world, not liberty.— H. L. Mencken, *Minority Report* 1956

1652 The protected man doesn't need luck; therefore it seldom visits him.— Alan Harrington, *Life in the Crystal Palace*, 1959

1653 The Xerox machine is one of the biggest threats to national security ever devised.— Thomas Moorer, in *Time*, June 17, 1985

Seduction

1654 It is not enough to conquer; one must know how to seduce.— Voltaire, *Mérope*, 1743

1655 He said it was artificial respiration, but now I find I am to have his child.— Anthony Burgess, *Inside Mr. Enderby*, 1963

1656 To seduce a woman famous for strict morals, religious fervor and the happiness of her marriage: what could possibly be more prestigious?— Christopher Hampton, *Dangerous Liaisons*, 1989

Sex

1657 Is it not strange that desire should so many years outlive performance?— William Shakespeare, *Henry IV, Part II*, 1597–98

1658 There are two things I have always loved madly: they are women and celibacy.— Sébastien-Roch Nicolas Chamfort, *Maximes et pensées*, 1796

1659 Sex is the lyricism of the masses.— Charles Baudelaire, *Intimate Journals*, 1887

1660 Wherever the religious neurosis has appeared on earth so far, we find it connected with three dangerous prescriptions as to regimen: solitude, fasting, and sexual abstinence.— Friedrich Nietzsche, *Beyond Good and Evil*, 1886

1661 To be womanly is one thing, and one only; it is to be sensitive to man, to be highly endowed with the sex instinct; to be manly is to be sensitive to woman.— Jane Harrison, *Alpha and Omega*, 1915

1662 Instead of this absurd division into sexes they ought to class people as static and dynamic.— Evelyn Waugh, *Decline and Fall*, 1928

1663 Part of the public horror of sexual irregularity so-called is due to the fact that everyone knows himself essentially guilty.— Aleister Crowley, *The Confessions of Aleister Crowley*, 1929

1664 The man experiences the highest unfolding of his creative powers not through asceticism but through sexual happiness.— Mathilde von Kemnitz, *The Triumph of the Immortal Will*, 1932

1665 Most successes are unhappy. That's why they are successes— they have to reassure themselves about themselves by achieving something that the world will notice.— Agatha Christie, *Remembered Death*, 1945

1666 Sex is one of the nine reasons for reincarnation. The other eight are unimportant.— Henry Miller, *Sexus*, 1949

1667 Tamed as it may be, sexuality remains one of the demonic forces in human consciousness— pushing us at intervals close to taboo and dangerous desires.— Susan Sontag, *Styles of Radical Will*, 1969

1668 Sex is a black tarantula and sex without religion is like an egg without salt.— Luis Buñuel, in *New York Times Magazine*, March 11, 1973

1669 Sex is not some sort of pristine, reverent ritual. You want reverent and pristine, go to church.— Cynthia Heimel, *Sex Tips for Girls*, 1983

1670 Being a sex symbol has to do with an attitude, not looks. Most men think it's looks, most women know otherwise.— Kathleen Turner, in *Observer*, April 27, 1986

1671 Really, sex and laughter do go very well together, and I wondered — and I still do— which is more important.— Hermione Gingold, *How to Grow Old Disgracefully*, 1988

1672 To ask women to become unnaturally thin is to ask them to relinquish their sexuality.— Naomi Wolf, *The Beauty Myth*, 1990

1673 Understand that sexuality is as wide as the sea. Understand that your morality is not law. Understand that we are you. Understand that if we decide to have sex whether safe, safer, or unsafe, it is our decision.— Derek Jarman, *At Your Own Risk: A Saint's Testament*, 1992

Shame

1674 With memory set smarting like a reopened wound, a man's past is not simply a dead history, an outworn preparation of the present: it is a still quivering part of himself, bringing shudders and bitter flavors and the tinglings of a merited shame.— George Eliot, *Middlemarch*, 1871

1675 The more things a man is ashamed of, the more respectable he is.— George Bernard Shaw, *Man and Superman*, 1905

1676 The basis of shame is not some personal mistake of ours, but the ignominy, the humiliation we feel that we must be what we are without any choice in the matter, and that this humiliation is seen by everyone.— Milan Kundera, *Immortality*, 1991

Silence

1677 Under all speech that is good for anything there lies a silence that is better. Silence is deep as Eternity; speech is shallow as Time.— Thomas Carlyle, *Critical and Miscellaneous Essays*, 1839

1678 Silence is the universal refuge, the sequel to all dull discourses and all foolish acts, a balm to our every chagrin, as welcome after satiety as after disappointment.— Henry David Thoreau, *A Week on the Concord and Merrimack Rivers*, 1849

1679 That man's silence is wonderful to listen to.— Thomas Hardy, *Under the Greenwood Tree*, 1872

1680 Among all nations there should be vast temples raised where people might worship in Silence and listen to it, for it is the voice of God.— Jerome K. Jerome, *Diary of a Pilgrimage*, 1891

1681 Everything has it wonders, even darkness and silence, and I learn, whatever state I may be in, therein to be content.— Helen Keller, *The Story of My Life*, 1903

1682   Decency is Indecency's conspiracy of silence.— George Bernard Shaw, *Man and Superman*, 1903

1683   True penitence condemns to silence. What a man is ready to recall he would be willing to repeat.— Francis H. Bradley, *Aphorisms*, 1930

1684   Silences have a climax, when you have got to speak.— Elizabeth Bowen, *The House in Paris*, 1936

1685   A small silence came between us, as precise as a picture hanging on the wall.— Jean Stafford, *Boston Adventure*, 1944

1686   Recognize the cunning man not by the corpses he pays homage to but by the living writers he conspires against with the most shameful weapon, Silence, or the briefest review.— Edward Dahlberg, *Alms for Oblivion*, 1964

1687   Speech and silence. We feel safer with a madman who talks than with one who cannot open his mouth.— Emile M. Cioran, *The New Gods*, 1969

1688   It takes more time and effort and delicacy to learn the silence of a people than to learn its sounds. Some people have a special gift for this. Perhaps this explains why some missionaries, notwithstanding their efforts, never come to speak properly.— Ivan Illich, *Celebration of Awareness*, 1969

1689   Learn to get in touch with silence within yourself and know that everything in life has a purpose.— Elisabeth Kübler-Ross, in *Yoga Journal*, November 1, 1976

1690   To communicate through silence is a link between the thoughts of man.—

Marcel Marceau, in U.S. News and World Report, February 23, 1987

1691   One of the hardest things in life is having words in your heart that you can't utter.— James Earl Jones, *Voices and Silences*, 1993

Simplicity

1692   The noble simplicity in the works of nature only too often originates in the noble shortsightedness of him who observes it.— G. C. Lichtenberg, *Aphorisms*, 1765–99

1693   The art of art, the glory of expression and the sunshine of the light of letters, is simplicity.— Walt Whitman, *Leaves of Grass*, 1855

1694   Simplicity is an acquired taste. Mankind, left free, instinctively complicates life.— Katherine F. Gerould, *Modes and Morals*, 1920

1695   No endeavor that is worthwhile is simple in prospect; if it is right, it will be simple in retrospect.— Edward Teller, *The Pursuit of Simplicity*, 1980

Sincerity

1696   A little sincerity is a dangerous thing, and a great deal of it is absolutely fatal.— Oscar Wilde, The Picture of Dorian Gray, 1891

1697   I have long since come to believe that people never mean half of what they say, and that it is best to disregard their talk and judge only their actions.— Dorothy Day, *The Long Loneliness*, 1952

Skepticism

1698   What has not been examined impartially has not been well examined. Skepticism is therefore the first step toward truth.— Denis Diderot, *Pensées Philosophiques*, 1746

1699   A wise skepticism is the first attribute of a good critic.— James Russell Lowell, *Among My Books*, 1870

1700   Scepticism is the beginning of Faith.— Oscar Wilde, *The Picture of Dorian Gray*, 1891

1701   The fact that a believer is happier than a skeptic is no more to the point than the fact that a drunken man is happier than a sober one. The happiness of credulity is a cheap and dangerous quality. —George Bernard Shaw, *Androcles and the Lion*, 1916

1702   Skepticism is the chastity of the intellect.— George Santayana, *Skepticism and Animal Faith*, 1923

1703   The path to sound credence is through the thick forest of skepticism. —George Jean Nathan, *Materia Critica*, 1924

1704   The civilized man has a moral obligation to be skeptical, to demand the credentials of all statements that claim to be facts.— Bergen Evans, *The Natural History of Nonsense*, 1946

Slavery

1705   Better to reign in hell, than serve in heaven.— John Milton, *Paradise Lost*, 1667

1706   Slaves lose everything in their chains, even the desire of escaping from them.— Jean-Jacques Rousseau, *The Social Contract*, 1762

1707   If you put a chain around the neck of a slave, the other end fastens itself around your own.— Ralph Waldo Emerson, *Essays, First Series*, 1841

1708   There is no king who has not had a slave among his ancestors, and no slave who has not had a king among his.— Helen Keller, *The Story of My Life*, 1903

1709   Men would rather be starving and free than fed in bonds.— Pearl S. Buck, *What America Means to Me*, 1943

Sleep

1710   No man can become a saint in his sleep.— Henry Drummond, *The Greatest Thing in the World*, 1890

1711   The last refuge of the insomniac is a sense of superiority to the sleeping world.— Leonard Cohen, *The Favorite Game*, 1963

Society

1712   The open society, the unrestricted access to knowledge, the unplanned and uninhibited association of men for its furtherance; these are what may make a vast, complex, ever growing, ever changing, ever more specialized and expert technological world.— J. Robert Oppenheimer, *Science and the Common Understanding*, 1953

1713   The anthropologist respects history, but he does not accord it a special value. He conceives it as a study complementary to his own: one of them unfurls the range of human societies in time, the other in space.— Claude Lévi-Strauss, *The Savage Mind*, 1962

1714   There is only one way left to escape the alienation of present day society: to retreat ahead of it.— Roland Barthes, *The Pleasure of the Text*, 1975

1715   Today Americans are overcome not by the sense of endless possibility but by the banality of the social order they have erected against it.— Christopher Lasch, *The Culture of Narcissism*, 1979

1716   We pass the word around; we ponder how the case is put by different people, we read the poetry; we meditate over the literature; we play the music; we change our minds; we reach an understanding. Society evolves this way.— Lewis Thomas, *The Medusa and the Snail*, 1979

1717   We still have discrimination because society isn't doing a good enough job.— Judith Martin, *Miss Manner's Guide to Excruciatingly Correct Behavior*, 1982

Solutions

1718   Good resolutions are simply checks that men draw on a bank where they have no account.— Oscar Wilde, *The Picture of Dorian Gray*, 1891

1719   It is living and ceasing to live that are imaginary solutions. Existence is elsewhere.— André Breton, *Manifesto of Surrealism*, 1924

1720   Utility is our national shibboleth: the savior of the American businessman is fact and his uterine half-brother, sta-

tistics.— Edward Dahlberg, *The Carnal Myth*, 1968

Speech

1721   Men of few words are the best men.— William Shakespeare, *Henry V*, 1599

1722   He's a wonderful talker, who has the art of telling you nothing in a great harangue.— Molière, *Le Misanthrope*, 1666

1723   The world would be happier if men had the same capacity to be silent that they have to speak.— Baruch Spinoza, *Ethics*, 1677

1724   Blessed is the man who, having nothing to say, abstains from giving us wordy evidence of the fact.— George Eliot, *The Impressions of Theophrastus Such*, 1879

1725   We shall probably have nothing to say, but we intend to say it at great length.— Don Marquis, *The Almost Perfect State*, 1927

Statistics

1726   Statistics is the art of lying by means of figures.— Wilhelm Stekel, *Marriage at the Crossroads*, 1931

1727   Statistics are the triumph of the quantitative method, and the quantitative method is the victory of sterility and death.— Hilaire Belloc, *The Silence of the Sea*, 1941

Strategy

1728   Delays have dangerous ends.—William Shakespeare, *Henry VI, Part I,* 1592

1729   In the end it is how you fight, as much as why you fight, that makes your cause good or bad.—Freeman Dyson, *Disturbing the Universe,* 1979

Strength

1730   Soft countries give birth to soft men.—Herodotus, *The History,* ca. 450 B.C.

1731   The gods are on the side of the stronger.—Tacitus, *Histories,* ca. 100

1732   Strengthen me by sympathizing with my strength, not my weakness.—Amos Bronson Alcott, Table Talk, 1877

1733   Go within every day and find the inner strength so that the world will not blow your candle out.—Katherine Dunham, in *American Visions,* February, 1937

1734   But the trouble is not as you think now, that we have put up obstacles too high for you to jump. It is that we have put up no obstacles at all. The great strength is in you.—Isak Dinesen, *Out of Africa,* 1938

1735   A weak man is just by accident. A strong but non-violent man is unjust by accident.—Mahatma Gandhi, *Non-Violence in Peace and War, Volume 1,* 1942

1736   The turning point in the process of growing up is when you discover the core of strength within you survives all

hurt.—Max Lerner, *The Unfinished Country,* 1950

Stupidity

1737   There are only two ways by which to rise in this world, either by one's own industry or by the stupidity of others.—Jean de LaBruyere, *Les Characteres,* 1688

1738   Just as the performance of the vilest and most wicked deeds requires spirit and talent, so even the greatest demand a certain insensitivity which under other circumstances we would call stupidity.—G. C. Lichtenberg, *Aphorisms,* 1765 — 99

1739   It is stupidity rather than courage to refuse to recognize danger when it is close upon you.—Arthur Conan Doyle, *The Memoirs of Sherlock Holmes,* 1894

1740   The great and almost only comfort about being a woman is that one can always pretend to be more stupid than one is and no one is surprised.—Freya Stark, *The Valleys of the Assassins,* 1934

1741   Indeed, the sole criticism of him was that he prolonged beyond the point of decency, his look of nuptial rapture and the vagueness which rendered him, in conversation, slightly stupid.—Jean Stafford, *Boston Adventure,* 1944

1742   The hardest thing to cope with is not selfishness or vanity or deceitfulness, but sheer stupidity.—Eric Hoffer, *The Passionate State of Mind,* 1954

1743   Strange as it may seem, no amount of learning can cure stupidity, and formal education positively fortifies it.—Stephen Vizinczey, in *Sunday Telegraph,* March 2, 1975

1744   We have not been scuffling in this waste-howling wildness for the right to be stupid.— Toni Cade Bambara, *The Salt Eaters*, 1980

1745   I'm patient with stupidity, but not with those who are proud of it.— Edith Sitwell, in *Reader's Digest*, February 1, 1993

Style

1746   When he killed a calf he would do it in a high style, and make a speech.— John Aubrey, *Brief Lives*, 1813

1747   Which, of all defects, has been the one most fatal to a good style? The not knowing when to come to an end.— Arthur Helps, *Companions of My Solitude*, 1852

1748   Every man is the builder of a temple, called his body, to the god he worships, after a style purely his own, nor can he get off by hammering marble instead. We are all sculptors and painters, and our material is our own flesh and blood and bones.— Henry David Thoreau, *Walden*, 1854

1749   Oh, never mind the fashion. When one has a style of one's own, it is always twenty times better.— Margaret Oliphant, *Miss Marjoribanks*, 1866

1750   An ethical sympathy in an artist is an unpardonable mannerism of style.— Oscar Wilde, *The Picture of Dorian Gray*, 1891

1751   An author arrives at a good style when his language performs what is required of it without shyness.— Cyril Connolly, *Enemies of Promise*, 1938

1752   A good style should show no sign of effort. What is written should seem a happy accident.— William Somerset Maugham, *The Summing Up*, 1938

1753   The evolution of the capitalist style of life could be easily — and perhaps most tellingly — described in terms of the genesis of the modern Lounge Suit.— Joseph A. Schumpeter, *Capitalism, Socialism and Democracy*, 1942

1754   Style is not something applied. It is something that permeates. It is of the nature of that in which it is found, whether the poem, the manner of a god, the bearing of a man. It is not a dress.— Wallace Stevens, *Opus Posthumous*, 1951

1755   In the final analysis, "style" is art. And art is nothing more or less than various modes of stylized, dehumanized representation.— Susan Sontag, *Against Interpretation*, 1966

1756   Fashions fade, style is eternal.— Yves Saint Laurent, in *New York*, April 13, 1975

1757   Eclecticism is the word. Like a jazz musician who creates his own style out of the styles around him, I play by ear.— Ralph Ellison, *The Essential Ellison*, 1978

Success

1758   Success plus Self-esteem equals Pretensions.— William James, *The Principles of Psychology*, 1890

1759   Human nature is the same everywhere; it deifies success, it has nothing but scorn for defeat.— Mark Twain, *Joan of Arc*, 1896

1760   Success makes men rigid and they tend to exalt stability over all the other virtues; tired of the effort of willing they become fanatics about conservatism.— Walter Lippmann, *A Preface to Politics*, 1913

1761   The logic of worldly success rests on a fallacy: the strange error that our perfection depends on the thoughts and opinions and applause of other men!— Thomas Merton, *The Seven Story Mountain*, 1948

1762   The penalty of success is to be bored by the people who used to snub you.— Nancy Astor, in *Sunday Express*, January 12, 1956

1763   The formula for achieving a successful relationship is simple: you should treat all disasters as if they were trivialities but never treat a triviality as if it were a disaster.— Quentin Crisp, *Manners from Heaven*, 1984

1768   God is the immemorial refuge of the incompetent, the helpless, the miserable. They find not only sanctuary in His arms, but also a kind of superiority, soothing to their macerated egos: He will set them above their betters.— H. L. Mencken, *Minority Report*, 1956

1769   When suffering knocks at your door and you say there is no seat for him, he tells you not to worry because he has brought his own stool.— Chinua Achebe, *Arrow of God*, 1967

1770   Suffering isn't ennobling, recovery is.— Christiaan Barnard, in *New York Times*, April 28, 1985

1771   It is not suffering as such that is most deeply feared but suffering that degrades.   Susan Sontag, *AIDS and Its Metaphors*, 1989

Suffering

1764   One does not love a place the less for having suffered in it unless it has all been suffering, nothing but suffering.— Jane Austen, *Persuasion*, 1818

1765   There are no bonds so strong as those which are formed by suffering together.— Harriet Ann Jacobs, *Incidents in the Life of a Slave Girl, Written By Herself*, 1861

1766   Although the world is full of suffering, it is full also of the overcoming of it.— Helen Keller, *Optimism*, 1903

1767   Suffering is the substance of life and the root of personality, for it is only suffering that makes us persons.— Miguel de Unamuno, *The Tragic Sense of Life*, 1913

Survival

1772   The survival of the fittest, which I have here sought to express in mechanical terms, is that which Mr. Darwin has called "natural selection, or the preservation of favored races in the struggle for life."— Herbert Spencer, *Principles of Biology*, 1864–67

1773   People are inexterminable — like flies and bedbugs. There will always be some that survive in cracks and crevices— that's us.— Robert Frost, in *Observer*, March 29, 1959

1774   He was as fitted to survival in this modern world as a tapeworm in an intestine.— William Golding, *Free Fall*, 1959

1775   In the name of Hippocrates, doctors have invented the most exquisite form of torture ever known to man: survival.— Luis Buñuel, *My Last Sigh*, 1983

1776   Survival is nothing more than recovery.— Dianne Feinstein, in *Boston Globe*, May 29, 1983

1777   Perhaps catastrophe is the natural human environment, and even though we spend a good deal of energy trying to get away from it, we are programmed for survival amid catastrophe.— Germaine Greer, *Sex and Destiny*, 1984

1778   In a world where change is inevitable and continuous, the need to achieve that change without violence is essential for survival.— Andrew Young, *A Way Out of No Way*, 1994

but to those who have suffered like themselves.— Catharine Esther Beecher, *Woman Suffrage and Women's Professions*, 1871

1783   The perception of the comic is a tie of sympathy with other men, a pledge of sanity, and a protection from those perverse tendencies and gloomy insanities in which fine intellects sometimes lose themselves.— Ralph Waldo Emerson, *Letters and Social Aims*, 1876

1784   There is something terribly morbid in the modern sympathy with pain. One should sympathize with the color, the beauty, the joy of life. The less said about life's sores the better.— Oscar Wilde, *The Picture of Dorian Gray*, 1891

Suspicion

1779   Suspicion always haunts the guilty mind; the thief doth fear each bush an officer.— William Shakespeare, *Henry VI, Part III*, 1592

1780   We are paid for our suspicions by finding what we suspected.— Henry David Thoreau, *A Week on the Concord and Merrimack Rivers*, 1849

1781   Suspicion is one of the morbid reactions by which an organism defends itself and seeks another equilibrium.— Nathalie Sarraute, *The Age of Suspicion*, 1950

Tact

1785   Talk to every woman as if you loved her, and to every man as if he bored you, and at the end of your first season you will have the reputation of possessing the most perfect social tact.— Oscar Wilde, *A Woman of No Importance*, 1893

1786   Tact is after all a kind of mind reading.— Sarah Orne Jewett, *The Country of the Pointed Firs and Other Stories*, 1896

1787   A man may lack everything but tact and conviction and still be a forcible speaker; but without these nothing will avail. Fluency, grace, logical order, and the like, are merely the decorative surface of oratory.— Charles Horton Cooley, *Human Nature and the Social Order*, 1902

Sympathy

1782   The delicate and infirm go for sympathy, not to the well and buoyant,

Talent

1788 If you have great talents, industry will improve them: if you have but moderate abilities, industry will supply their deficiency.— Joshua Reynolds, speech, December 11, 1769

1789 Who in the same given time can produce more than others has vigor; who can produce more and better, has talents; who can produce what none else can, has genius.— Johann Kasper Lavater, *Aphorisms on Man*, 1788

1790 Coffee is good for talent, but genius wants prayer.— Ralph Waldo Emerson, *Journal*, 1841

1791 Talent isn't genius and no amount of energy can make it so. I want to be great, or nothing. I won't be a commonplace dauber, so I don't intend to try any more.— Louisa May Alcott, *Little Women*, 1868

1792 Everybody is so talented nowadays that the only people I care to honor as deserving real distinction are those who remain in obscurity. Thomas Hardy, *The Hand of Ethelberta*, 1876

1793 The best friend is likely to acquire the best wife, because a good marriage is based on the talent for friendship.— Friedrich Nietzsche, *Human, All Too Human*, 1878

1794 It is a very rare thing for a man of talent to succeed by his talent.— Joseph Roux, *Meditations of a Parish Priest*, 1886

1795 The gift of teaching is a peculiar talent, and implies a need and a craving in the teacher himself.— John Jay Chapman, *Practical Agitation*, 1898

1796 There is no substitute for talent. Industry and all the virtues are of no avail.— Aldous Huxley, *Point Counter Point*, 1928

1797 To note an artist's limitations is but to define his talent.— Willa Cather, *Not Under Forty*, 1936

1798 If a man has a talent and cannot use it, he has failed. If he has a talent and uses only half of it, he has partly failed. If he has a talent and learns somehow to use the whole of it, he has gloriously succeeded.— Thomas Wolfe, *The Web and the Rock*, 1939

1799 Genius is talent provided with ideals.— William Somerset Maugham, *A Writer's Notebook*, 1949

1800 Talent is nothing but a prolonged period of attention and a shortened period of mental assimilation.— Konstantin Stanislavsky, *The Art of the Stage*, 1950

1801 Any writer, I suppose, feels that the world into which he was born is nothing less than a conspiracy against the cultivation of his talent.— James Baldwin, *Notes of a Native Son*, 1955

1802 Money demands that you sell, not your weakness to men's stupidity, but your talent to their reason.— Ayn Rand, *Atlas Shrugged*, 1957

1803 Talent is only a starting point in this business. You've got to keep on working that talent. Someday I'll reach for it and it won't be there.— Irving Berlin, in *Theatre Arts*, February, 1958

1804 Only the really plain people know about love. The very fascinating ones try so hard to create an impression that they soon exhaust their talents.— Katharine Hepburn, in *Look*, February 18, 1958

1805 Talent is like a faucet; while it is open, you have to write. Inspiration?—

a hoax fabricated by poets for their self-importance.— Jean Anouilh, in *New York Times*, October 2, 1960

1806   Middle age snuffs out more talent than ever wars or sudden deaths do.— Richard Hughes, *The Fox in the Attic*, 1961

1807   It takes little talent to see what is under one's nose, a good deal of it to know in what direction to point that organ.— W. H. Auden, *The Dyer's Hand*, 1962

1808   Our affluent society contains those of talent and insight who are driven to prefer poverty, to choose it, rather than to submit to the desolation of an empty abundance. It is a strange part of the other America that one finds in the intellectual slums.— Michael Harrington, *The Other America*, 1962

1809   I don't think success is harmful, as so many people say. Rather, I believe it indispensable to talent, if for nothing else than to increase the talent.— Jeanne Moreau, *The Egotists*, 1963

1810   Everyone has talent at twenty-five. The difficulty is to have it at fifty.— Edgar Degas, *The Notebooks of Edgar Degas*, 1976

1811   An idea can turn to dust or magic, depending on the talent that rubs against it.— William Bernbach, in *New York Times*, October 6, 1982

1812   Like a kick in the butt, the force of events wakes slumberous talents.— Edward Hoagland, in *Guardian* , August 11, 1990

1813   I remember always the need to know myself, because if I avoid knowing who I am deep inside, then I can't express what I have to say through the talent that I have.— Judith Jamison, *Dancing Spirit*, 1993

1814   Talent in cheaper than table salt. What separates the talented individual from the successful one is a lot of hard work.— Stephen King, in *Independent on Sunday*, March 10, 1996

Taste

1815   Good taste is either that which agrees with my taste or that which subjects itself to the rule of reason. From this we can see how useful it is to employ reason in seeking out the laws of taste.— G. C. Lichtenberg, *Aphorisms*, 1765–99

1816   If the study to which you apply yourself has a tendency to weaken your affections, and to destroy your taste for those simple pleasures in which no alloy can possibly mix, then that study is not befitting the human mind.— Mary Wollstonecraft Shelley, *Frankenstein*, 1818

1817   Taste is nothing but an enlarged capacity for receiving pleasure from works of imagination.— William Hazlitt, *Sketches and Essays*, 1839

1818   To achieve harmony in bad taste is the height of elegance.— Jean Genet, *The Thief's Journal*, 1949

1819   Taste has no system and no proofs.— Susan Sontag, *Against Interpretation*, 1961

1820   I base most of my fashion taste on what doesn't itch.— Gilda Radner, *It's Always Something*, 1989

1821   Taste is more to do with manners than appearances. Taste is both myth and reality; it is not a style.— Stephen Bayley, *Taste*, 1991

Taxes

1822   To tax and to please, no more than to love and to be wise, is not given to men. — Edmund Burke, *On American Taxation*, 1775

1823   If a thousand men were not to pay their tax-bills this year, that would not be a violent and bloody measure, as it would be to pay them, and enable the State to commit violence and shed innocent blood. — Henry David Thoreau, *On the Duty of Civil Disobedience*, 1849

1824   When everybody has got money they cut taxes, and when they're broke they raise 'em. That's statesmanship of the highest order. — Will Rogers, *Autobiography of Will Rogers*, 1949

1825   Government expands to absorb revenue and then some. — Tom Wicker, in *New York Times Magazine*, March 17, 1968

1826   The rich aren't like us — they pay less taxes. — Peter De Vries, *Washington Post*, July 30, 1989

Technology

1827   Technology, the knack of so arranging the world that we don't have to experience it. — Max Frisch, *Homo Faber*, 1957

1828   Technology is not in itself opposed to spirituality and to religion. But it presents a great temptation. — Thomas Merton, *Conjectures of a Guilty Bystander*, 1968

1829   Technology brings you great gifts with one hand, and it stabs you in the back with the other. — C. P. Snow, in *New York Times*, March 15, 1971

1830   Technology is so much fun but we can drown in our technology. The fog of information can drive out knowledge. — Daniel J. Boorstin, in *New York Times*, July 8, 1983

1831   We try to picture what the products will be and then say, what technology should we be working on today to help us get there? — John Sculley, in *Inc. Magazine*, January, 1988

Television

1832   Why should people go out and pay to see bad films when they can stay at home and see bad television for nothing? — Samuel Goldwyn, in *Observer*, September 9, 1956

1833   The time of the rack and the screws is come. Summer television has set in with its usual severity. And the small screen, where late the sweet birds sang, is now awash with repeats, reruns, rejects, replacements and reversions to the primitive. — Harriet Van Horne, in *New York World-Telegram and Sun*, June 2, 1958

1834   Every time you think television has hit its lowest ebb, a new program comes along to make you wonder where you thought the ebb was. — Art Buchwald, *Have I Ever Lied to You?*, 1968

1835   Television is the first truly democratic culture — the first culture available to everyone and entirely governed by what the people want. The most terrifying thing is what people do want. — Clive Barnes, in *New York Times*, December 30, 1969

1836 The difference between writing a book and being on television is the difference between conceiving a child and having a baby made in a test tube.— Norman Mailer, in *Village Voice*, January 21, 1971

1837 All television ever did was shrink the demand for ordinary movies. The demand for extraordinary movies increased. If any one thing is wrong with the movie industry today, it is the unrelenting effort to astonish.— Clive James, in *Observer*, June 16, 1979

1838 The printed page conveys information and commitment, and requires active involvement. Television conveys emotion and experience, and it's very limited in what it can do logically. It's an existential experience there and then gone.— Bill Moyers, in *New York Times*, January 3, 1982

1839 The sense of national catastrophe is inevitably heightened in a television age, when the whole country participates in it.— R. W. Apple, Jr., in *New York Times*, January 29, 1986

1840 Thank God we're living in a country where the sky's the limit, the stores are open late and you can shop in bed thanks to television.— Joan Rivers, in *International Herald Tribune*, May 31, 1989

1841 Television is actually closer to reality than anything in books. The madness of TV is the madness of human life.— Camille Paglia, in *Harper's*, March, 1991

Theories

1842 The great tragedy of Science — the slaying of a beautiful hypothesis by an ugly fact.— T. H. Huxley, *Collected Essays*, 1895

1843 As a rule we disbelieve all facts and theories for which we have no use.— William James, *The Will to Believe*, 1897

1844 Theories that go counter to the facts of human nature are foredoomed.— Edith Hamilton, *The Roman Way*, 1932

Thought

1845 Except our own thoughts, there is nothing absolutely in our power.— René Descartes, *Discourse on the Method*, 1637

1846 The secret thoughts of a man run over all things, holy, profane, clean, obscene, grave, and light, without shame or blame.— Thomas Hobbes, *Leviathan*, 1651

1847 Liberty of thought is the life of the soul.— Voltaire, *Essay on Epic Poetry*, 1727

1848 Perspicuity is the framework of profound thought.— Marquis de Vauvenargues, *Reflections and Maxims*, 1746

1849 One cannot demand of a scholar that he show himself a scholar everywhere in society, but the whole tenor of his behavior must none the less betray the thinker, he must always be instructive.— G. C. Lichtenberg, *Aphorisms*, 1765–99

1850 In every work of genius we recognize our own rejected thoughts: they come back to us with a certain alienated majesty.— Ralph Waldo Emerson, *Essays, First Series*, 1841

1851 How hard it is to make your thoughts look anything but imbecile fools when you paint them with ink on paper.— Olive Schreiner, *The Story of an African Farm*, 1883

1852 Thoughts are the shadows of our sensations— always darker, emptier, simpler than these.— Friedrich Nietzsche, *The Gay Science*, 1887

1853 The mind is not a hermit's cell, but a place of hospitality and intercourse.— Charles Horton Cooley, *Human Nature and the Social Order*, 1902

1854 It is not what we learn in conversation that enriches us. It is the elation that comes of swift contact with tingling currents of thought.   Agnes Repplier, *Compromises, The Luxury of Conversation*, 1904

1855 To think hard and persistently is painful.— Louis D. Brandeis, *Business — A Profession*, 1914

1856 How many of our daydreams would darken into nightmares, were there a danger of their coming true!— Logan Pearsall Smith, *Afterthoughts*, 1931

1857 No man ever looks at the world with pristine eyes. He sees it edited by a definite set of customs and institutions and ways of thinking.— Ruth Benedict, *Patterns of Culture*, 1934

1858 To reflect is to disturb one's thoughts.— Jean Rostand, *Pensées d'un Biologiste*, 1939

1859 The human mind prefers to be spoon-fed with the thoughts of others, but deprived of such nourishment it will, reluctantly, begin to think for itself — and such thinking, remember, is original thinking and may have valuable results.— Agatha Christie, *The Moving Finger*, 1942

1860 A thinker who cannot set forth

weighty thoughts in simple and clear language should be suspected, primarily, of lacking talent for thought.— Jacob Klatzkin, *In Praise of Wisdom*, 1943

1861 He can't think without his hat.— Samuel Beckett, *Waiting for Godot*, 1955

1862 It is a far, far better thing to have a firm anchor in nonsense than to put out on the troubled seas of thought.— John Kenneth Galbraith, *The Affluent Society*, 1958

1863 The aim of those who try to control thought is always the same. They find one single explanation of the world, one system of thought and action that will (they believe) cover everything; and then they try to impose that on all thinking people.— Gilbert Highet, *Man's Unconquerable Mind*, 1964

1864 It is love of candor that makes men radical thinkers.— Eric Bentley, *Thirty Years of Treason*, 1971

1865 Every thought derives from a thwarted sensation.— Emile M. Cioran, *The Trouble with Being Born*, 1973

1866 First thoughts have tremendous energy. The internal censor usually squelches them, so we live in the realm of second and third thoughts, thoughts on thought, twice and three times removed from the direct connection of the first fresh flash.— Natalie Goldberg, *Writing Down the Bones*, 1986

Tolerance

1867 The only true spirit of tolerance consists in our conscientious toleration of each other's intolerance.— Samuel Taylor Coleridge, *The Friend*, 1809

1868   Tolerance is composed of nine parts of apathy to one of brotherly love.— Frank Moore Colby, *The Colby Essays*, 1926

1869   Tolerance is a very dull virtue. It is boring. Unlike love, it has always had a bad press. It is negative. It merely means putting up with people, being able to stand things.— E. M. Forster, *Two Cheers for Democracy*, 1951

1870   The peak of tolerance is most readily achieved by those who are not burdened with convictions.— Alexander Chase, *Perspectives*, 1966

Tradition

1871   Even a god cannot change the past.— Aristotle, *Nicomachean Ethics*, 4th c. B.C.

1872   Originality and genius must be largely fed and raised on the shoulders of some old tradition.— George Santayana, *The Life of Reason*, 1905–06

1873   Tradition means giving votes to the most obscure of all classes, our ancestors. It is the democracy of the dead.— Gilbert K. Chesterton, *Orthodoxy*, 1908

1874   Almost always tradition is nothing but a record and a machine-made imitation of the habits that our ancestors created. The average conservative is a slave to the most incidental and trivial part of his forefathers' glory.— Walter Lippmann, *A Preface to Politics*, 1914

1875   No progress of humanity is possible unless it shakes off the yoke of authority and tradition.— André Gide, *Journals*, March 17, 1931

1876   Traditionalists are pessimists about the future and optimists about the past.— Lewis Mumford, *Technics and Civilization*, 1934

1877   Tradition is a guide and not a jailer.— William Somerset Maugham, *The Summing Up*, 1938

1878   Tradition! We scarcely know the word anymore. We are afraid to be either proud of our ancestors or ashamed of them. We cling to a bourgeois mediocrity which would make it appear we are all Americans, made in the image and likeness of George Washington.— Dorothy Day, *The Long Loneliness*, 1952

1879   As soon as tradition has come to be recognized as tradition, it is dead.— Allan Bloom, *The Closing of the American Mind*, 1987

1880   The assumption must be that those who can see value only in tradition, or versions of it, deny man's ability to adapt to changing circumstances.— Stephen Bayley, *Commerce and Culture*, 1989

1881   In America nothing dies easier than tradition.— Russell Baker, in *New York Times*, May 14, 1991

Treaties

1882   Treaties are like roses and young girls. They last while they last.— Charles de Gaulle, in *Time,* July 12, 1963

1883   You cannot shake hands with a clenched fist.— Indira Gandhi, in *Christian Science Monitor*, May 17, 1982

Trouble

1884   Each man must have his "I"; it is more necessary to him than bread; and if he does not find scope for it within the existing institutions he will be likely to make trouble.— Charles Horton Cooley, *Human Nature and the Social Order,* 1902

1885   One of the basic causes for all the trouble in the world today is that people talk too much and think too little. They act impulsively without thinking. I always try to think before I talk.— Margaret Chase Smith, Speech, June 7, 1953

1886   A man who makes trouble for others is also making trouble for himself.— Chinua Achebe, *Things Fall Apart,* 1959

1887   Most of the trouble in this world has been caused by folks who can't mind their own business, because they have no business of their own to mind, any more than a smallpox virus has.— William S. Burroughs, *The Adding Machine,* 1985

Trust

1888   For somehow this is tyranny's disease, to trust to friends.— Aeschylus, *Prometheus Bound,* 5th c. B.C.

1889   I wonder men dare trust themselves with men.— William Shakespeare, *Timon of Athens,* 1607

1890   Trust men, and they will be true to you; treat them greatly, and they will show themselves great.— Ralph Waldo Emerson, *Essays, First Series,* 1841

1891   There are men whose presence infuses trust and reverence.— George Eliot, *Romola,* 1863

1892   Trust everybody, but cut the cards.— Finley Peter Dunne , *Casual Observations,* 1900

1893   Never trust the artist. Trust the tale. The proper function of the critic is to save the tale from the artist who created it.— D. H. Lawrence, *Studies in Classic American Literature,* 1924

1894   It is impossible to go through life without trust: that is to be imprisoned in the worst cell of all, oneself.— Graham Henry Greene, *The Ministry of Fear,* 1943

1895   We have to distrust each other. It's our only defense against betrayal.— Tennessee Williams, *Camino Real,* 1953

1896   How desperately we wish to maintain our trust in those we love! In the face of everything, we try to find reasons to trust. Because losing faith is worse than falling out of love.— Sonia Johnson, *From Housewife to Heretic,* 1981

Truth

1897   Truth is great and its effectiveness endures.— Ptahhotpe, *The Maxims of Ptahhotpe,* ca. 2350 B.C.

1898   The way of truth is like a great road. It is not difficult to know; the evil is only that men will not seek it.— Mencius, *Discourses,* ca. 300 B.C.

1899   The first reaction to truth is hatred.— Tertullian, *Apologeticus,* ca. 197

1900   Truth hast a quiet breast.— William Shakespeare, *Richard II,* 1595

1901 The dignity of truth is lost with much protesting.— Ben Jonson, *Catiline's Conspiracy*, 1611

1902 It is a pleasure to stand upon the shore, and to see ships tost upon the sea: a pleasure to stand in the window of a castle, and to see a battle and the adventures thereof below: but no pleasure is comparable to standing upon the vantage ground of truth.— Francis Bacon, *Essays*, 1597–1625

1903 A man may be in as just possession of truth as of a city, and yet be forced to surrender.— Thomas Browne, *Religio Medici*, ca. 1635

1904 Follow not truth near the heels, lest it dash out thy teeth.— George Herbert, *Jacula Prudentum*, 1651

1905 Even truth needs to be clad in new garments if it is to appeal to a new age.— G. C. Lichtenberg, *Aphorisms*, 1765–99

1906 The teller of a mirthful tale has latitude allowed him. We are content with less than absolute truth.— Charles Lamb, *The Last Essays of Elia*, 1833

1907 I tell the honest truth in my paper, and I leave the consequences to God.— James Gordon Bennett, in *New York Herald*, May 10, 1836

1908 God offers to every mind its choice between truth and repose. Take which you please; you can never have both.— Ralph Waldo Emerson, *Essays, First Series*, 1841

1909 Truth is not always in a well. In fact, as regards the more important knowledge, I do believe that she is invariably superficial. The depth lies in the valleys where we seek her, and not upon the mountain-tops where she is found.— Edgar Allan Poe, *The Murders in the Rue Morgue* 1841

1910 It takes two to speak truth — one to speak, and another to hear.— Henry David Thoreau, *A Week on the Concord and Merrimack Rivers*, 1849

1911 It has always been desirable to tell the truth, but seldom if ever necessary. It is a melancholy truth that even great men have their poor relations.— Charles Dickens, *Bleak House*, 1852

1912 Truths and roses have thorns about them.— Henry David Thoreau, *Walden*, 1854

1913 Truths are first clouds; then rain, then harvest and food.— Henry Ward Beecher, *Life Thoughts*, 1858

1914 The highest compact we can make with our fellow is—"Let there be truth between us two forevermore."— Ralph Waldo Emerson, *The Conduct of Life*, 1860

1915 The ultimate aim of the human mind, in all its efforts, is to become acquainted with Truth.— Eliza Farnham, *Woman and Her Era*, 1864

1916 Truth has rough flavors if we bite it through.— George Eliot, *Armgart*, 1871

1917 It is the customary fate of new truths to begin as heresies and to end as superstitions.— Thomas Henry, *The Coming of Age*, 1880

1918 He who sees the truth, let him proclaim it, without asking who is for it or who is against it.— Henry George, *The Land Question*, 1881

1919 Not when truth is dirty, but when it is shallow, does the enlightened man dislike to wade into its waters.— Friedrich Nietzsche, *Thus Spoke Zarathustra*, 1883

1920 Man discovers truth by reason only, not by faith.— Leo Tolstoy, *On Life*, 1887

1921 We must prepare and study truth under every aspect, endeavoring to ignore nothing, if we do not wish to fall into the abyss of the unknown when the hour shall strike.— Helena Petrova Blavatsky, in *La Revue Theosophique*, March 21, 1889

1922 The way of paradoxes is the way of truth. To test Reality we must see it on the tight-rope. When the Verities become acrobats we can judge them.— Oscar Wilde, *The Picture of Dorian Gray*, 1891

1923 It is always the best policy to speak the truth, unless of course you are an exceptionally good liar.— Jerome K. Jerome, in *Idler*, February, 1892

1924 When in doubt, tell the truth.— Mark Twain, *Following the Equator*, 1897

1925 An epigram is a flashlight of a truth; a witticism, truth laughing at itself.— Minna Thomas Antrim, *Naked Truth and Veiled Allusions*, 1901

1926 As there is no worse lie than a truth misunderstood by those who hear it, so reasonable arguments, challenges to magnanimity, and appeals to sympathy or justice, are folly when we are dealing with human crocodiles and boa-constrictors.— William James, *The Varieties of Religious Experience*, 1902

1927 The People have a right to the Truth as they have a right to life, liberty and the pursuit of happiness.— Frank Norris, *The Responsibilities of the Novelist*, 1903

1928 Truth generally lies in the coordination of antagonistic opinions.— Herbert Spencer, *Autobiography*, 1904

1929 "The true," to put it briefly, is only the expedient in the way of our thinking, just as "the right" is only the expedient in the way of our behaving.— William James, *Pragmatism*, 1907

1930 The truth is a snare: you cannot have it, without being caught. You cannot have the truth in such a way that you catch it, but only in such a way that it catches you.— Soren Kierkegaard, *The Papers of Søren Kierkegaard*, 1909

1931 He who wishes to teach us a truth should not tell it to us, but simply suggest it with a brief gesture, a gesture which starts an ideal trajectory in the air along which we glide until we find ourselves at the feet of the new.— José Ortega y Gasset, *Meditations on Quixote*, 1911

1932 Heaven knows what seeming nonsense may not tomorrow be demonstrated truth.— Alfred North Whitehead, *Science and the Modern World*, 1925

1933 Truth is meant to save you first, and the comfort comes afterward.— Georges Bernanos, *The Diary of a Country Priest*, 1937

1934 The truth that makes men free is for the most part the truth which men prefer not to hear.— Herbert Agar, *A Time for Greatness*, 1942

1935 Some minds remain open long enough for the truth not only to enter but to pass on through by way of a ready exit without pausing anywhere along the route.— Elizabeth Kenny, *And They Shall Walk*, 1943

1936 Truthfulness so often goes with ruthlessness.— Dodie Smith, *I Capture the Castle*, 1948

1937 Intense feeling too often obscures the truth.— Harry S Truman, speech, October 19, 1948

1938   Truth never damages a cause that is just.— Mahatma Gandhi, *Non-Violence in Peace and War, Volume 2*, 1949

1939   For truth there is no deadline.— Heywood C. Broun, in *Saturday Review*, February 13, 1954

1940   Crushing truths perish by being acknowledged.— Albert Camus, *The Myth of Sysyphus*, 1955

1941   Duration is not a test of truth or falsehood.— Anne Morrow Lindbergh, *Gift From the Sea*, 1955

1942   In every generation there has to be some fool who will speak the truth as he sees it.— Boris Pasternak, in *New York Times*, February 2, 1959

1943   Not only are there as many conflicting truths as there are people to claim them; there are equally multitudinous and conflicting truths within the individual.— Virgilia Peterson, *A Matter of Life and Death*, 1961

1944   Truth isn't always beauty, but the hunger for it is.— Nadine Gordimer, in *London Magazine*, May 1963

1945   The truth is always something that is told, not something that is known. If there were no speaking or writing, there would be no truth about anything. There would only be what is.— Susan Sontag, *The Benefactor,* 1963

1946   Sometimes, surely, truth is closer to imagination or to intelligence, to love than to fact? To be accurate is not to be right.— Shirley Hazzard, *The Evening of the Holiday*, 1965

1947   The truth is balance. However the opposite of truth, which is unbalance, may not be a lie.— Susan Sontag, *Against Interpretation*, 1966

1948   In the society of men the truth resides now less in what things are than in what they are not.— R. D. Laing, *The Politics of Experience*, 1967

1949   Youthful arrogance [believes] the truth, once found, would be simple as well as pretty.— James D. Watson, *The Double Helix*, 1968

1950   I tore myself away from the safe comfort of certainties through my love for truth — and truth rewarded me.— Simone de Beauvoir, *All Said and Done*, 1974

1951   Spilling your guts is just exactly as charming as it sounds.— Fran Lebowitz, *Social Studies*, 1977

1952   As scarce as truth is, the supply has always been in excess of the demand.— Josh Billings, in *Rocky Mountain News*, June 5, 1980

1953   I have never seasoned a truth with the sauce of a lie in order to digest it more easily.— Marguerite Yourcenar, in *New York Times*, May 5, 1980

1954   Truth is used to vitalize a statement rather than devitalize it. Truth implies more than a simple statement of fact. "I don't have any whiskey," may be a fact but it is not a truth.— William S. Burroughs, *The Adding Machine*, 1985

1955   Truth knows no color; it appeals to intelligence.— James Cone, *Speaking the Truth*, 1986

1956   The truth is not simply what you think it is; it is also the circumstances in which it is said, and to whom, why, and how it is said.— Václav Havel, *Disturbing the Peace*, 1986

1957   The truth is not so good a story.— Marion Zimmer Bradley, *The Firebrand*, 1987

1958   The truth is really an ambition which is beyond us.— Peter Ustinov, in *International Herald Tribune*, March 12, 1990

1959   The clichés of a culture sometimes tell the deepest truths.— Faith Popcorn, *The Popcorn Report*, 1991

Tyranny

1960   The worst of tyrants, an usurping crowd.— Homer, *The Iliad*, ca. 700 B.C.

1961   In every tyrant's heart there springs in the end / This poison, that he cannot trust a friend.— Aeschylus, *Prometheus Bound*, ca. 490 B.C.

1962   We are more wicked together than separately. If you are forced to be in a crowd, then most of all you should withdraw into your self.— Seneca, *Epistolae Morales*, 1st c.

1963   The face of tyranny is always mild at first.— Jean-Baptiste Racine, *Britannicus*, 1669

1964   You need neither art nor science to be a tyrant.— Jean de La Bruyère, *Characters*, 1688

1965   Tyranny, like hell, is not easily conquered.— Thomas Paine, in *The American Crisis*, 1776–83

1966   Tyrants seldom want pretexts.— Edmund Burke, *Letter to a Member of the National Assembly*, 1791

1967   The tyrant grinds down his slaves and they don't turn against him; they crush those beneath them.— Emily Brontë, *Wuthering Heights*, 1847

1968   Whatever crushes individuality is despotism, by whatever name it may be called.— John Stuart Mill, *On Liberty*, 1859

1969   The evils of tyranny are rarely seen but by him who resists it.— John Hay, *Castilian Days*, 1871

1970   You have not converted a man because you have silenced him.— John Morley, *On Compromise*, 1874

1971   People complain of the despotism of princes; they ought to complain of the despotism of man.— Joseph de Maistre, *Study on Sovereignty*, 1884

1972   Dictators ride to and fro upon tigers which they dare not dismount. And the tigers are getting hungry.— Winston S. Churchill, *While England Slept*, 1936

1973   Tyranny is always better organized than freedom.— Charles Péguy, *Basic Verities*, 1943

1974   Except as its clown and jester, society does not encourage individuality, and the State abhors it.— Bernard Berenson, *Aesthetics and History*, 1948

1975   The benevolent despot who sees himself as a shepherd of the people still demands from others the submissiveness of sheep.— Eric Hoffer, *The Ordeal of Change*, 1964

1976   The more a regime claims to be the embodiment of liberty, the more tyrannical it is likely to be.— Ian Gilmour, *Inside Right*, 1977

Understanding

1977   Men credit most easily the things which they do not understand. They believe most easily things which are obscure.— Tacitus, *Histories*, ca. 104

1978   Men hate what they cannot understand.— Moses Ibn Ezra, *Shirat Yisrael*, 12th c.

1979   If you do not understand a man you cannot crush him. And if you do understand him, very probably you will not.— Gilbert K. Chesterton, *All Things Considered*, 1908

1980   He neither knew anything, nor wished to know anything. His instinct told him that it was better to understand little than to misunderstand a lot.— Anatole France, *The Revolt of the Angels*, 1914

Value

1981   I wouldn't have turned out the way I was if I didn't have all those old-fashioned values to rebel against.— Madonna, in *Time*, December 17, 1990

1982   Although a system may cease to exist in the legal sense or as a structure of power, its values (or anti-values), its philosophy, its teachings remain in us. They rule our thinking, our conduct, our attitude to others.— Ryszard Kapuściński, in *Independent on Sunday*, September 1, 1991

Vanity

1983   A vain man may become proud and imagine himself pleasing to all when he is in reality a universal nuisance.— Baruch Spinoza, *Ethics*, 1677

1984   Nothing can exceed the vanity of our existence but the folly of our pursuits.— Oliver Goldsmith, *The Good Natur'd Man*, 1768

1985   Vanity is as ill at ease under indifference as tenderness is under a love which it cannot return.— George Eliot, *Daniel Deronda*, 1876

1986   What is the vanity of the vainest man compared with the vanity which the most modest possesses when, in the midst of nature and the world, he feels himself to be "man"!— Friedrich Nietzsche, *The Wanderer and His Shadow*, 1880

1987   Wounded vanity knows when it is mortally hurt; and limps off the field, piteous, all disguises thrown away. But pride carries its banner to the last; and fast as it is driven from one field unfurls it in another.— Helen Hunt Jackson, *Ramona*, 1884

1988   The vanity of men, a constant insult to women, is also the ground for the implicit feminine claim of superior sensitivity and morality.— Patricia Meyer Spacks, *The Female Imagination*, 1975

Vice and Virtue

1989   Our virtues are most often but our vices disguised.— François Duke de La Rochefoucauld, VI, *Maxims*, 1665

1990   I prefer an accommodating vice to an obstinate virtue.— Molière, *Amphitryon*, 1666

1991   Vice came in always at the door of necessity, not at the door of inclination.— Daniel Defoe, *Moll Flanders*, 1721

1992   Virtue by premeditation isn't worth much.— G. C. Lichtenberg, *Aphorisms*, 1765–99

1993 However great an evil immorality may be, we must not forget that it is not without its beneficial consequences. It is only through extremes that men can arrive at the middle path of wisdom and virtue.— Karl Wilhelm, Baron von Humboldt, *Limits of State Action*, 1792

1994 The less a man thinks or knows about his virtues, the better we like him.— Ralph Waldo Emerson, *Essays, First Series*, 1841

1995 There are nine hundred and ninety-nine patrons of virtue to one virtuous man.— Henry David Thoreau, *On the Duty of Civil Disobedience*, 1849

1996 There is never an instant's truce between virtue and vice.— Henry David Thoreau, *Walden*, 1854

1997 The ascetic makes a necessity of virtue.— Friedrich Nietzsche, *Human, All Too Human*, 1878

1998 There are men so incorrigibly lazy that no inducement that you can offer will tempt them to work; so eaten up by vice that virtue is abhorrent to them, and so inveterably dishonest that theft is to them a master passion.— William Booth, *In Darkest England and the Way Out*, 1890

1999 Every vice you destroy has a corresponding virtue, which perishes along with it.— Anatole France, *The Garden of Epicurus*, 1894

2000 A crime persevered in a thousand centuries ceases to be a crime, and becomes a virtue. This is the law of custom, and custom supersedes all other forms of law.— Mark Twain, *Following the Equator*, 1897

2001 I sometimes wish you had not so many lofty virtues. I assure you little sins are far less dangerous and uncomfortable.— Baroness Emmuska Orczy, *The Scarlet Pimpernel*, 1905

2002 A new philosophy generally means in practice the praise of some old vice.— Gilbert K. Chesterton, *All Things Considered*, 1908

2003 What men and women need is encouragement. Instead of always harping on a man's faults, tell him of his virtues. Try to pull him out of his rut of bad habits.— Eleanor H. Porter, *Pollyanna*, 1912

2004 It is queer how it is always one's virtues and not one's vices that precipitate one into disaster.— Rebecca West, *There Is No Conversation*, 1935

2005 Man seems to be capable of great virtues but not of small virtues; capable of defying his torturer but not of keeping his temper.— Gilbert K. Chesterton, *Autobiography*, 1936

2006 Children should be taught not the little virtues but the great ones. Not thrift but generosity and an indifference to money; not caution but courage and a contempt for danger; not a desire for success but a desire to be and to know.— Natalia Ginzburg, *The Little Virtues*, 1962

2007 Nothing in our times has become so unattractive as virtue.— Edward Dahlberg, *Alms for Oblivion*, 1964

2008 Virtue is simply happiness, and happiness is a by-product of function. You are happy when you are functioning.— William S. Burroughs, *Painting and Guns*, 1992

Victory

2009   Victory shifts from man to man.— Homer, *The Iliad,* ca. 700 B.C.

2010   Those who know how to win are much more numerous than those who know how to make proper use of their victories.— Polybius, *History,* ca. 125 B.C.

2011   Of war men ask the outcome, not the cause.— Seneca, *Hercules Furens,* ca. 50

2012   When there is no peril in the fight, there is no glory in the triumph.— Pierre Corneille, *Le Cid,* 1636

2013   The tragedy of life is not that man loses but that he almost wins.— Heywood Broun, *Pieces of Hate, and Other Enthusiasms,* 1922

2014   In a serious struggle there is no worse cruelty than to be magnanimous at an inopportune time.— Leon Trotsky, *The History of the Russian Revolution,* 1933

2015   There are not fifty ways of fighting, there is only one: to be the conqueror.— André Malvaux, *L'Espoir,* 1937

2016   Victory has a hundred fathers, but defeat is an orphan.— Galeazzo Ciano, *Diary,* "September 9, 1942," 1946

2017   No one can guarantee success in war, but only deserve it.— Winston S. Churchill, *Their Finest Hour,* 1949

Violence

2018   Violence does, in truth, recoil upon the violent, and the schemer falls into the pit which he digs for another.—

Arthur Conan Doyle, *The Adventures of Sherlock Holmes,* 1891

2019   In violence, we forget who we are.— Mary McCarthy, *On the Contrary,* 1961

2020   Violence is the repartee of the illiterate.— Alan Brien, in *Punch,* February 7, 1973

2021   A man who lives with nature is used to violence and is companionable with death. There is more violence in an English hedgerow than in the meanest streets of a great city.— P. D. James, *Devices and Desires,* 1989

2022   That even an apocalypse can be made to seem part of the ordinary horizon of expectation constitutes an unparalleled violence that is being done to our sense of reality, to our humanity.— Susan Sontag, *AIDS and Its Metaphors,* 1989

Vulgarity

2023   Vulgarity in a king flatters the majority of the nation.— George Bernard Shaw, Man and Superman, 1903

2024   The vulgar man is always the most distinguished, for the very desire to be distinguished is vulgar.— Gilbert K. Chesterton, *All Things Considered,* 1908

War

2025   Men grow tired of sleep, love, singing and dancing sooner than war.— Homer, *The Iliad,* ca. 700 B.C.

2026   Let him who desires peace prepare for war.— Vegetius, *De Rei Militari,* ca. 375

2027   One should always have one's boots on, and be ready to leave.— Michel Eyquem de Montaigne, *Essays,* 1580

2028   There is nothing so subject to the inconstancy of fortune as war.— Miguel de Cervantes, *Don Quixote,* 1605–15

2029   God is always with the strongest battalions.— Frederick the Great, letter, May 8, 1760

2030   With men, the state of nature is not a state of peace, but war.— Immanuel Kant, *Perpetual Peace,* 1795

2031   War is a kind of superstition; the pageantry of arms and badges corrupts the imagination of man.— Percy Bysshe Shelley, *A Philosophical View of Reform,* 1819

2032   War is a game in which princes seldom win, the people never.— Charles Caleb Colton, *Lacon,* 1820–22

2033   So long as war is the main business of nations, temporary despotism — despotism during the campaign — is indispensable.— Walter Bagehot, *Physics and Politics,* 1872

2034   Against war it may be said that it makes the victor stupid and the vanquished revengeful.— Friedrich Nietzsche, *Human, All Too Human,* 1878

2035   A war, even the most victorious, is a national misfortune.— Helmuth von Moltke, letter, 1880

2036   Capitalism carries within itself war, as clouds carry rain.— Jean Jaurès, *Studies in Socialism,* 1902

2037   In the arts of peace Man is a bungler.— George Bernard Shaw, *Man and Superman,* 1903

2038   Make wars unprofitable and you make them impossible.— A. Philip Randolph, *The Messenger,* 1919

2039   Violence seldom accomplishes permanent and desired results. Herein lies the futility of war.— A. Philip Randolph, *The Truth About Lynching,* ca. 1922

2040   Probably no nation is rich enough to pay for both war and education.— Abraham Flexner, *Universities,* 1930

2041   Give capital thirty days to think it over and you will learn by that time that there will be no war. That will stop the racket — that and nothing else.— Smedley D. Butler, in *The Forum and Century,* September, 1934

2042   Don't tell me peace has broken out, when I've just bought fresh supplies.— Bertolt Brecht, *Mother Courage,* 1939

2043   As long as there are sovereign nations possessing great power, war is inevitable.— Albert Einstein, in *Atlantic Monthly,* November, 1945

2044   The next World War will be fought with stones.— Albert Einstein, in *Living Philosophies,* 1949

2045   After each war there is a little less democracy to save.— Brooks Atkinson, *Once Around the Sun,* 1951

2046   War is an invention of the human mind. The human mind can invent peace.— Norman Cousins, *Who Speaks for Man?* 1953

2047   The grim fact is that we prepare for war like precocious giants and for peace like retarded pygmies.— Lester B. Pearson, news summaries, March 15, 1955

2048 War will never cease until babies begin to come into the world with larger cerebrums and smaller adrenal glands.— H. L. Mencken, *Minority Report*, 1956

2049 War is, after all, the universal perversion.— John Rae, *The Custard Boys*, 1960

2050 War is the province of chance. In no other sphere of human activity must such a margin be left for this intruder. It increases the uncertainty of every circumstance and deranges the course of events.— Carl von Clausewitz, *War, Politics and Power*, 1962

2051 Every war is its own excuse.— Karl Shapiro, *The Bourgeois Poet*, 1964

2052 You can no more win a war than you can win an earthquake.— Jeanette Rankin, in H. Josephson, *Jeanette Rankin: First Lady in Congress*, 1974

2053 The Falklands thing was a fight between two bald men over a comb.— Jorge Luis Borges, in *Time*, February 14, 1983

2054 Throughout human history, the apostles of purity, those who have claimed to possess a total explanation, have wrought havoc among mere mixed-up human beings.— Salman Rushdie, in *Independent on Sunday*, February 4, 1990

2055 The Gulf War was like teenage sex. We got in too soon and out too soon.— Tom Harkin, in *Independent on Sunday*, September 29, 1991

Waste

2056 The torment of human frustration, whatever its immediate cause, is the knowledge that the self is in prison, its vital force and "mangled mind" leaking away in lonely, wasteful self-conflict.— Elizabeth A. Drew, *Poetry: A Modern Guide to Its Understanding and Enjoyment*, 1959

2057 Alone, even doing nothing, you do not waste your time. You do, almost always, in company. No encounter with yourself can be altogether sterile: Something necessarily emerges, even if only the hope of some day meeting yourself again.— Emile M. Cioran, *The New Gods*, 1969

2058 The best way to fill time is to waste it.— Marguerite Duras, *Practicalities*, 1987

Weakness

2059 We are born weak, we need strength; helpless, we need aid; foolish, we need reason. All that we lack at birth, all that we need when we come to man's estate, is the gift of education.— Jean-Jacques Rousseau, *Emile*, 1762

2060 Three failures denote uncommon strength. A weakling has not enough grit to fail thrice.— Minna Thomas Antrim, *At the Sign of the Golden Calf*, 1905

2061 The weakness of most men / they do not know how to become a stone or tree.— Aimé Césaire, *First Problem*, 1946

Wealth

2062 Riches are a good handmaiden, but the worst mistress.— Francis Bacon,

De Dignitate et Augmentis Scientiarum, 1623

2063 Superfluous wealth can buy superfluities only. Money is not required to buy one necessary of the soul.— Henry David Thoreau, *Walden*, 1854

2064 Wealth is in applications of mind to nature; and the art of getting rich consists not in industry, much less in saving, but in a better order, in timeliness, in being at the right spot.— Ralph Waldo Emerson, *The Conduct of Life*, 1860

2065 Man is the only animal which esteems itself rich in proportion to the number and voracity of its parasites.— George Bernard Shaw, *Man and Superman*, 1903

2066 Their capacity for identification is not an expression of inner poverty but of inner wealth.— Helene Deutsch, *The Psychology of Women*, 1944–5

2067 Wealth is the relentless enemy of understanding.— John Kenneth Galbraith, *The Affluent Society*, 1958

Widows

2068 It's a delicious thing to be a young widow.— John Vanbrugh, *The Relapse*, 1696

2069 Never marry a widow unless her first husband was hanged.— James Kelly, *Scottish P:roverbs*, 1721

Wisdom

2070 It is not enough to acquire wis-

dom, it is necessary to employ it.— Cicero, *De Finibus*, ca. 45 B.C.

2071 Man is wise only while in search of wisdom; when he imagines he has attained it, he is a fool.— Solomon Ibn Gabirol, *Choice of Pearls*, ca. 1050

2072 The first key to wisdom is this— constant and frequent questioning. By questioning, we arrive at the truth.— Pierre Abélard, *Sic et Non*, ca. 1120

2073 Such is the nature of men, that howsoever they may acknowledge many others to be more witty, or more eloquent, or more learned; yet they will hardly believe there be many so wise as themselves.— Thomas Hobbes, Leviathan, 1651

2074 What is strength without a double share of wisdom?— John Milton, *Samsom Agonistes*, 1671

2075 Wise men are not wise at all hours, and will speak five times from their taste or their humor, to once from their reason.— Ralph Waldo Emerson, *The Conduct of Life*, 1860

2076 He dares to be a fool, and that is the first step in the direction of wisdom.— James G. Huneker, *Pathos of Distance*, 1913

2077 Every man is a damn fool for at least five minutes every day. Wisdom consists in not exceeding the limit.— Elbert Hubbard, *Roycroft Dictionary and Book of Epigrams*, 1923

2078 It requires wisdom to understand wisdom; the music is nothing if the audience is deaf.— Walter Lippmann, *A Preface to Morals*, 1929

2079 We thought, because we had power, we had wisdom.— Stephen Vincent Benét, *Litany for Dictatorships*, 1935

2080   Wisdom is knowing when you can't be wise.— Paul Engle, *Poems in Praise*, 1959

2081   Wisdom consists of the anticipation of consequences.— Norman Cousins, in *Saturday Review*, April 15, 1978

2082   We need to haunt the house of history and listen anew to the ancestors' wisdom.— Maya Angelou, in *New York Times*, August 25, 1991

Wit

2083   It is not enough to possess wit. One must have enough of it to avoid having too much.— André Maurois, *Conversation*, 1927

2084   Wit is a treacherous dart. It is perhaps the only weapon with which it is possible to stab oneself in one's own back.— Geoffrey Bocca, *The Woman Who Would Be Queen*, 1954

Wives

2085   Wives are young men's mistresses, companions for middle age, and old men's nurses.— Francis Bacon, *Essays*, 1597–1625

2086   London is full of women who trust their husbands. One can always recognize them. They look so thoroughly unhappy.— Oscar Wilde, *Lady Windermere's Fan*, 1892

2087   Any intelligent woman who reads the marriage contract, and then goes into it, deserves all the consequences.— Isadora Duncan, *My Life*, 1927

2088   The only guy that shouldn't have nothing to do with picking out a wife is the guy that's going to marry her.— John Steinbeck, *Sweet Thursday*, 1954

Words

2089   Give me the right word and the right accent, and I will move the world.— Joseph Conrad, *A Personal Record*, 1912

2090   How often misused words generate misleading thoughts.— Herbert Spencer, *Principles of Ethics*, 1892–93

Work

2091   Let me not forget again that I came not here for friendly sympathy or for anything else but to work, and to work hard. Let me do that faithfully and well.— Charlotte Forten Grimké, *Journal of Charlotte Forten*, 1953

2092   Work spares us from three great evils: boredom, vice, and need.— Voltaire, *Candide*, 1759

2093   Where the whole man is involved there is no work. Work begins with the division of labor.— Marshall McLuhan, *Understanding Media*, 1964

2094   I didn't want to work. It was as simple as that. I distrusted work, disliked it. I thought it was a very bad thing that the human race had unfortunately invented for itself.— Agatha Christie, *Endless Night*, 1967

Writing

2095 In quoting of books, quote such authors as are usually read; others you may read for your own satisfaction, but not name them.—John Selden, *Table Talk*, 1686

2096 The style of an author should be the image of his mind, but the choice and command of language is the fruit of exercise.—Edward Gibbon, *Memoirs of my Life*, 1796

2097 The reason there are so few good books are written is that so few people that can write know anything.—Walter Bagehot, *Literary Studies*, 1879

2098 Genuine polemics approach a book as lovingly as a cannibal spices a baby.—Walter Benjamin, *One-Way Street*, 1928

2099 The art of storytelling is reaching its end because the epic side of truth, wisdom, is dying out.—Walter Benjamin, *The Storyteller*, 1936

2100 Like all writers, he measured the achievements of others by what they had accomplished, asking of them that they measure him by what he envisaged or planned.—Jorge Luis Borges, *Ficciones*, 1944

2101 For your born writer, nothing is so healing as the realization that he has come upon the right word.—Catherine Drinker Bowen, *Adventures of a Biographer*, 1946

2102 Creative writers are always greater than the causes that they represent.—E. M. Forster, *Two Cheers for Democracy*, 1951

2103 If I had to give young writers advice, I would say don't listen to writers talking about writing or themselves.—Lillian Hellman, in *New York Times*, February 21, 1960

2104 Writing is conscience, scruple, and the farming of our ancestors.—Edward Dahlberg, *Alms for Oblivion*, For Sale, 1964

2105 Writing is nothing more than a guided dream.—Jorge Luis Borges, *Doctor Brodie's Report*, 1972

2106 Self-plagiarism is style.—Alfred Hitchcock, in *Observer*, August 8, 1976

2107 Writers and travelers are mesmerized alike by knowing of their destinations.—Eudora Welty, *One Writer's Beginnings*, 1984

2108 There are few things as toxic as a bad metaphor. You can't think without metaphors.—Mary Catherine Bateson, *A World of Ideas*, 1989

Youth

2109 When a man is young he is insufferable. When he is old he plays the saint and becomes insufferable again.—Nikolai Gogol, *The Gamblers*, 1842

2110 For God's sake give me the young man who has brains enough to make a fool of himself.—Robert Louis Stevenson, *Virginibus Puerisque*, 1881

2111 The troubles of the young are soon over; they leave no external mark. If you wound the tree in its youth the bark will quickly cover the gash; but when the tree is very old, peeling the bark off you will see the scar there still.—Olive Schreiner, *The Story of an African Farm*, 1883

2112　I remember my youth and the feeling that never came back any more — the feeling that I could last forever, outlast the sea, the earth, and all men. — Joseph Conrad, *Youth,* 1898

2113　Young men have a passion for regarding their elders as senile. — Henry Adams, *The Education of Henry Adams,* 1907

2114　I suppose it's difficult for the young to realize that one may be old without being a fool. — William Somerset Maugham, *The Circle,* 1921

2115　Don't laugh at a youth for his affections: he's only trying on one face after another till he finds his own. — Logan Pearsall Smith, *Afterthoughts,* 1931

2116　The hatred of the youth culture for adult society is not a disinterested judgment but a terror-ridden refusal to be hooked into the, if you will, ecological chain of breathing, growing, and dying. It is the demand, in other words, to remain children. — Midge Decter, *The New Chastity and Other Arguments Against Women's Liberation,* 1972

INDEX OF PERSONS

References are to subjects and entry numbers

INDEX OF KEY WORDS
IN CONTEXT

References are to entry numbers

ing men 501; of prevent-
ing people 1445; of Rem-
brandt 841; of statesman-
ship 788; of storytelling
2099; of telling you nothing 1722; of writing something 1010; style is a. 1755;
there is no great a. 142; to
choose a. 167; toward
their a. 148; transmits
these truths 1627; where-
with a critic tries 378;
work of a. 151, 155, 156
articles written about me
383
articulated minutely a.
1628
artificial and impermanent
1287; respiration 1655
artist and his audience 155;
has ethical sympathies
141; is a dreamer 144; is a
man of action 145; is an
educator 163; performed
by the a. 154; scratch an a.
142; support the a. 160;
sympathy in an a. 1750;
trust the a. 1893; virtue
for an a. 159; you are an a.
1342
artist's attitude 294; fame
378
artistic ability 165; plan
273; temperament is a
disease 143
artists few are a. 369; great
a. 147; limitations 1797;
love to immerse them-
selves 162; of a large and
wholesome vitality 143; of
the future 163; reactions
of a. 148;ideas 160
arts crooked a. 803; of
peace 2037; popular a.
442; would perish 886
arty and specious 934
ascendant power 1262
ascending and descending
1156
ascent making her a. 645
ascetic makes a necessity of
virtue 1997
asceticism not through a.
1664
ashamed man is a. 1675; of
them 1878; of 487
ask an impertinent question 1544; for when we already know 82; for your
own 1306; him his opin-

ion 1618; right to a. 1154;
the one who loves 980;
the outcome 2011; women
to become 1672
asked most frequently
1543; to lend money 721
asking a lamppost 380; a
working writer 380; from
the other 1243; of them
2100; prayer is not a.
1495; without a. 1918
asleep that I dream 483
aspect of the universal
scheme 42; under every a.
1921
aspiration ambition and a.
106; to have no a. 827
assassin you are an a. 410
assassination is the extreme 1589; is the quick-
est way 1580
assembly that a man enters
555
assert itself in trifles 1474
assertion and aggression
668
assigns to woman 665
assimilation mental a. 1800
assists the circulation 83
associated energy a. 1151;
with it 667
associates support from
their a. 813
association of men 1712;
mere a. 1629
associations seemed to be
melted 1300
assuming a loud tone 170
assumption must be 1880
assure you little sins 2001
assured end 959
astonish effort to a. 1837
asylum lunatic a. 1366
athletes underwent 1547
atoms chemical a. 676
attached to comfort 969
attaching our drowning
selves 489
attack I shall a.,178
attain the highest excellence 601
attains its full value 1315;
through words 1140
attempt at self-understanding 1432
attempts action he a. 555;
to liberate himself 1345
attendant spirit 1352
attended by a bodyguard of
lies 1523

attention pay a. 365; period
of a. 1800
attitude and reactions 148;
artist's a. 294; not looks
1670; similar to that 148;
toward everything 294
attraction mystery and a.
1647; that moves human-
ity 1505
attractions one of the a.
166
attractive by comparison
1161; power makes you a.
1471; trade of historian so
a. 853; virtues for attractive vices 1564
attracts the weak 772
attribute commendable a.
109; of a good critic 1699
audacity increase it's a.
1103; of imagination 967
audience artist and his a.
155; awareness of an a.
745; is deaf 2078
augment official power 240
aura of distrust 1018
austere critic 1582
authentic work of art 155
author arrives at a good
style 1751; should be the
image 2096; that wrote it
1550
authorities whom we do
not control 1270
authority and tradition
1875; fixed by a. 472;
highest a. 601; is recent
169; rejection of a. 171
authors as are usually read
2095; phrase 918
autobiography deepest part
of a. 1432
autocracy democracy is not
a. 709
autonomy individual a.
712; of perception 161
avail nothing will a. 1787;
of no a. 1795
available to everyone 1835
average conservative is a
slave 1874; man simply
spends 1131; of faculties
494; people talk about
things 926
aversions appetites and a.
754
avidly read the newspapers
a. 1013
avoid foreign collision 445;
having too much 2083;

saint 1710; a stone or tree
2061; acquainted 1915;
clear 815; fanatics 1790;
obscure 1078; so accus-
tomed 620; the moral 1168
becomes a genius 737; a
virtue 2000; an affectation
290; insufferable again
2109
becoming light 289
bed lying in b. 919; shop in
b. 1840
bedbugs flies and b. 1773
bedded in his people 318
bedfellows never be b. 599
beehive of our knowledge
1059
been the one most fatal 1747
beer another b. 99; exactly
to his taste 1239; is the
Danish national drink 99
befitting the human mind
1816
before going to sleep 919;
he develops taste 974; I
learn 769; killing other
good 1311; marriage 1240;
the world 1073; they're
plumbers 1220; you finish
1240; you have 1030
befouled that it may be b.
194
beg in the streets 1101
began in mystery 1165
begin as blasphemies 1590;
as heresies 1917; to cherish them 620; to question
667; to think 311
beginning not the end 480;
of faith 1700; ridiculous b.
812; to happen 158; to live
1156; to tire 969
begins in mysticism 1444;
to repeat itself 572; with a
wail 1149; with the divi-
sion of labor 2093; with
the idea 1643
begun to whisper 313
behave like free spirits 1155
behaving way of our b.
1929
behavior can be regulated
1321; good b. 761; must
none the less betray 1849
behind leaving b. 1258; the
complicated details 1044;
to be b. 1022
beholder eye of the b. 168
being a sex symbol 1670; by
nature winged insects

1059; engulfed in doubt
479; human b. 999, 1230,
1352; in close contact
1177; inconvenienced by
few rivals 1326; no other
human b. 101; on televi-
sion 1836; the piano
player 382
beings creation of living b.
367; free b. 42; human b.
45, 2054; living b. 367
belief abandon a b. 210;
consists in accepting 202;
define b. 220; easy of b.
200; forced into b. 1553;
give up the b. 205; in a
devil 214; in a supernatural 765; in facts 584; in
God 214; in some other
thing 199; in the occur-
rence 598; in themselves
818; infantile b. 212; is not
true 1514; may be larger
than a fact 218; our na-
tional b. 217; robust is our
b. 508; suspension of b.
1430; that politics can be
scientific 1451; that the
truth once found 1949;
which determines the
consequences 206
beliefs faithful to one's b.
215; fixed by authority
472; man bears b. 203;
reaches of his b. 257;
strong in their b. 221;
swallow more b. 211;
transfer my b. 219; we
thought were ours 216;
what exactly those b. were
221
believe as Lenin said 268;
as much as we can 596;
easier to b. 208; every-
thing if we could 596; for
us to b. 299; hard to b.
209; if we take 96; in it
1349; in miracles 930; in
my soul 761; in prayer
1496; in the collective
wisdom 945; it indispen-
sable 1809; it to be true
1430; most easily 1977; or
to disbelieve 201; that
dreams do come true 484;
that people 1697; that she
is invariably superficial
1909; that the world 286;
their wish 1429; those
who are seeking the truth

481; what is pleasant 213;
what is true 213; what
they read 449; what they
wish 1512
believed as many 204
believer is happier 1701; to
the b. 790
believes consequences it b.
206; first thing that he b.
538; that the value 1412
believing object of b. 220;
we are born b. 203; worth
b. 209
belong to a suppressed minority 1296
belongs in the modern university 1104; to the past
1375
below adventures thereof b.
1902; the surface 197
benefactor Adam our b.
937; of our race 795
beneficial consequences
1993
benefit in making a few
failures 586; supposed to
b. 1131
benevolent despot 1975
bent on doing evil 749
beset by partisan appeals
1359
besetting vice of democracies 1527
best always the b. 1524; and
greatest 841; and the very
worst 233; defense against
death 1164; distributed
commodity 306; evolu-
tions 163; friend 1793;
history 841, 881; ideas are
common property 894;
intentions 1001; men 1721;
of all 1317, 1367; of it in
this world 429; policy
1923; repartee 1207; re-
venge 1578; scientist 1643;
servants 686; service 1363;
the emperor can do 250;
they think b. 1033; time
919; to disregard 1697;
very b. 1624; way 2058;
what I like b. 1550; wife
1793; with the b. 537
bestows upon it a silent
completeness 420
betray easier to b. 224; is to
b. 568; the thinker 1849;
whatever you can still b.
225; you 223
betrayal can only happen

225; defense against b. 1895

betrayed to be b. 1193; yourself 925

better a little b. 526; a witty fool 680; ask the one who loves 980; building 1412; death is b. 394; given unsought is b. 1181; in prayer 1495; left to the best-trained 301; less said about life's sores the b. 1784; order 2064; organized 1973; part of valor is discretion 335; place 564; proof 660; side 1218; silence that is b. 1677; than a mouthful of arguments 1276; than fish 1063; than life today 1347; than the man who commands 1283; thing 1862; to be a fool 402; to be first 192; to entertain 916; to have a war 1045; to understand little 1980; twenty times b. 1749; we like him 1994; you have the b. 131

betters above their b. 1768; their b. 226

between a man in prayer 1572; a saint 1568; destruction 1576; friends 1364; it and anything else 1169; learning 1125; lies in b. 1165; ourselves 275; the artist and his audience 155; the political ideas 968; the possible 993; the thoughts 1690; truth and repose 1908; wish and reality 960

beverage harmless b. 97

bewail it senseless 768

beware the fury 1376; the politically obsessed 1456

bewildered utterly b. 157

beyond the limitations 275; the point of decency 1741; this is voluntary submission 1534

biases the judgment 1030

big adventure 406; as they can pay for 1565; experiments 1103; ideas 915; men 807; story 1022

biggest library 1055; threats 1653

bill presented to us by our children 796

billion years 1154

bills terrific b. 569

bind old and new 1626

binds until it strangles 632

birds sang 1833

birth and death 1150; lack at b. 2059; to soft men 1730

bit of life 416

bite it through 1916

bitter and husky 1028; flavors 1674; moments 1615

bitterest pain among men 1049

bitterness source of b. 1308

bittersweet mixture 1427

black brown or fair 1185; tarantula 1668

blacks whites on b. 1463

blade knife all b. 1556

blame shame or b. 1846

blames his memory 1025

blasphemies begin as b. 1590

bleed makes the hand b. 1556

blessed is the man 1724; or cursed 52

blessing of idleness 937

blessings here on earth 113

blind belief 199; instruments 1382; kingdom of the b. 1605; obeisance 264; wife 1223; willingness to sacrifice 556

bliss ignorance is not b. 953

blockbusting fiction 1551

blood and bones 1748; circulation of their b. 83; innocent b. 1823; life b. 389; pool of b. 468

bloody measure 1823

bloom in their turn 245

blow strike the first b. 93; your candle out 1733

blunders are often made 550

blunt that trivial instinct 734

blushing without b. 1137

boa-constrictors crocodiles and b. 1926

board wish on b. 437

boast of a man 597

boatmen do not know 1633

body and soul 189; called his b. 1748; exists 934; mind and a b. 934; mind and b. 416; of the world

197; shapes itself to the b. 182; sins once 1422

bodyguard of lies 1523

bogey men 300

bold virtue is b. 752

boldly defend 1146

bolts pleasure 1423

bombardment of 970

bondage fear of b. 1173

bonds fed in b. 1709; so strong 1765

bones blood and b. 1748; interred with their b. 751

book as lovingly 2098; friends, discourse of my b. 231; learning 504; not the b. 1551; of the teacher 293; on the peculiar situation 1219; or painting 101; read a b. 1548; really knocks me out is a b. 1550; reviewing 379; that's at least funny 1550; which must inspire 293; writes a whole b. 15; writing a b. 1836

books anything in b. 1841; are not made 229; author's b. 251; betters here my b. 226; burning b. 1552; classes of b. 233; contain a person 1551; expend more money for b. 230; good b. 2097; in a true spirit 1547; not all b. 228; of which the backs and covers 227; quoting of b. 2095; reading of certain b. 248; study of mankind is b. 232; that of b. 1617; the same b. 234; they read 385; which contain no lies 843; won't stay banned 252

boon to people 1070

boots on 2027

borders on the chaos 266

bore first is being a b. 239; people who b. 235

bored as if he b. 1785; by the people 1762; people 941; when he is trying 236

boredom abyss of b. 238; and cruelty 941; crime is b. 239; may dictate 1453; vice and need 2092

boring about somebody else's happiness 825; it is b. 1869

born a genius 737; always

b. with 173; believing 203; charming fresh 305; in a man 29; into which he was born b. 1801; man that is b. 787; to action 48; to own 1458; weak 2059; writer 2101

borne willingly 1612

borrow from others 1336; their opinions 1355

bosses of our mass media 1015

both commonly succeed 434; himself in b. 1491; morality and invigoration 1325; the power it confers 1647; war and education 2040

bottle of gin 974

bottling the common-sense 1190

bottom stupid at b. 388

bought as furniture 1551; fresh supplies 2042; and placed it 1459; it at any price 126

boundaries limits or b. 1203

bourgeois ideas 1569; mediocrity 1878

bourgeoisie lives of the b. 1161; the b. 1588

boy fault in a b. 1138; who suffers 460

boys teenage b. 794

braces one up 366

brain cognition of the b. 1064; damage 500; of the b. only 146; weak b. 997

brains enough 2110; everything but b. 98; integrity and force 288

branch of the art of lying 1522

brand of beer 1239

brave good and the b. 1208; man braver 343; on a battlefield 353; or else be killed 353; very b. 347; when he observes 349

bravely told 1140

bravery never goes out of fashion 345

bravest sight in the world 797

breached occasionally 1397

bread beauty as well as b. 189; more necessary to him than b. 1884; steal b. 1101

breadth what beauty 653

break of day 1548; with one's past 975; with the work of art 156

breakdown of policy 696

breakfast before b. 204

breaks promises 1202

breast quiet b. 1900

breathe any greatness 63; easily 143

breathing growing 2116; space 1647

bred by the gap 960

breed sad sorrows 1611

breeds reptiles 1357

breeze undecided b. 919

brewery work in the b. 1239

bricks with which he built 1412

bridges sleep under b. 1101

bridle passions with logic 1372

brief gesture 1931; strive to be b. 1078

briefcase lawyer with his b. 1110

briefest review 1686

briefly defined b. 598; put it b. 1929

bright and interesting 1456

brighter than ignorance 1353

brilliant and warm-blooded 96; more b. 432

bringing shudders and bitter flavors 1674; up a family 297; us into our own 1575

brings to bear 1111; to human perception 1627; us nearer to destruction 1076; you great gifts 1829

briskly doing something 915

Britain as an extension 1014

Britain's mistake 565

broad deep knowledge 1062

broadest and most prevalent error 549

broad minded people are b. 100

broke they're b. 1824

broken and painful 274; friendships 722; out 2042

brother be my b. 104

brotherly love 1868

brothers and sisters 1486

brought death into the world 795; his own stool 1769

brown or fair 1185

brunt of life 325

brushstroke in someone else's painting 321

brutal truth 1189

budget federal b. 1455; meat b. 915

bugle blown by a b. 358

build easy to b. 207; himself a throne 1610

builder of a temple 1748

building better b. 1412; in the b. 1412; public b. 1187

builds it daily 278

built such high standards 1176; when it is b. 368; which he b. 1412

bull at the red cloth 613

bullets some with b. 95

bungler man is a b. 2037

buoyant well and b. 1782

burden irksome b. 713; it imposes 1647

burdened with convictions 1870

bureaucracy consists of functionaries 241; is not an obstacle 243; is sure to think 240; saves us from b. 247; the rule of no one 244; understand the b. 241

bureaus official b. 242

buried a whole world 571; alive 51; the hatchet 1393

burn they won't b. 252

burning books 1552; conviction 489; of an author's books 251; restless urge 165

burps history just b. 865

burst old rules 1626

bury itself 1374

bush fear each b. 1779

business creed 563; difficult b. 536; drive b. 1144; executives 509; from his b. 562; get rich in b. 317; I learned in b. 561; news b. 1022; of nations 2033; official b. 240; starting point in this b. 1803; talking b. 562; their own b. 1887; to be complimentary 850; to conceal 450; to lay bare the facts 850

businesses successful b. 563

businessman American b. 1720

busy as waltzing mice 915; life 411; thinking about myself 1299

butt kick in the b. 1812

butterflies to the b. 1132

buy a canary 457; superfluities only 2063

buying second-hand furniture 1235; something 883

by-product of function 2008

bywords of the modern world 1209

Caesar might be great 1277

cage around its gilt c. 182

calamities are of two kinds 525

calamity worst c. 1290

calculate the worth 520

calculation of the evils 759

calf killed a c. 1746

call a spade a spade 1167; him up on the phone 1550; his muscles into action 1313; our character 276; the temple of fame 1525; you darling 1209

called an acute knowledge 932; by no meaner name 447; it may be c. 1968; natural selection 1772

callous absolutely c. 327

callousness toward them 1139

calls it enslavement 663

came in contact 302; not here for friendly sympathy 2091

camp is a vision 558

campaign presidential c. 1455

campaigning weather 75

can calculate the worth 520; find no purpose 1157; love lightly 1370; never have both 1908; only be of value 1069; only form the minds 578;see things under ground 625

can't be right 1322; be wise 2080; lead a cavalry charge 1120; think without his hat 1861

canary buy a c. 457

candle blow your c. 1733

candor that makes men radical thinkers 1864

cannibal spices a baby 2098; uses knife and fork 1504

cannot accept the doctrine 1430; afford to be thrown out 1440; be a good commander 1351; be creative of virtue 1097; be forced 1553; be free 1345; be legislated 1321; be reasoned with 470; be sent into exile 1292; create experience 575; demand of a scholar 1849; enter into the idea 469; ever prosper 748; get white flour 1405; give us dispensation 396; have it 1930; have power for good 1476; help fearing 1501; hope to obtain excellence 540; keep an idea 1141; live without some knowledge 1157; love a reserved person 1184; open his mouth 1687; play innocents 699; rest till it be employed 938; retain an identity 1082; return 1985; ride two horses 887; cannot set forth 1860; shake hands 1883; soar until the millstones are lifted 1303; stifle a predilection 1331; train a horse 462; trust a friend 1961; understand 1271, 1978

canonization natural c. 399

can't express what I have to say 1813; mind their own business 1887; think with out metaphors 2108

capable of defying his torturer 2005; of every wickedness 765; of great virtues 2005; of suggesting 48

capacities and strengths 570

capacity for identification 2066; for receiving pleasure 1817; must be shown 1102; to be silent 1723; to dream dreams 970; to empathize 1486; to pause 718; worth and c. 1440

capital mistake 1030; surplus c. 493

capitalism carries within itself war 2036

capitalist society 1502; style of life 1753

caprice often takes the

form 260; prejudice or accident 1145

captain quality in the c. 1285

captive held c. 653

car keys 794

cardinal virtues 690

card-indexes consulted 1269

cards cut the c. 1892

care and love 1486; ceased to c. 631; nothing about 708; of children 301; of freedom 857

career political c. 1440, 1441

careerism or of a poet trying 1428

careful in the choice 522; when you told somebody 561

careless of his life 351

cares hopes joys 1300

caricature prejudice and c. 149

carried to the extreme 760

carries its banner 1987; within itself 1129, 2036

case facts of the c. 850; in any c. 957; is put by different people 1716

cases in select c. 187

cash customers have to sit 789; out of c. 1179; solid c. 886

caste did not originate 1289; fatal to c. 911

castle window of a c. 1902

castles in the air 207

casts a most becoming light 289; a vivid light 841; its wealth 1633

casualty first c. 1516

catapult set in motion 1008

catastrophe education and c. 852; is clearly visible 1162; is inevitably heightened 1839; is the natural human environment 1777

catastrophes see c. 810

catch way that you c. 1930

catchword can obscure 1086

Catholic Church 1573

Catholicism never was C. 1569

caught without being c. 1930

cauldron of their talk 1300

cause for alarm 1153; good

or bad 1729; immediate c. 2056; in our c. 44; not the c. 2011; of human error 547; that is just 1938; the philanthropist 983; them and those who profit 1584
caused angels to fall 1464; by folks 1887
causes for all the trouble 1885; much woe 1003; of war 1535; selected c. 841; that they represent 2102; which are unpenetrated 440
caution but courage 2006
cautions us what not to do 1352
cavalry charge 1120
cease to be loved 1197; to be popular 763; to exist 1982; to exist 580; until babies begin 2048
ceased to care 631; to communicate 1175; to constitute a threat 530; to fear 631
ceases to be a crime 2000; to be a mannerism 290; to be dangerous 166; to be true 210
ceasing to live 1197, 1719
celebration of the body of the world 197
celibacy has no pleasures 1227; women and c. 1658
cell hermit's c. 1853; cell worst c. 1894
cellar ivory c. 1619
cemetery of dead ideas 1632
censor and the inquisitor 252; can decapitate 910; usually squelches them 1866
censorship extreme form of c. 1589
center is giving way 178; office as a social c. 68
centers of dominance 1324
centuries a thousand c. 2000; ago 865
century by century 1076; desires of the c. 726; interest of our c. 370; nineteenth c. 404; philosophy of one 1411; twentieth c. 416
cerebrums and smaller adrenal glands 2048
ceremonies may be

breached 1397; of reconciliation 1398
certain alienated majesty 1850; dangers 1129; errors of such ingenuity 1141; greatness to find him 807; in any case 957; insensitivity 1738; other sets of people are human 1518; selected causes 841; talent 726; unless he is c. 81; certain we can be absolutely c. 256
certainly be exquisite 784; not death 1408; one of the most revolutionary doctrines 1591; that just to be alive 1159
certainties through my love for truth 1950
certainty doubt is to c. 482; general c. 254; his own c. 257; in our daily existence 259; is absurd 477; knew for a c. 1000; love of c. 255; of profaning it 194; utters a c. 258
certainty's constant companion 552
chagrin every c. 1678
chain alliance is like a c. 105; around the neck 1707; iron c. 200; of breathing 2116
chains do not hold a marriage together 1246; everything in their c. 1706
challenge of filling the space 1011
challenges strength to him who c. 906; to magnanimity 1926
champagne fighting is like c. 353
chance contributions that fell 1300; matter of c. 263; province of c. 2050
chances of a single life 959; too many c. 1202; were very high 561
change against c. 1320; and behave like free spirits 1155; existence being c. 259; for its own sake 265; his life 922; in conscience 329; is inevitable 1778; less things c. 1600; obeisance to c. 264; of ideas 896; or we will die 264; our minds 1716; reform

and c. 1650; small c. 743; the heart 1321; the past 1871; travel and c. 261; without violence 1778
changeable always is woman 640
changed human thought 1591; my ideas 898
changeful proverbially called c. 260
changing circumstances 1880; ever more specialized 1712
chaos and whim 267; form out of c. 162; immerse themselves in c. 162; madness and c. 269; of memories 266; revolutionary c. 268; submitting to c. 856; triumph over c. 164
chaotic borders on the c. 266; diversity 1639
chaotically limitless 663
chapel wooden c. 1525
character compromise of their c. 1458; contributes to beauty 279; his own c. 275; isn't inherited 278; judges of c. 734; melancholy c. 1614; one's c. 273; person's c. 277; too is a process 271; we call our c. 276; words and his c. 274
characteristic mannerism or c. 290
characteristics personal c. 620
charge cavalry c. 1120
charity begins at home 280; in their age 282; is no excess 1464; is the power 281; separates the rich from the poor 283
charity-boy air of a c. 270; said 1231
charlatanism of some degree 1118
charm at one period 311; exemplary c. 287; is a glow 289; need today is c. 288; power to c. 285
charmed even when they abuse us 778
charmer is aware 290
charming as it sounds 1951; fresh 305; in falling in love 1182; little personal characteristics 620; makes a person c. 290; manners 377; others find c. 290

climb out beyond 275; upward on the miseries 107
cling to a bourgeois mediocrity 1878
clings to the popular judgment 557
cloak wearing a shabby c. 122
clock faultless as a c. 1044; that is always running down 1294; which is always slow 320
close contact 1177; propinquity 1175; to death 595; to taboo 1667; upon you 1739
closed gap is c. 198
closeness to others 1257
closer and closer in touch 1341; to imagination 1946; to reality 1841; to the ants 1132
cloth at the red c. 613
clothes divested of their c. 1281
clothing firing 1303
clouds carry rain 2036; first c. 1913; in an undecided breeze 919; rose in c. 904
clown and jester 1974
coal sack 1405
cock crowing on its own dunghill 1333
coffee is good for talent 1790
cognition of the brain 1064
cohabit marry to c. 1245
cohesion recognizable c. 1330
coincided with and helped to shape 1258
coincides with the effectiveness 1593
coins and pieces of paper 1308
cold comfortless and distasteful 720; impartial intellect 1076; unproductive thinking 658
collapse temporary c. 1203
collection of facts 582
collective wisdom 945
collectively with a glum 677
collector's passion 266
college no dramatic c. 29
collide felt them c. 904
collision foreign c. 445
color knows no c. 1955; of my mind 898; of the skin 1497; the beauty 1784

colors are distilled 986
columns advice c. 664
comb over a c. 2053
combat electoral c. 1455
combination stable c. 904
combinations new c. 927
combines reflection c. 1050; the maximum 1236
come back to us 1850; downstairs 892; in danger 1464; into the world 2048; to an end 1747; to be looked upon 762; to believe 1697; to speak properly 1688; to that state 940; when you want them 484
comedy naturally wears itself out 1092
comes a time 1058, 1644; from the dirty 779; from the refusal 990; into the world 884; of swift contact 1854; to judging 1046; to the top 939
comfort about being a woman 1740; attached to c. 969; comes afterward 1933; of certainties 1950; of your dreams 499; the conservative 1103
comfortable vanity 587
comfortless and distasteful 720
comforts the military mind 817
comic perception of the c. 1783
coming into contact 1567; that close to death 595; to my house 1000
command of language 2096
commander good c. 1351
commands man who c. 1283
commemorates a robbery 1388
commendable attribute 109; philanthropy is c. 983
commerce more brilliant than c. 432; of minds 917
commit violence 1823
commitment information and c. 1838; ideas 614; to some 614
committee is organic 245; personality in any c. 246
committees will bloom 245
commodity in the world 306; marketable c. 1347

common affairs of life 822; denominator 23; enemy 1330; ground of truth 895; have in c. 818; not so c. 308; origin 116; property 894; quality of human nature 340; sense 306, 308, 494, 1190, 1411, 1628; strength 1575; transactions and daily intercourse 1145; womanhood 644
commonly succeed 434
commonplace dauber 1791
commonplaces of existence 1147
communicate ceased to c. 1175; through silence 1690
communicated to great masses of people 474
communicates some of its strength 906
communication art is c. 160
community betrayed your c. 925; has a right 693; ordinary c. 1139; small anarchist c. 118
compact highest c. 1913
companion constant c. 552; to make him feel 1172
companionable with death 2021
companions for middle age 2085
company almost always in c. 2057
comparable to standing 1902
compared herself to a rotten herring 312; with our own private opinion 1528; with the vanity 1986
comparison advantageous c. 96; attractive by c. 1161
comparison with the dreams 963
comparisons without c. 106
compel the soul 201
compelled to do 1538; to use one 1167
compensates for the trouble 838
compete with man 659
complain of the despotism 1971
complains of moral indigestion 1423

complement inevitable c. 243

complementary to his own 1713

complete intimacy 1257

completely and cheerfully 756; and swept away 1192; conscious 834; completeness silent c. 420

complex ever growing 1712; is made over into the simple 474; the inexplicable 630; things are; communicated 474

complicate simplicity 1509

complicated details 1044; situation 145

complicates life 1694

compliment to his intelligence 1359

complimentary business to be c. 850

compliments instead of c. 377

composed of nine parts 1868; when it is c. 368

comprehend and accept 1340; its own ignorance 948

compressed into tiny tablets 1019; within the skull 205

compromise of their character 1458

comrade dangerous c. 628

conceal the facts 450

concealment of it will do 1192

conceit arrogance 1385; spoils the finest genius 731

conceive the things 1147

conceives it as a study 1713

conceiving a child 1836

concentrated power 1483

concentrates it c. 1537

concentration on disaster 1015

concept theatrical c. 745

conceptions bind old and new 1626

concern them 1445

concerned with it 784

concerning international relations 1399

concludes one c. 1245

concrete not for the c. 354

concurrence no great c. 1125

condemns to silence 1683

condition new social c. 329; pleasant c. 477; social c. 1616; that directs 1616

conditionally true 1131

conditioning totality of their c. 660

conditions actions or c. 39; modern c. 788; of middle-class life 1463

conduct our attitude 1982; perilous to c. 1559; their own affairs 1043; was double 447

confederacy against him 725

conferences to scare up a war 452

confers power it c. 1647

confession is always weakness 1646; of the deficiency it indicates 1298

confined powers 69

conflicting points of view 995; truths 1943

conformist by being a c. 317

conformists live c. 319

conformity is the ape 313; recognition and c. 1209; ruined by c. 316

confounding their enemies 1221

confront an unbridled desire 439

confronted history 859; with the impossibility 215

confused and clamorous 788; easily c. 110

confusion form of c. 30

confusions courage of their c. 359

conjectures price upon c. 905

connect which we c. 600

connected with strength 1497; with three dangerous prescriptions 1660

connection between the political ideas 968; of the first fresh flash 1866

connections between it and anything else 1169

conquer must c. 322; not enough to c. 1654

conquered and peopled 324; not easily c. 1965

conqueror to be the c. 2015; you are a c. 410

conquerors into silent footnotes 860; must expect 323

conquest for its c. 140; is the missionary of valor 346; right of c. 443

conquests and all to the success 832

conscience be their guide 1105; change in c. 329; courage without c. 328; is not the vessel 329; man calls his c. 330; of the human race 834; of what must be 1056; quiet c. 325; scruple 2104; self-esteem 331; social c. 1565; without judgment 326

conscientious stupidity 955; toleration 1867

conscious design 1000; mind 970; of itself 834; that you are ignorant 947

consciously over-compensates 608

consciousness human c. 1667; of others 1521; of possessing 731; of the truth 8

consequence as a c. 1455; of no c. 1177

consequences anticipation of c. 2081; beneficial c. 1993; deserves all the c. 2087; estimate of c. 206; knowledge of c. 1620; to God 1907

conservatism fanatics about c. 1760

conservative adopts them 1545; is a slave 1874; nor depress the radical 1103; the day after 1599

consider are those which they inflict 771; it criticism 80; most important 1627

considerable and often 474

consideration with c. 310

considered a process 865; in its deepest meaning 151

considering it as true 220

consistency or a consistent expediency 1099; laugh at himself 1093

consists in nearly deceiving 1522; in our conscientious toleration 1867; in redou-

crowd in a c. 1962; usurping c. 1960; will always save Barabbas 528
crowing cock c. 1333
crown for the c. 1247; wears a c. 1606
crowns exertion 1457; upon the heads 885
crucial but an indispensable 1426; moment of decision 818
crucified who is to be c. 528
crude requirement 1237; violence 1148
cruel are c. 941; never more c. 1175
cruelest lies 1136
cruelty boredom and c. 941; sources of c. 634; worse c. 2014; crusade war a c. 69
crush him 1979; those beneath them 1967
crushes individuality is despotism 1968
crushing truths perish 1940
crutch of dogma 472
crystal facet of the c. 151
crystallize into new forms of life 268
crystallizes the optical illusion 504
cuckolds bachelors or c. 175
cult patriotism is its c. 1334
cultivate among their dupes 954; time to c. 1299
cultivation of his talent 1801
cultural exchange 1347; strength 1486
culture and their values 318; clichés of a c. 1959; democratic c. 1835; for adult society 2116; for all 499; in this c. 382; is properly described 384; is the name 385; old c. 158; to leisure 969; tyranny of his c. 161
cultures two c. 662
cumbersome and costly 1245
cunning man 1686
cunningly Americans know 1551
cure for birth 1150; of all diseases 395; our own c. 395; stupidity 1743

curiosity has withered 1323; is in great and generous minds 386; is one of the lowest 388; is the life blood 389; origin in c. 384; without really satisfying 1169
curious man 1642
curiously boring 825
currents of thought 1854
curse of labor 937; of senility 940; which lies upon marriage 1243
cursed with a nature 52
curtain lace c. 1459
custom is despot of mankind 835; supersedes all other forms 2000
customary fate of new truths 1917
customer at the shop door 103
customers have to sit 789
customs and institutions 1857; may be creative of vice 1097; of the day 1547
cut annual c. 915; taxes 1824; the cards 1892; the claws 1649; us out of the blessing 937
cuts its way through 1633; without wounding 1348
cutting edge 59
cynicism is after all 392; is intellectual dandyism 390; prides himself on c. 393; sin I know is c. 391

daily admission of one's weakness 1495; by the way 278; existence 259; intercourse 1145; life 388, 1633, 1633
damage brain d. 500
damages a cause 1938
damn fool for at least five minutes 2077
dancer good d. 1413
danceth without music 874
dancing fencing and d. 1104; singing and d. 2025
dandyism without the coxcomb's feathers 390
danger come in d. 1464; contempt for d. 2006; is not that military spending 700; makes a brave man braver 343; of an ethics 556; of contagion 13; of success 982; of their

coming true 1856; recognize d. 1739; that real talent or goodness 731; theory as a d. 1501
dangerous about extremists 615; and uncomfortable 2001; and unpredictable 1463; art is d. 166; ceases to be d. 166; comrade 628; desires 1667; ends 1728; genius is d. 1264; more d. 955; most d. 683; nothing is more d. 912; nowadays 365; prescriptions 1660; quality in the captain 1285; quality 1701; thing 1070, 1126, 1696; till our fears 637; to come by 1517; to take liberties 710; to the life 614; to truth 1135; to write the truth 1517; truths that are d. 1630; untruths 1134
dangers certain d. 1129; that come from trusting 988
Danish national drink 99
dare not dismount 1972; to avouch for them 39; to conceive 1147; trust themselves 1889
dares to be a fool 2076
daring adventure or nothing 1155; less d. 343
dark alleys in their hearts 803
darken into nightmares 1856
darker emptier 1852; than knowledge 1353
darkness and silence 1681; plunges into d. 1073
darling call you d. 1206
dart treacherous d. 2084
Darwin has called natural selection 1772; or Hegel 920
dash out thy teeth 1904
dastardly pitiless selfish 341
dauber commonplace d. 1791
daunted me more than the morning 312
dawn of one's strength 1548
day after the revolution 1599; break of d. 1548; every d. 1230, 1733; in virtual environments 931; news every d. 1019; of his

death 357; present d. 1714; some d. 2057; times a d. 416; when he shall no longer cast a shadow 387; witty every d. 364

daydreams would darken 1856

days before the world again plunges 1073; catching d. 267; in the house three d. 188; these d. 453

dead audience is d. 2078; by their late twenties 1428; cities 1331; democracy of the d. 1873; general 817; history 1674; ideas 1632; in fact its d. 134; it is d. 1879; like the d. 397; love is d. 113; man without ambition is d. 113; mechanized specialized actions 416; once I am d. 869; play upon the d. 836; relic of the d. 401; selves 893; skin 1258; son of the d. 400; than to be d. 402; thing 862; troublemakers 319; who do not return 398

deadliest form of democracy 709

deadline there is no d. 1939

deadly sin 391; sins 1303

deaf husband 1223

deal good d. 1127, 1238, 1452, 1696, 1807

dealer in hope 1113

dealing justly 1035; with human crocodiles 1926

dear deceit of beauty 185; my d. 310

death afraid of d. 423; and rebirth 1576; and vulgarity 404; as for d. 417; as for ourselves 418; at the proper time 403; bed on my d. 408; birth and d. 1150; cancels everything 399; certainly not d. 1408; close to d. 595; companionable with d. 2021; consolations about d. 421; counter to d. 1201; day of his d. 357; defense against d. 1164; diminishes a little 418; dispensation from d. 396; even d. 600; fear of d. 413, 1166, 1616; inevitability of d. 1157; into the world 795; is better

394; is not the enemy 422; is the cure of all diseases 395; is the obscene mystery 421; is to the finish 407; life and d. 1109; mattered not 419; not merely ends life 420; of one's own free choice 403; of public opinion 1532; on an installment plan 304; only by your d. 414; other people's d. 417; reveals the eminent 405; sense of d. 421; should not be 415; sign of d. 196; sterility and d. 1727; terrifies men 416; timely d. 411; to know d. 1152; ultimately is the victor 407; waiting docilely for d. 940

deaths sudden d. 1806

debt of gratitude 795, 796

debts repay their d. 1355

decade even of the d. 726

decapitate ideas 910

decay grief d. 819; its own d. 1626

decaying trees 1339

decays upon growing familiar 64

deceit of beauty 185

deceived ready to be d. 1248

deceiving your friends 1522

decency is indecency's conspiracy 1682; point of d. 1741

decent fellows like himself 1311

decently bury itself 1374

decide to have sex 1673

decided to have it all for yourself 426

deciphering and interpreting 154

decision it is our d. 1673; making isn't a matter 425; moment of d. 818; without information 1362

decisions concerning international relations 1399; good d. 427; healthier your d. 426; of our life 424

declare peace 1395; the inhabitants 248

declared when war is d. 1516

declares that it is his duty 487

decorative surface of oratory 1787

decree how it is to be imparted 132

decrees judicial d. 1321

deed for love 544

deeds as well as d. 1081; everybody with our d. 95; fact and in d. 1140; great d. 812; have denied beliefs 216; requires spirit and talent 1738

deep a debt 795; as eternity 1677; feelings 1070; inside 1813; knowledge 1062; places of the imagination 968; thinking and high imagining 734

deepest definition of youth 262; impulses 1573; meaning 151; part of autobiography 1432; truths 1959

deeply believe 484; feared 1771; impressed on men so d. 1569

defeat is an orphan 2016; knowledge of d. 429; post-mortems on d. 431; scorn for d. 1759; to defeat 76

defeats itself 854

defect grave d. 1407

defects of all d. 1747

defend it to the last 1146; yourself 777

defending power of d. 281

defends from chaos 267; itself and seeks another equilibrium 1781

defense adequate d. 913; against betrayal 1895; against death 1164; of morals 1320

deficiencies moral d. 185

deficiency it indicates 1298; supply their d. 1788

define belief not as the object 220; failures to understand d. 806; his talent 1797

defined as the subject 1253; briefly 598; by our ideas 931; in psychological terms 608; judgment is therewith d. 1029

definite and inexorable ruler 441; set of customs 1857; understanding 1146

definition of youth 262

definitions of virtue 1324

deflated in favor of strong 438

defying his torturer 2005

degenerate man 1029

deglutition human d. 1028

degrades suffering that d. 1771

degree of some d. 1118; of wisdom 513

dehumanized representation 1755

deifies success 1759

deign to turn into an idea 928

deigns to speak 138

delay if you d. 53

delays have dangerous ends 1728

delicacy to learn the silence 1688

delicate and infirm 1782; emotions 34

delicious thing to be a young widow 2068

delight civilized d. 27; in war 1285; it can d. 1647

delightful thing to think 1403

delighting in such exercises 1313; their friends 1221

delights from the sentiments 1425

deliver more than I promise 1511; us from the pain 1616

deliverance liberation is not d. 707

deludes the thoughtless 121

delusion will be no greater 552

demagogues spring up 1094

demand a certain insensitivity 1738; excess of the d. 1952; for guarantees 255; for ordinary movies 1837; freedom 1473; it is the d. 2116; of a scholar 1849; popular d. 828; the credentials 1704; to be stood for 922

demanding freedom 717

demands from others 1975; of its own convenience 791; personal progress 592; that you sell 1802

democracies in d. 432; vice of d. 1527

democracy can afford 954; is not autocracy 709; is

the recurrent suspicion 433; means government by the uneducated 133; obstacle to d. 243; of idolaters 241; of the dead 1873; offers you d. 435; to save 2045; under d. 434

democratic culture 1835; nations 1401; source 1077

demonic forces 1667

demonstrated truth 1932

demonstrations for impressions 1622

denied it can only be d. 421; that dogma draws a circle 475

denominator lowest common d. 24

denunciation of the young 83

deny man's ability 1880; than to d. 208; the sentiments 884

denying unbelief in d. 202

depart from traditions 1115

depend only on your own good taste 372; upon it 1058; upon their separation 1451

dependence of one fact 1620

depending on the talent 1811

depends on the thoughts 1761

depose my state d. 742

depository of power 1472

deprived of such nourishment 1859

depth lies in the valleys 1909

deranges the course of events 2050

derivative from this pure activity 1635

derived genuine pleasure 1459

derives from a thwarted sensation 1865

descending ascending and d. 1156

describe a fool 687

described in terms of the genesis 1753; not as having its origin 384

desert of uniformity 468

deserve it 2017; to live 1311

deserved good-fortune 534; to be called 447

deserves a slight whip 459; all the consequences 2087

deserving real distinction 1792

design conscious d. 1000; drawn from the convolutions 986

designed for a war 1443

designs crooked d. 1382

desirable to tell the truth 1911

desire always being told about d. 438; and prize 342; for a son 617; for knowledge 1464; for power 1464; for success 2006; of escaping 1706; of greatness 800; of knowledge 1051; rival is d. 438; should so many years 1657; to be and to know 2006; to be distinguished 2024; to seek power 1465; unbridled d. 439

desired beauty is d. 194; results 2039

desires dangerous d. 1667; of the century 726; peace 2026

desolation of an empty abundance 1808

despairingly acutely miserable 1159

despairs one who d. 349

desperate know to be d. 281

desperately numerous 242; we wish to maintain 1896

despicable more d. 636

despise one's neighbor 1570

despite the continuing expansion 979

despot of almost any man 1475; of mankind 835; who sees himself 1975

despotism during the campaign 2033; form of d. 244; individuality is d. 1968; of princes 1971

destinations knowing of their d. 2107

destinies opposed d. 442

destiny is an absolutely definite 441; is made known 424; of the human race 302; offers 69

destroy life becomes the equivalent 1492; vice you d. 1999; wish to d. 811; your taste 1816

destroyed appetite 1007

destroys base people 1302;

discovery is not ignorance 1074; of cosmic truths 1156

discrepancy between a man's words 274

discriminated against 660

discrimination still have d. 1717

disdainful self confident and d. 271

disease fatal d. 934; infantile d. 1332; just a d. 872; not a d. 87; that affects amateurs 143; to trust to friends 1888; which can afflict 509

diseases cure for all d. 395

disenfranchised I am not d. 231

disentangles activity which d. 1313

disguised as a god 809; vices d. 1989

disguises thrown away 1987

dishonest inveterably d. 1998

dishonor will not trouble me 869

disillusion embraces only his own d. 198

disintegrate first thing to d. 1089

disinterested intellectual curiosity 389; judgment 2116; virtue 549

dislike to wade into its waters 1919

disliked advice is not d. 78

dislikes values and d. 300

dismiss anything which reaches beyond 1260

dismount dare not d. 1972

disobey orders you d. 1286

disorder an implied order 1017; and stress 610; by authorities 1270; is not as useful 1055

disordered movements 293; wits are d. 1048

disoriented easily d. 1337

dispassionately understands them d. 850

dispensation from death 396

disregard their talk 1697

dissembled it can only be d. 121

disseminate through a medium 1521

dissenting opinions 1361

dissipated in futile imaginings 123

dissolves in time 156

distance at a d. 437; greater d. 1572

distant and unfamiliar 474; early warning system 158

distasteful comfortless and d. 720

distilled from the experiences 986

distinct ideas 899

distinction between good and evil 766; deserving real d. 1792; to achieve d. 1188

distinctly an acquired taste 618

distinguish between live ones 914

distinguished always the most d. 2024; from panic 355

distinguishes between the possible 993

distorted slightly d. 1134

distortion radical d. 474

distraction they offer 1015

distractions of all kinds 499; uncertain of its d. 167

distressing sight 1337

distributed commodity 306

distrust and fear 1018; each other 1895; everyone 466; great men 468; it 1414; more lonely than d. 465

distrusted work 2094; you will be d. 467

disturb one's thoughts 1858

diversity of our sense-experience 1639

diverted to inner meditation 123

divested of their clothes 1281

divide it with 820

divided by a sharp line 1491; roughly d. 853

dividends if ignorance paid d. 498; steal their own d. 1458

divine a discrepancy 274; guidance 42; principle of our race 47; see the D. 1341; service 1413; still d. 1338

divined newly d. 1626

divinity kind of d. 776

division into sexes 1662; of labor 2093

doctor advised me 85

doctors have invented 1775

doctrinaire philosophers 1415

doctrine for his servant 877; of the Kingdom of Heaven 1591; that in poetry 1430

doctrines revolutionary d. 1591

documents more d. 849

Dodge Dart 1604

doers no good d. 40

does not encourage individuality 1974; not find scope 1884; not guarantee freedom 950; not know 777, 908, 1345; not possess 647

doesn't always go with everything else 883; matter as it passes 1396; need luck 1652; wish 1538

dog in the fight 1312; spends it 1131

dogma a program 220; crutch of d. 472; draws a circle 475; has been the fundamental principle 469

dogmas facts and not d. 1372; hold d. 471; makes d. 606

dogmatic hypothetical into the d. 474; most d. 473

dogs bark loudest 338; feels about d. 380

doing evil 749; me good 1000; not worth d. 25; nothing 2057; the important job 701; thing that needs d. 52; us harm 802; worth d. 25

dollars all their cares 1300; melted down into d. 1300; slab with d. 1300

domain of aesthetic judgment 1029

domestic policy 697

dominance in any society 1324

dominated by the creative urge 654

done a great deal 544; at home 504; by people 775; harm has been d. 679; nothing is ever d. 49; or learned 644; reading it

1550; some things 554;
the thing before 344; to
make herself beautiful
193; to our sense of reality
2022; what was d. 62;
with its sin 1422; work is
d. 1001
don't abuse your friends 80;
ask for facts 581; buy a canary 457; know 366, 498,
951; laugh at a youth 2115;
tell me peace has broken
out 2042; turn against
him 1967; worry about
your enemies 532; believe
in miracles 930; fear life
1166; have 561, 1070, 1233,
1827, 1954; intend to try
any more 1791; like people
590; listen to writers
2103; think I'd have the
strength 1163; understand
now 1231; want to quit
1455
doomed force is d. 695; to
failure 589; to mediocrity
1266; to retrace my steps
1130; to try and learn 1130
door knocks at your d.
1769; next d. 280, 1570; of
necessity 1991; shop d.
103
doors lock d. 875
dope field 100
double conduct was d. 447;
share 2074; that goes d.
669
doubleness act with d. 447
doubt above all to d. 1631;
and has fears 482; as far
as possible 476; engulfed
in d. 479; honest d. 478; I
have no d. 302; is not a
pleasant condition 477; is
the beginning 480; is to
certainty 482; of his own
certainty 257; secret d.
608; those who have
found it 481; when in d.
1924
doubts discouragements
and d. 23
down drag d. 1250; looked
d. 1368; to the day 387
downfall national d. 1040
downhill from toil to
pleasure 1419
downstairs from their
ivory towers 892
downward mobility 1453

dozen facts 581
drag an executive 562;
down the gods 1250
dragged on by their favorite 541
drama is action 50; drama
of life 1149
dramatic action 60; college
29; flourishes 701
dramatist only wants more
liberties 849
draught washy d. 1028
draw an ape 136; on a bank
1718; on their accumu-
lated wisdom 818;
strength from heaven
1496
drawn around it 475; from
the convolutions 986; his
teeth 1649; to the hand
701
draws a circle 475; its
means 728; noble delights
1425
dread of loneliness 1173
dreadful injustice 982
dreadfully married 882;
unjust world 1233
dream and a mockery 469;
dreams 970; guided d.
2105; of lying 1226; of the
actual world 144; stems
the d. 58; when I am
awake 483
dreamed of it 744
dreamer consenting to
dream 144
dreams and ideas 376; are
loose 875; comfort of
your d. 499; do come true
484; in our d. 939; life d.
898; of fevered imagina-
tions 963; of terror 1168;
pass into the reality of action 58; their own d. 976
dreamt in my life dreams
898
dress it is not a d. 1754
dressed indecently d. 566
dressing up 38
drift like clouds 919
drink as much 97; national
d. 99
drinking eating and d. 678
drip with the oil of forbearance 461
drive business home 1144;
if a man doesn't d. 100;
drive out knowledge 1830
driven from one field 1987;

him to a revenge 120; lives
1161; to justice 1048; to
prefer poverty 1808; to
the most 215
drivers taxi d. 1220
drives out thought 1310
drop drown in every d. 454
drown in every drop 454;
in our technology 1830
drowning selves 489
drum drives out thought
1310
drunk being very d. 174
drunkards habitual d. 96
drunken man is happier
1701
dry duty of analyzing 1455;
shriveled kernel 838
dryness of the mouth 1007
due to man's being unreasonable 1170; to the ambition 1415; to the fact 1663;
to their feeling 367
dukes lords and d. 226
dull apt to be d. 1407; as
their readers 228; dis-
courses 1678; monoto-
nous years 75; play 363;
that he be d. 698; virtue
1869
dunces are all in confederacy 725
dunghill on its own d. 1333
dupes among their d. 954
duplicate himself 617
duration is not a test 1941
dust or magic 1811
duties are sacrilege 837;
double your d. 1229; to
perform 486
duty is to augment 240; it
is his d. 487; largely consists of pretending 490;
moral d. 1168; of analyz-
ing 1455; to worship 485;
toward others 489; we
owe 845; well performed
488
dwarfs giants or d. 6
dwells within others 764
dying growing and d. 2116;
scorned 603; worth d. for
412
dynamic static and d. 1662

each asking from the other
1243; man 318, 1884; new
generation 1401; other's
intolerance 1867
eager to be concerned 784

certainty's 552; is the corollary 552; of the senses 1557; prevalent e. 549; said about e. 552; strange e. 1761; study of e. 551

errors and absurdities 1403; of life 1170; of such ingenuity 1141; succession of e. 553

escape his own 393; narrow e. 502; the alienation 1714

escaping from them 1706

especially if it is about women 782

essence of learning lines 38; of science 1544; perversion of its e. 1566

essential basic e. 32; for survival 1778; hailed as e. 787; sense 1629; to persuade 1311

essentially guilty 1663; human 1558

essentials of patriotism 1385

establishing the truth 837

estate man's e. 2059; real e. 1156, 1386

esteem customs of the day e. 1547

esteems itself rich 2065

esthetic pride and pleasure 409

estimable most e. 339

estimate of consequences 206; the wisdom 493

estrangement feeling of e. 1537

eternal style is e. 1756; trinity 633; verities 329

eternally creative source 1575

eternity causes to appear 196; deep as e. 1677; manifestation of e. 196

ethical making men e. 501; sympathies 141

ethics abstracted from life 556

even a fool understands 679; a god cannot change 1871; higher levels 965; to live is an act of courage 333; when they abuse us 778; when they bring gifts 516

event there is no e. 1615

events and actions 790; are not a matter 263; course

of e. 2050; force of e. 1812; in the past 853; men and e. 859; which ought not 855

ever least tolerant 764

evergreens don't stagnate 264

ever-receding nature 198

every action he attempts 555; assembly 555; chagrin 1678; child 295; day 1733; death 418; field 16; every generation 1942; great advance 171; great advance 967; hour 387; human being 1352; innovation 1501; man 307, 387, 571, 787, 1218, 1261, 1563, 1748, 1785, 2077; man's 4371 mind 1908; moment of the flight 966; mystery from sex 1192; natural philosopher 1414; ordinary community 1139; passion borders 266; question 1044, 1542; society honors 319; sort of psychic phenomena 970; thought derives 1865; time you think 1834; truth find 964; tyrant's heart 1961; vice you destroy 1999; war is its own excuse 2051; woman 1785

everybody has got money 1824; is constantly graded 297; is content to hear 877; is so talented nowadays 1792; needs beauty 189; right against e. 1322; trust e. 1892

everybody's a mad scientist 269

everyday life 1199

everyone available to e. 1835; becomes brave 349; blames his memory 1025; but you 224; has a small part 1491; has talent at twenty-five 1810; humiliation is seen by e. 1676; in whom the impulse 466; is dragged on 541; seems to crave 1209

everything action is e. 44; appears as art 273; begins in mysticism 1444; believe e. 596; but brains 98; but tact 1787; but truth 399; cover e. 1863; else in the

house 883; except genius 733; face of e. 1896; has been said 1069; has it wonders 1681; in life 1689; in their chains 1706; is an artist's attitude 294; is being compressed 1019; know e. 956; names are e. 1084; price of e. 492; questions e. 479; recalls to me 966; settles e. 1533; should fear e. 1466; that happens is a necessity 1346; thinks he knows e. 1441; to imagine is e. 962; to see e. 463; ultimately fails 21

everywhere and anywhere 486; in society 1849; man now sees e. 8; society e. 315; surveys are e. 1016

evidence all the e. 1030; corollary of e. 552; of the fact 1724; evidence sense of e. 1359

evidently consoling to reflect 1570

evil alone has oil 773; because it is evil 758; do all the e. 769; doing e. 749; face of e. 774; good and e. 750, 754, 766; good or e. 775; he does 755; immorality 1993; is done 775; is not necessary 765; is only 1898; know the e. 769; knowledge of e. 1297; love e. 769; man 746; men by their own nature 748; men never do e. 756; monstrously flourish 767; no explanation for e. 768; often attracts the weak 772; power for e. 1476; productive of e. 760; still an e. 770; that dwells 764; that lies in ourselves 764; that men do 751; totality of e. 613; weed 954

evil-minded tempt the e. 566

evils flow from ourselves 757; great e. 2092; knowledgeable of e. 747; lesser of two e. 770; of tyranny 1969; that mankind 771; which police 759

evolution and every 592; of the capitalist 1753

evolutions best e. 163

evolves this way 1716

exact proportion 413

exactly as charming 1951; those beliefs were 221; to his taste 1239

exaggerated love of the e. 558

exaggeration element of e. 557

examined impartially 1698

example of the routineer 242

examples of women 643

exceed that of the latter 759; the vanity 1984

exceeding the limit 2077

excelled in learning 643

excellence encourages one 559; highest e. 601; love of e. 601; makes people nervous 560; obtain e. 540

excellent campaigning weather 75; native word 888

except as its clown and jester 1974; by stealth 1404; genius 733; he be first a historian 1435; he can see what must be 1435; our own thoughts 1845

exceptionally good liar , 1923

excess of commitment 614; of the demand 1952; power in e. 1464

excesses inhuman e. 215

exchange cultural e. 1347

excitable and lying old lady 844

exciting poetically e. 1430

excluded from the realm 1399

exclusively of wicked men 762

excuse its own e. 2051; what e. is there 387

executive drag an e. 562

executives are like joggers 562; in their work 509

exemplary charm 287

exempt from fear 622

exercise fruit of e. 2096; it who surveys 273; noble e. 1547; of power 1491; of the human will 1362; which the 1547

exercises as call 1313

exert power 1474

exertion with rest 1457

exhaust their talents 1804

exhausted mind and body are e. 416

exhibit their tyranny 1527

exhilarating as to be shot 1309

exile sent into e. 1292

exiled truth 195

exist cease to e. 580; in the legal sense 1982; without 513

existence absurdity of e. 8; commonplace of e. 1147; daily e. 259; ground of e. 923; is elsewhere 1719; loneliness in e. 1177; segment of e. 1075; undeniable e. 964; existence vanity of our e. 1984

existential experience 1838

existing institutions 1884

exists for me 934; my body e. 934

exit without pausing 1935

expanding and contracting 1154; the field 952

expands in proportion 361

expands to absorb revenue 1825

expanse of water 824

expansion or even explosion 979

expect it to obey a whisper 462; justice 1038; no mercy 323; that mankind 77; them to consider 80; to rule others 170

expectation constitutes 2022; of power 1490; uncertainty and e. 253

expected to regulate 320

expects to be paid 1389

expediency consistent e. 1099

expedient in the way 1929; invents an e. 145

expend more money for books 230

expense grudge no e. 1186; of all others 1484

experience cannot create e. 575; don't have to e. 1827; emotion and e. 1838; existential e. 1838; glut of e. 1271; hardly is e. 572; in ascending 1156; in history 576; indispensable e. 1426; is a good teacher 569; isn't interesting 572;

learn by e. 574; loneliness I e. 1174; love 1195; mixed with e. 978; of course fades 595; of finding 216; of politics 1449; of the soul 1064; open to e. 1643; quality of our e. 1091; record of e. 183; some of his 2; transmit an e. 568

experiences life e. 662; of the senses 986; relationships and e. 570; string our e. 1087; the highest 1664

experiment to find a way to live 269; write off an e. 1644

experimentation reflection and 1050

experiments mean revolutions 1438; without trembling 1103

expert technological world 1712

expert's advice 1122

experts on secrecy 1647

explain away 404; the demands 791

explaining things to them 1256

explains why some 1688

explanation for evil 768; of the world 1863; total e. 2054

explicitly referring e. 1199

exploding cigar 1205; in her face 958

exploits curiosity 1160

exploring illusion that I am e. 1130

explosion of information 979

exposing the follies 1092

express in mechanical terms 1772; what I have to say 1813; your own original ideas 925

expresses man who e. 903

expression glory of e. 1693; of energy 1151; of ideas 1082; of inner poverty 2066; of the value 495

expressions makes use of his e. 918

exquisite form 1775; must certainly be e. 784

extension of conversation 1014; of history 1014; of one's limits 1203

extent of man's knowledge

fields open f. 1474
fiend dope f. 100
fight between life and death 407; between two bald men 2053; dog in the f. 1312; for it 708; for principles 1042; how you f. 1729; nor fly 623; peril on the f. 2012; to the death 222; with weakness 871
fighting is like champagne 353; ways of f. 2015
fights interval between f. 1392
figure wax f. 276
figures incorrect f. 1255; means of f. 1726
fill time 2058
filled with beauty 187; with men 471
filling the space 1011
film and television 1015; invention of f. 36
films bad f. 1832
final analysis 1755; forming 277; wisdom of life 19
finally be passed back 300
financial equality 665
find a fool 688; a way to live 269; an effective 964; as we f. 43; difficult to f. 807; greatness to f. 807; hard to f. 838; her ignorance 958; him desperately numerous 242; in the Paganism 1338; it connected 1660; not only sanctuary 1768; now I f. 1655; one single explanation 1863; ourselves at the feet 1931; out what life is 795; reasons to trust 1896; sympathy 588; that I can f. 1024; the inner strength 1733; the same reason 181; what we f. 1072
finding experience of f. 216; him not sufficiently alone 1172; out who we are 1158; pleasure 1243; what we suspected 1780; you haven't got 366
finds himself engaged 370; his own 2115; in the intellectual 1808; the issue 145
fine art 1413; intellects 1783
finest genius 731; one's f. 1170
finish death is to the f. 407; saying it 1240

finishes place where it f. 86
fire of thought 440
fires fused in the f. 206
firing rent taxes 1303
firm anchor in nonsense 1862
first attribute 1699; call promising 811; casualty 1516; duties 837; encountered 300; Eros is the f. 543; fresh flash 1866; from the f. 48; great benefactor 795; half of life 1158; husband 1234; impressions 43; in the world made gods 624; is being a bore 239; key to wisdom 2072; kiss from a woman 408; part of politics 503; passion and the last 386; reaction to truth 1899; requirement 698; season 1785; sight 188, 1185; step 1501, 1698; syllable 79; thing 538, 1089; this direction 919; thoughts 1866; time as tragedy 865; truly democratic culture 1835; truth of aesthetics 1920; wife 1234; with an ugly woman 192
fish for it 1633; keep any better than f. 1063
fisherman good f. 1137
fist clenched f. 1883
fit if our shoes f. 1054; of absence of mind 324; thing he is f. for 1167; to participate in society 305
fitness is questioned 1288
fitted nature f. 1261; to interpret correctly 1341; to survival 1774
fittest survival of the f. 1772
fixed by authority 472; idea ends in madness 902
flare up 119
flash fresh f. 1866
flashes of vision 921
flashlight of a truth 1925
flatter themselves 619
flatters the majority 2023
flattery and admiration 671; corrupts both 670
flavor ignorant of f. 677; of it doesn't 595
flavors bitter f. 1674; if we bite it through 1916
flesh and blood 1748

flies and bedbugs 1773
flight of my ideas 966
flights eccentric f. 727
flirt with their own husbands 673
floor off the f. 1251
flour white f. 1405
flourish monstrously f. 767
flourished civilizations once f. 863
flourishes dramatic f. 701; most f. 1366
flow from duty 488
flowers of reason 1557; wilts and dies 245
flows a river of contempt 671
fluency grace logical order 1787
fluid prejudice 846
flunk the course 379
flux to which 420
fly fight nor f. 623
foe by a f. 514
foes all our f. 529; as well as by his friends 524; half his f. 691
fog of information 1830
folks who can't 1887
follies and weaknesses 1092; of all the f. 564; that we are one 588
follow a leader 1119; not truth 1904; precedent 242
follows a sentimental reaction 330
folly according to his f. 685; of our pursuits 1984; when we are dealing 1926
fond men are of justice 1046; of truth 1526
fondly believe their wish 1429
food and eating 678; clothing firing 1303; harvest and f. 1913; nourishing f. 298; on which it lives 1092; to fill us 677
fool be made serviceable 685; better to be a f. 402; bolts pleasure 1423; can be brave 353; court f. 686; damn f. 2077; dares to be a f. 2076; even a f. 679; find a f. 688; from his friends 518; he is a f. 2071; in me 1202; is a greater fool 681; is the slowest 682; made a f. 1225; not made a f. 502; of himself

127; question in his h.
387; there springs 1961;
thudding h. 1007; to the
h. 523; without words
1495; won her h. 377;
words in your h. 1691;
wrapped in a woman's
hide 641

hearts do not forgive 1398;
in their h. 803; senti-
ments of our h. 884; will
bear 96

heat laws of h. 485; strange
h. 1111

heaven draw strength from
h. 1496; earth or in h. 412;
knows what 1932; serve in
h. 1705; thank h. 886

heavy ground of existence
923

hedgerow than in the
meanest streets 2021

heels putting on high h.
170; truth near the h. 1904

Hegel Darwin or H. 920

height of elegance 1818

heightened in a television
age 1839

held captive 653; in reverence 1533; together 1330

hell go to h. 1499; headed
for h. 1570; on earth 1255;
reign in h. 1705; there is a
h. 1536; to belong 1296;
tyranny like h. 1965

help him forget them 1218;
in the smuggling 1088; to
preserve it 1097

helped to shape 1258

helpless the miserable 1768;
we need aid 2059

helps us to make a decision
1362

heresies begin as h. 1917

hermit's cell 1853

hero is still worshipable
1338; needs a h. 1117;
show me a h. 829; with
coward's legs 360

heroes and bogey men 300;
and its villains 830; are
created 828; deteriorate
36; fame of h. 832;
quickly as of h. 353; to
have no h. 827

heroic dimension 831

heroism madness or h.
902

hero-worship is strongest
1280

herring encased in a block
of ice 312

herself to do to h. 193

hesitate to embrace it 1440

heterosexual or homosexual 1220

hibernation is a covert
preparation 54

hidden beauty of the world
1424; in the soul 296; rage
cannot be h. 121; under
185; when h. 339

hide he does not h. 34;
woman's h. 641

hierarchy of values 1625

high chances were very h.
561; for you to jump 1734;
heels 170; imagining 734;
price 905; respect for
your nerves 310; stan-
dards 1176; style 1746

higher nature 1218; than itself 1265

highest authority 601; compact we can make 1914;
degree prophylactic 551;
excellence 601; form of
living 58; order 1824;
things are achieved 18;
unfolding 1664

highly endowed 1661; paid
ambassadors 457

himself creating h. 370; he
exposes h. 34; place for h.
114; who prides h. 393

hindmost with his heads h.
254

hindsight 20-20 h. 1624

hip pocket 674

Hippocrates in the name of
H. 1775

historian essentially wants
849; is a prophet 847; or a
traveler 1435; so attractive
853

historian's first duties 837;
business 850

historians talent of h. 840

historical books 843; group
1330; sense 385

histories contain instruction 838

history anthropologist respects h. 1713; as a story
656; become a bad word
866; becomes more 852;
can be well written 833;
can begin 1587; can en-
dure h. 842; confronted
h. 859; dead h. 1674; de-

feats itself 854; does not
long entrust 857; experi-
ence in h. 576; extension
of h. 1014; good h. 62,
1391; house of h. 2082;
human h. 2054; is a
gallery of pictures 839; is
after all nothing 836; is
like an old man 1337; is
not what you thought
854; is principally 855; is
the study 851; is the transformation 860; is to be regarded 834; is written
846; just burps 865; long
run of h. 252; name in h.
1575; of a country 62; of
mankind 1415; of the
world 1532; on the run
1012; only through h. 834;
page of h. 804; pat h. 975;
personal h. 1454; repeat
itself 865; revolutions in
h. 1583; secular and
church h. 60; selects its
heroes 830; that excitable
844; that we learn 848;
their culture 318; treats
almost exclusively 762;
was all there was 864; we
owe to h. 845; you don't
know 861

hit its lowest ebb 1834

hither and thither 254

hoax fabricated by poets
1805

hold a marriage together
1246; it in your hands
1519; on to that 383

hole there is a h. 1456

Hollywood gossip 664

holy duty toward others
489; passion of friendship
721; profane clean 1846

homage pays h. 1686

home and lie awake 1240;
charity begins at h. 280;
done at h. 504; must go h.
1618; sitting quietly at h.
70; stay at h. 1832; take it
h. 916; to the full period
1144; when you get it h.
883

homey taste of lies was h.
1143

homosexual heterosexual
or h. 1220

honest doubt 478; man
478, 1343; men 282, 867,
868; truth 1907

ideals foreign word i. 888; in our i. 891; talent provided with i. 1799

ideas and feelings 376; are fatal to caste 911; are powerful things 922; are refined 917; artists' i. 160; best i. 894; big i. 915; bourgeois i. 1569; but grief 921; cannot be resisted 1561; change of i. 896; changed my i. 898; commitment to i. 614; dead i. 1632; decapitate i. 910; distinct, i. 899; drift like clouds 919; expression of i. 1082 ; flight of my i. 966; fought for i. 921; identity of i. 1082; improve 918; in human affairs 920; mind with i. 970; move rapidly 924; nasty i. 542; new i. 927; of chivalry 1569; of our educated class 968; offensive i. 1088; original i. 925; originating 895; other people's i. 51; people find i. 914; rose in clouds 904; staccato i. 915; talk about i. 926; taste in i. 996; that were true 907; the slow way 923; to hang i. 1083; too are a life 897; twenty years later 735; won't go to jail 252

identification is not an expression 2066

identified as an animal 606; with the majority 1209

identity gives man an idea 933; is a bag and a gag 934; of ideas 1082

idiocy form of i. 1387

idiots with ideas 735

idle hour 940; people are often bored 941

idleness blessing of i. 937; in our dreams 939; is an appendix 935; is either enforced 736; is its rust 938; like kisses 936

idolatry organization of i. 241; our i. 1334

idols aristocracy of i. 241; national i. 241

ignominy the i. 1676

ignorance allied with power 957; and conscientious stupidity 955; brighter than i. 1353; child of i. 1598; exploding in her face 958; gives one a large range 949; horizon of i. 952; in action 946; individual i. 945; inhibited by i. 1449; is a voluntary 944; is an evil weed 954; is not bliss 953; is one of the surest proofs 1024; its own i. 948; no sin but i. 942; obstacle to discovery is not i. 1074; of good and evil 750; of the past 950; paid dividends 498; perpetual i. 1358; weight of its i. 479

ignorant age 251; and to be i. 1631; fool 681; know everything 956; man so i. 943; of flavor 677; people 1573; shepherds 863; than knowledgeable 747; you are i. 947

ignore it is childish 768; nothing 1921; our impertinent 1636; try to i. 383

ignored they are i. 580

ill at ease 1985; provider 139

illiterate repartee of the i. 2020

illnesses trials and i. 87

illogical belief 598

illusion is an anodyne 960; many have given the i. 318; of knowledge 1074; of real creation 101; optical i. 504; that I am exploring 1130; that my vision 972

illusions are often in truth 959; of fancy 285; specious i. 1382

image and likeness 1878; of knowledge 1068

image-junkies citizens into i. 197

images effect 917

imaginary solutions 1719

imagination audacity of i. 967; created the illusion 972; creatures of i. 1145; destroys i. 969; devoid of i. 190; functioning of the i. 355; is the outreaching 970; lady's i. 65; men's i. 964; never have i. 546; not invention 964; nourishes his i. 159; of man 2031; of the senses 966; operating 880; or to intelligence 1946; people without i. 969; places of the i. 968; revolts the i. 274; schools for the i. 1107; slipstreams of i. 923; speak to the i. 69; to lift her work 965; uncorking the i. 1190; works of i. 1817

imaginations fevered i. 963; ruled by their i. 961

imagine a society 135; an ending 1452; himself pleasing 1983; is everything 962; myself on my death-bed 408; what it is to have a man's form 646

imagined to be 1185

imagines and every sort 970; he has attained it 2071

imagining high i. 734

imaginings in futile i. 123

imbecile fools 1851

imbecility into what the mob regards 1251

imitation great by i. 801; of the habits 1874; of the reality 140

immediate cause 2056

immediately add its second 1029; destroys 1488

immemorial refuge 1768

immense belief in themselves 818; riches 1506

immorality may be 1993

immortal periods 284

immortality installs the poet in his i. 399

immunity protective i. 1139

impact of a new idea 913; of military virtues 346

impairs its quality 240

imparted to be i. 132

impartial intellect 1076

impartiality is not neutrality 1047

impartially and without 850; examined i. 1698

imperfection accuse a government of i. 783; is the greatness 815

imperfections freedom from its i. 950

impermanent artificial and i. 1287

impertinent interference 1636; question 1544

formed 1023; reporters became j. 1018; tell lies to j. 449; unemployed or j. 1220

joy brought by the certainty 194; full of j. 1160; of life 1784; sorrow than to j. 1613; value of a j. 820

joyfulness with j. 403

joys affections virtues 1300; of life 253

Judah sons of J. 47

judge does God j. 124; events and actions 790; from the vast numbers 784; of a man by his foes 424; only their actions 1697; we can j. 1922

judges of character 734; one's actions 878

judging always j. 1026; for themselves 1027; the crimes 1046

judgment bad j. 1033; biases the j. 1030; blames his j. 1025; but a terror-ridden refusal 2116; conscience without j. 326; feeling without j. 1028; gives you 1034; good j. 377; initiative and for j. 1031; is therewith defined 1029; perception and j. 161; popular j. 557; proofs of j. 1924; untempered 1028

judgment-days full of j. 555

judgments value j. 583

judicial decrees 1321

jump over it 14; too high for you to j. 1734

jumps from admiration to love 65

jungle law of the j. 1446

just a disease 872; absurdly j. 461; as little 1054; as well get himself killed 609; average of faculties 494; by accident 1735; cause that is j. 1938; coins and pieces of paper 1308; if the world were j. 1037; in being a father 618; mind 411; possession 1903; to be alive 1159; weapon 1348

justice among men 1043; begins next door 280; can have 957; driven to j.

1048; interested in j. 1369; is as measured 1044; love of j. 534; partiality for j. 1047; strictest j. 981; sympathy or j. 1926; war for j. 1045; what stings is j. 1041; when it comes to judging 1046; where might is right 1038

justified and approved 1488

justify them in the law courts 1372

justly dealing j. 1035; undervalued by others 1298

keen as their resentment 684; vision 901

keenly feel his solitude more k. 1192

keep a guard over your eyes 223; an idea 1141; any better than fish 1063; house 1221; love we k. 1191; on working 1803; our faces toward change 1155; out of prison 1534; silence 652; the promises 1510; things under his feet 270; up such a regime 193

keeping his temper 2005

keeps his balance 1442; his own wounds green 1577; its own secrets 1646

kept for those days 1073

kernel scarcely compensates 838

key to wisdom 2072

keyhole of nature 1642

keys car k. 794

kick in the butt 1812

kid straggle into the kitchen 974

kidneys weak k. 997

kill a man 410; courage to k. 224; everybody 95; everyone 410; I will k. you 104; millions of men 410; one another 49; things that can k. 90

killed a calf 1746; for one 609; or else be k. 353

killing before k. 1311; cleanly 409

kills for an idea 609

kind fear of any k. 1394; force of any k. 201; of anxious fear 1180; of callousness 1139; of divinity 776; of habit 984; of mind reading 1786; of piety

1413; of superiority 1768; of superstition 2031; of taste 996; of technological leapfrog game 259

kindness and generosity 296; and lies 1142

kinds distractions of all k. 499; of loneliness 1177; of slaves 535; of two k. 525; triumph over all k. 87

king among his 1708; can least afford 686; man is k. 1605; of those 742; scratch a k. 688; should have bought it 126; vulgarity in a k. 2023; who has not had a slave 1708

Kingdom of Heaven 1591

kingdom of the blind 1605

kings is mostly rapscallions 1609; thieves called k. 885

kiss first k. 408

kissed you get k. 595

kisses to be sweet 936

kitchen in the morning 974

knack of so arranging the world 1827

knave honest man a k. 1343

knew anything 1980; before 1058; for a certainty 1000; how women 651; how 787; that she had encountered 1177

knife all blade 1556; and fork 1504

knocks at your door 1769; me out 1550

know about economics 498; about love 1804; afraid of what I k. 1056; anything 1980; both the power it confers 1647; death 1152; does not k. 777; don't need to k. 27; enough to get by 1542; everything 956; for our pleasure 27; from what they k. 1070; here that the law 1107; him by this sign 725; his worth 270; history you don't k. 861; how to become a stone or tree 206; how to fish 1633; how to make proper use 2010; how to seduce 1654; how to win 2010; if our shoes fit 1054; in what direction 1807; is nothing 962; less 655; manuscripts to k. 1618; more about women

limitless and therefore unmanageable 653; expanse 824

limits forever be l. 979; or boundaries 1203

limps off the field 1987

line of wonder 1066; sharp l. 1491

linen clean l. 673

lines learning l. 38

link between the thoughts 1690

links weak l. 105

lion claws of the l. 1649

lips as the outlets 223

listen anew 2082; particularly l. 1350; to writers 2103; to your own being 925; wonderful to l. 1679

literature great l. 28; is my Utopia 231; is the art of writing 1010; is the result 1428; meditate over the l. 1716; moral duty of l. 1168; realism in l. 1167; when it is passionate 1021

litigation brings to bear 1111

little adventure too l. 1144; agreement 1436; bit of life 416; careless 351; diminishes a l. 418; hope for a peaceful world 1399; learn so l. 1231; learning 1126; less democracy to save 2045; man's pleasure 468; more than the faculty 732; ones 448; pains 645; personal characteristics 620; prized 1315; room is left 587; security 822; sharp staccato ideas 915; sincerity 1696; sins 2001; than to misunderstand 1980; think too l. 1885; time 181, 301; to the extent 832; too l. 933; too self confident 271; virtues 2006; while 1220; wooden chapel 1525

littleness his own l. 805

live according to its dictates 1410; ceasing to l. 1197, 1719; conformists 319; content 870; do not deserve to l. 1311; even to l. 333; every day 931; find a way to l. 269; for a single aim 1156; for those who l. 421; for thousands of

years 18; fully 595; in a state 1460; in a world 866; in houses 1565; in prison 1615; in the best 1367; in the realm 1866; in the world 1499; like gods 1211; man could not l. 1614; manfully 342; on charity 282; on the momentum 827; ones 914; over again 1163; pleasantly 1397; under continual threat 442; up to them 1042; with you 916; without 1157

lived for fifty years 571; forever 910; long enough 795; might have l. 910; some thirty years 79; to my age 311; who ever l. 1429

lively sense 1333

lives after them 751; impoverish our l. 84; in fear 621; in whose l. 1615; of the bourgeoisie 1161; on which it l. 1092; outside our l. 1258; period of our l. 311; political l. 1447; with nature 2021

liveth in hope 874

living and ceasing to live 1719; and its decaying trees 1339; beauty of l. 1308; beings 367; highest form of l. 58; I like l. 1159; in a country 1840; in constant fear 638; on a site 863; pain of l. 1616; standard of l. 499; valued l. 401; well 1578; writers 1686

loan of his public opinion 1359

loath to die 397

loathing seizes him 8

local politics 1448

lock doors 875; too much l. 1241

locking of false gods 837

locks up its spoons 1284

lofty things from low 1052; virtues 2001

logic and metaphysics 1171; ice of l. 923; mind all l. 1556; of worldly success 1761

logical being l. 1170; order 1787

logically uniform system

1639; what it can do l. 1838

London is full of women 2086; women in L. 673

loneliness I experienced 20; in existence 1177; is greater 1173; is more lonely 465; is never more cruel 1175; is part 1176

lonely and introspective 687; more l. 465; often l. 1176; wasteful self-conflict 2056

long as there are sovereign nations 2043; as war is the main business 2033; consult too l. 1144; dull monotonous years 75; enough to find out 795; entrust the care 857; experience of politics 1449; forgotten 563; martyrdom 656; retain either 1469; run of history 242; since come to believe 1697; time since we've had any 930; time 883

longer cast a shadow 387; longer no l. 667; the shore line 1066

longing of the soul 1495

longings for beauty 197

look at life one way 1153; beyond it 14; funny on a horse 1120; like a ruin 1187; man's l. 43; of nuptial rapture 1741; on every new theory 1501; so thoroughly unhappy 2086; to its definitions 1324; up his manuscripts to know 1618

looked down upon 1368; upon 762, 763, 768

looking for someone 1196; for the modern equivalent 563; ridiculous 1093; through a keyhole 1642

looks at the world 1857; attitude not l. 1670; like money wasted 1551

loose in the streets 875

loose-leaf notebook 1071

Lord make my enemies ridiculous 519; work of our L. 1342; would do if He knew 605

lords and dukes 226

lose afford to l. 686; is to l. 430; liberty 1465; nothing to l. 1579, 1586; sight of

miseries or credulities of
mankind 107
misfortune national m.
2035; no mercy in m. 323;
support in m. 1308; to
ourselves 525; voluntary
m. 944
misleading thoughts 2090
miss a big story 1022;
would not m. 567
misshapen somehow m.
1456
missing something m. 1456
mission in their m. 818
missionaries explains why
some m. 1688
missionary foreign m. 193;
of valor 346
mistake Britain's m. 565; it
for a universal one 1426;
me my dear 310; of mar-
rying 977; of ours 1676;
this is a m. 1137; to make
a habit 1232; to theorize
1030
mistakes a lot of m. 1166;
invented m. 554; it for
happiness 758; people's
m. 851
mistress jealous m. 139;
worst m. 2062
mistresses men's m. 2085
misunderstand a lot 1980
misunderstanding manu-
facturer of m. 999
misunderstandings pro-
found m. 1111
misunderstood by those
who hear it 1926; to be m.
1417
misused words 2090
mix possibly m. 1816
mixed with experience 978
mixed-up human beings
2054
mixture for all possible
1427; of the love 534
mob regards as profundity
1251
mobility upward or down-
ward m. 1453
mockery dream and a m.
469
mode of purification 1422
models the books 385
moderate abilities 1788
moderation recommends
m. 878
modern conditions 788;
conveniences 499; equiva-

lent 563; form of despot-
ism 244; life 587; lounge
suit 1753; man must de-
scend 14; man 238; soci-
ety 499; sympathy with
pain 1784; university 1104;
world is filled 471; world
1209, 1774
modes of stylized 1755
modest possesses 1986
modesty cultivate m. 1299;
is natural to man 1297; is
the lowest of the virtues
1298; only begins with the
knowledge 1297
molded people are m. 67
moment at the m. 1032;
every m. 966; he wants to
be 704; in a m. 65; may be
one's finest 1170; of abolition 156; of decision 818;
of unwariness 223
momentarily arrested 1017
moments bitter m. 1615
momentum of the past 827
money action for their m.
1307; and large armies
1305; and power 794; and
security 1304; can be
translated 1308; demands
that you sell 1802; everybody has got m. 1824; for
books 230; honor without
m. 872; in the hands of a
few 1489; indifference to
m. 2006; is not required
to buy 2063; is the most
important thing 1302; is
the root 1306; lend m.
721; marry for m. 1233;
neck but m. 1303; never
remains 1308; regard for
m. 1302; the more m.
1301; wasted 1551
money-handler rather than
money-maker 665
monotonous interval 1392
monotony irritating m. 824
monster green-eyed m.
1003; he is a m. 609
monstrously flourish 767
moral activity 1313; approbation 41; deficiencies
185; determination 441;
dilemmas 664; duty of literature 1168; indigestion
1423; indignation 1318;
obligation 1704; one be-
comes m. 1319; prejudices
1499; revolution 1598;

startlingly m. 1314; truly
m. 1434
morality and invigoration
1325; cannot be legislated
1321; comes with the sad
wisdom 1323; is not law
1673; is the best of all devices 1317; only m. 1075;
politics and m. 1439; sensitivity and m. 1988;
touched by emotion 1316
morally in the right 1592
morals defense of m. 1320;
in m. truth is but little
prized 1315; strict m. 1656
morbid in the modern
sympathy 1784; reactions
1781
more admirable 1221; and
more a race 852; and
more efficient 815; angry
at undeserved 534; as-
sured end 959; dangerous
912, 955, 1135; despicable
than respect 636; difficult
to be witty 364; easily acquired 884; great or more
brilliant 432; in the skies
625; interesting 557;
knows no m. 1052; lonely
than distrust 465; numer-
ous than those 2010; of
the same 265; or less 1755;
our egoism is satisfied
508; realistic perspective
570; revolutions occur
1600; satisfaction 1034;
than a school 1104; than
half of the people 433;
than I promise 1511; than
of reason 1145; than to
love 1822; things a man is
ashamed of 1675; to do
with manners 1821; use
from his enemies 518;
wicked together 1962;
witty 2073
morning early in the m.
1548; I spent with an old
lady 312; with outfits 974
morsel for human degluti-
tion 1028
mortal foes are m. 529;
things 783
mortally afraid of government 117; hurt 1987
mortals mere m. 250
mortuary word 539
most Americans 498; be-
coming light 289; by ob-

epochs 1329; business of n. 2033; democratic n. 1401; great n. 455; have present or past 1335; old n. 1338; possessing great power 2043; small n. 455, 566; wisdom of n. 493
nation's strength 1336
native word 888
natural anything else as n. 421; canonization 399; human environment 1777; knowledge 171; lay of the land 645; philosopher 1414; selection 1772; to man 1297; vicissitudes 570
naturally affirmative 208; has a somewhat melancholy character 1614; placed 656; wears itself out 1092
nature about us 1341; and development 653; and its teachings 1341; and quality 1091; and the world 1986; being by n. 1059; can afford 1636; cannot ever prosper 748; copy n. 1342; demands 592; enduring a n. 721; ever-receding n. 198; fitted him 1261; good n. 880, 1359, 1608; higher n. 1218; human n. 340, 900, 932, 1140, 1405, 1759, 1844; in her indifference 766; interests by n. 987; interpreted n. 1107; is just enough 1340; is not a state 2030; is still divine 1338; keyhole of n. 1642; laws of n. 1634; lives with n. 2021; may heal 189; mechanical in its n. 245; mind to n. 2064; nothing in n. 1325; observation of n. 1050; of a novel 1365; of fanaticism 613; of genius 735; of men 2073; of that 1754; presents 273; reality of n. 140; uses human imagination 965; which has to interfere 52; works of n. 1692
natures in their n. 1456; one of the n. 206; real n. 275; true n. 1543
near an approach to virtue 447; impotents 1507

nearer to destruction 1076
nearly always 388, 1283; as strong 1529; deceiving 1522
necessarily emerges 2057; not n. 1312; represent 1079
necessary allowed to become n. 1602; evil is not n. 765; if ever n. 1911; ingredient 1377; make philanthropy n. 983; of the soul 2063; part 83, 768; plagiarism is n. 918; that at least once in your life 476; to avoid starvation 1534; to employ it 2070; to him than bread 1884; to raise imbecility 1251
necessity does the work of courage 1344; door of n. 1991; everything that happens is a n. 1346; face of n. 890; liberate himself from n. 1345; makes an honest man 1343; of virtue 1997; out of n. 527; subject to n. 1345
neck from man's n. 1303; of a slave 1707
need and a craving 1795; of ancestors 1380; of valor 1037; only look 1324; someone to love 1196; strength 2059; to achieve that change 1778; to be professionals 1054; to be shoemakers 1954; to exert power 1474; to know 27, 254, 1813; to lead 1116; to minimize the poverty 1463; today is charm 288; total n. 774; vice and n. 2092; when we come 2059
needed for learning 876; to create incidents 1503; to sorrow 1613
needle-work and housewifry 643
needs a hero 1117; a second quality 1114; and it n. 807; most 298; things a child n. 298; to be clad 1905; to be maintained 695; to remain a mystery 290
needy raises the n. 283
negative it is n. 1869; judgment 1034
neglect intelligent n. 298
neglected mien 739

neighbor despise one's n. 1570; to be governed 117
neighbors call good 761
neither a past nor a future 291; art nor science 1964; can man or angels come 1464; fight nor fly 623; knew anything 1980; read nor write 284; their property nor their honor 870
Nero in the gentlest 1475
nerves destroys one's n. 1230; respect for your n. 310
nervous makes people n. 560
net for catching days 267
network of possible paths 254
neurosis guilt n. 1065; has appeared 1660; is to psychosis 482
neurotic is in doubt 482
neutral facts are never n. 583
neutrality impartiality is not n. 1047
never afraid 595, 1056; allow 1171; alters his opinion 1357; an instant's truce 1996; be a civilized country 230; be a free man 621; be a substitute 1031; be bedfellows 599; be if we are to live 1397; be thought 530; came back 2112; cease until babies begin 2048; come to speak properly 1688; contend with a man 1579; create one 242; dies 1398; do evil so completely 756; fallen 590; fearful 752; forget 809; found 1449; free 705; get the notion 1219; goes out of fashion 345; grown out 212; happened 853; happy 823; have both 1908; have enough of nature 1339; have imagination 546; hope more than you work 374; imagine 646; indiscreet 1541; inspired such achievements 284; its tool 1571; know 1253; learned to obey 1351; lose the awareness 172; make a statement 1430; make men free 1100; make up

their minds 775; make virtue 626; marry 651, 2069; mean half 1697; met a man 943; mind the fashion 1749; more cruel 1175; more powerful 284; more than an animal 809; neutral 583; possible to rule 1607; remains just coins 1308; repay their debts 1355; seasoned a truth 1953; simple 1515; skating over 923; stop investigating 1542; surrender 478; the people n. 2032; those we bore 235; to say n. 971; treat a triviality 1763; trust the artist 1893; understand 1256, 1439; very useful 431; want occasion 749; was Catholicism 1569; was yet philosopher 1409; we'll n. achieve 26; were the ideas of chivalry 1569; wholly successful 1345; without belief in a devil 214; won a battle 177; worth going through 311; written a line 1425

nevertheless retaining faith 856; within one's reach 1257

new age 1909; answers 730; audacity of imagination 967; combinations 927; country 69; facts burst old rules 1626; feet of the n. 1931; forms of life 268; garments 1905; generation 1401; history 1587; idea 900; ideas still waiting 927; in the world 861; journalist 1018; lover 1194; masters 1581; movement 150; novelty 1020; old and n. 1626; order of things 1559; order 573; philosophy 2002; problem 1067; program 1834; questions 738; rooms 723; scenery 571; social condition 329; source of power 1489; theory 1501; thinker 908; truths 1917

newly divined conceptions 1626

news business 1022; every day 1019; get the n. 523; is staged 1020; organizations

1023; reports information 1016

newspaperman even a n. 100

newspapers read the n. 1013; seen in the n. 1009

next common sense of the n. 1411; door 280, 1570; interpretation of the n. 1361; to a man 1226l world war 2044

nice man is a man of nasty ideas 542; man 1244

nicer things 303

nicest way 451

night awake all n. 1240

nightmares darken into n. 1856

nineteenth century 404

nipples of modern society 499

no fury like a woman searching 1194; gods say n. 441; great concurrence 1125; longer retreat 667; obstacles at all 1734; political system 1616; safety in regaining the favor 515; unhappier creature 545

nobility appendix to n. 935; the romance 1140

noble deeds are most estimable 339; delights 1425; exercise 1547; shortsightedness 1692; simplicity 1692; unquestionably n. 907; values 438

nobler instincts 1218; it would 907; nothing n. 1221

nobody can describe a fool 687; comes into the world 884; ever forgets 1393; is bored 236; is so constituted 486

none greater than wanting 564; have really walked alone 318; practice 877; to make them keep silence 652

nonetheless the poorest 1057

nonperson she was a n. 1177

nonsense may not 1932; solidified 309

nonstop music 1258

nonviolence is a powerful 1348

non-violent man 1735

noose that binds 632

nose by the n. 1317; under one's n. 1807

nostalgia a marketable commodity 1347

not a compliment 1359; a desire for success 2006; a disinterested judgment 2116; a good teacher 639; a hermit's cell 1853; a more mean 341; a pleasant condition 477; a radical 1546; a test of truth 1941; accident 941; accord it a special value 1713; administer 1043; all that could be said 511; always have clean hands 716; always tell us 1352; an extension 1203; as strong 684; asked to lend money 721; at all of martyrdom 1526; at the door 1991; aware 693; be a violent 1823; be allowed 1602; be made a fool of 1725; been examined 1698; been scuffling 1744; befitting the human mind 1816; being talked about 780; believe in the collective wisdom 945; burdened with convictions 1870; by faith 1920; by the sense 1715; caution 2006; dare 1147; difficult 1898; due 1415; easily 1965; enough 769, 1293, 1654, 2070, 2083; exceeding the limit 2077; expect justice 1038; feel himself quite secure 1649; feeling it incumbent 645; fifty ways of fighting 2015; find scope 1884; forget again 2091; free to love 1192; from the barrel of a gun 1486; given to men 1822; in itself opposed 1828; in our virtues 588; in sympathy 1106; in what it can borrow 1336; knowing 1747; long retain 1469; love a place 1764; made a fool 502; merely 1410; money 1489; much danger 731; my griefs 742; natural 1297; necessarily the size 1312; of small virtues 2005; only prophesy 1480; quite what he

reign in hell 1705; year of his r. 1608

reincarnation reasons for r. 1666

reined by scruple 1056

reject the conventions 667

rejected genius 740; thoughts 1850

rejecting nasty ones 303

rejection of authority 171

rejects replacements 1833

relation to the general development 7

relational power 1575

relations among states 1481; human r. 1142; international r. 1399; poor r. 1911

relationship between destruction 1576; is simple 1763

relationships and experiences 570

relative rank 1281

relatively easy to bear 1041; small part 367

released you get r. 114

relentless enemy 2067

relic of the dead 401

relied on to tell 158

relief to believe 213

relieve them of the trouble 472

religion faith is in r. 1383; is thus not simply morality 1316; lies for his r. 1568; myth or r. 1576; of science 1635; principle of my r. 469; sex without r. 1668; spirituality and to r. 1828

religious consolations 421; conviction 756; fervor 1656; intolerance 1570; man 1567; neurosis 1660

relinquish their sexuality 1672

reluctantly begin to think for itself 1859; most often 1543

remain a mystery 290; children 2116; in obscurity 1792; in us 1982; loyal 224; open long enough 1935; to be accomplished 1506

remaining faithful 215

remains nothing r. 1422; one of the demonic forces 1667; sorrow 1612

remarkable about it 1195; pattern 617

Rembrandt art of R. 841

remember always the need 1813; and what to forget 1269; it's as easy to marry 1232; my youth 2112; that it is still an evil 770; that we were so once 823; what you can r. 854

remind you of it 1220

reminded that it is not the master 1571

remorse awakenings of r. 41

removed from the direct connection 1866

render mediocrity 1262; the multitude 1382

rendered harmless 1483; her invisible 1177; him in conversation 1741

renders people more insensible 1537

renewed courage 927

rent taxes 1303

renunciation remains sorrow 1612

reopened wound 1674

repartee best r. 1207; of the illiterate 2020

repay their debts 1355

repeat does history r. 865; itself 572; willing to r. 1683

repeatedly meats served up r. 720

repeats reruns rejects 1833

repent of anything 761; too soon 1144

repentance road to r. 1222

replace to r. 1245

replacements and reversions 1833

replaces it with the right idea 918

reported analyzed 1020

reporters became journalists 1018; who cover politics 1455

reports news r. 1016

repose truth and r. 1908

represent a plurality of things 1079; causes that they r. 2102

representation dehumanized r. 1755

represented in the advertising 1238

represents health 1302

reproached afterwards r. 642

reptiles of the mind 1357

republic aristocracy in a r. 134; of mediocrity 1264

repudiates the suggestion 1347

reputation for good nature 1608; of possessing 1785

required of it without shyness 1751; to make a good fisherman 1137

requirement of a statesman 698; of polygamy 1237

requirements of romantic love 1604

requires a training 1547; active involvement 1838; spirit and talent 1738; the most disinterested 549; to be as constantly wound up 1294

requiring not a studious contemplation 922

reruns rejects 1833

resemble military tactics 1443

resentment keen as their r. 684

reserved for those whose 1454; for women 1399; person 1184

resides now less 1948; the strength 1324

resist participation 830

resistance power of r. 1537

resisted armies can be r. 1561

resists him who r. 1969

resolute minority 616

resolutions are simply checks 1718

resolve to steer 889

resort last r. 694

respect based on fear 636; for your nerves 310; in this r. 486; of other people's ideas 51; public opinion 1534; sincerity 521

respectability and children 1303

respectable more r. 1675; ordinarily r. 147

respects history 1713

respiration artificial r. 1655

respond simply 1482

response one r. 718

responsibility of directing

art nor s. 1964; cannot lead 979; essence of s. 1544; in the very act 1637; increases our power 1623; is a cemetery 1632; is a piece of impudence 1636; is always simple 1630; is knowledge 1634; is nothing 1628; is the attempt 1639; is the great antidote 1621; is the knowledge 1620; like life 1626; man of s. 1640; moves with the spirit 1641; religion of s. 1635; should leave off 1638; teaches 1631; tragedy of c. 1842; true s. 1627; when we say s. 1635; which cuts its way 1633; work of s. 1622

sciences are now under the obligation 1625; depend 1451

scientific man 1629; method 1624; politics can be s. 1451; training 385; value 567

scientist every s. 1644; is open to experience 1643; mad s. 269; what is a s. 1642

scoop here and there a s. 992

scope and increase its audacity 1103; for it 1884

scorn for defeat 1759

scorned than forgotten 603

scoundrel last refuse of a s. 1381; man over forty is a s. 1216

scourge terrible s. 459

scraps stolen the s 1080

scratch a king 688; an artist 142

screen for sexuality 1245; small s. 1833

scruple and the farming 2104; reined in by s. 1056

scuffling in this waste-howling wildness 1744

sculptors and painters 1748

sea outlast the s. 2112; tost upon the s. 1902; wide as the s. 1673

sea-coast with its wrecks 1339

search of wisdom 2071

searching for a new lover 1194; for the truth 1018

seas of thought 1862

season first s. 1785

seasoned a truth 1953

seat for him 1769; of beauty 183; of government 788

second and third thoughts 1866

second-hand furniture 1235

second-nature in a married man 1138

secrecy experts in s. 1647

secret constituting a s. 1016; doubt 608; preserve your s. 1645; thoughts of a man 1846; virtues 781

secrets keeps its own s. 1646; trade s. 1511

sect of Christianity 1566

sections of time 267

sector private s. 793

secular and church history 60

secure quite s. 1649

security future s. 1308; have we 822, in this world 1651; is an insipid thing 1648; money and s. 1304; national s. 1653; of being identified 1209; power and s. 678; to be found 1650

seduce a woman 1656; know how to s. 1654

seducing charms 127

see bad television 1832; everything 463; eye could actually s. 972; eye to eye 1221; how a good dinner 675; how it comes out 703; it on the tight-rope 1922; journalists as the manual workers 1021; now that I am asleep 483; ships tost 1902; taste and s. 938; that the increasingly dangerous 1463; the Divine 1341; the world 146; them when they please 362; there is a place 86; things under ground 625

seed scattering the s. 245

seeding of the self 1521

seeds of every passion 884

seeing ourselves in our interaction 1158; what they did 493

seek as well as what we find 1072; information 980; power 1465; simplicity

and distrust it 1413; where we s. 1909; will not s. 1898

seeker after truth 476

seekers office s. 1447

seeking out the laws of taste 1815; the truth 481; to become like each other; to escape 393; what he is s. 112

seeks another equilibrium 1781; good he s. 758

seem a happy accident 1752; attractive by comparison 1161; part of the ordinary 2022; strange as it may s. 1743; to be invincible 1032; to steal 1458

seemed to be melted 1300

seeming nonsense 1932

seemingly opposed 442

seems to be a compromise 1458; to be an experience 1156; valueless 963

seen in context 554; in the light 195; in the newspapers 1009; that great men are often lonely 1176

segment of existence 1075

seldom accomplishes permanent 2039; drive business home 1144; get anything 1581; had much support 813; if ever necessary 1911; visits him 1652; want pretexts 1966; win 2032

select cases 187

selected causes 841

selecting the most effective course 425

selection natural s. 1772

selections idealizations and s. 276

selective memory must be s. 1271

selects its heroes 830; what it does 1271

self confident and disdainful 271; in the consciousness 1521; is in prison 2056; narrow s. 827; one's s. 261

self-acceptance greater s. 570

self-confidence humor comes from s. 879

self-conflict wasteful s. 2056

self-control lacks s. 1202

makes us all s. 120; man is doing something 487; man so s. 131; more s. 1740; one 120; right to be s. 1744; slightly s. 1741; ugly and the s. 429

stupidity conscientious s. 955; except s. 913; men's s. 1802; no amount of learning can cure s. 1743; of others 1737; or malevolence 771; pains of s. 510; patient with s. 1745; rallies s. 1320; rather than courage 1739; sheer s. 1742; we would call s. 1738; well wadded with s. 901

style good s. 1751, 1752, 1848; high s. 1746; in that s. 1233; is art 1755; is eternal 1756; is not something applied 1754; lack of s. 1148; mannerism of s. 1750; of a generation 576; of an author 2096; of its architecture 728; of life 1753; of one's own 1749; out of the styles around him 1757; purely his own 1748; self-plagiarism is s. 2106; terms of s. 558; to one's character 273

styles of portrait painting 137

stylized dehumanized representation 1755

subject all things human are s. 420; in which we never know 1253; interested in the s. 1535; no living creature is s. 4; to necessity 1345; to the inconstancy 2028

subjects itself to the rule of reason 1815

subject's investment 220

submerged truth 939

submission to an unnecessary tyranny 1534

submissive woman 661

submissiveness of sheep 1976

submit to the desolation 1808

submitting to chaos 856

subordination inevitability of their s. 667

substance of life 1767

substantial merit 1104

substitute facts for appearances 1622; for initiative 1031; for talent 1795; for the one thing 1373; for thoroughness 1022; public opinion 1527

substitutes attractive virtues 1564

subtle thoughts 1410

subversive about love 1199

succeed and are right 434; by his talent 1794; in the other trades 1102; in their aim 1015

succeeded gloriously s. 1798

succeeds no man s. 109

success against the penalties 702; but a desire 2006; by his very s. 238; danger of s. 982; deifies s. 1759; in war 2017; is harmful 1809; lasting s. 317; makes men rigid 1760; mediocrity of s. 1144; of the tributes 832; penalty of s. 1762; plus self-esteem 1758; recognition 1209; rests on a fallacy 1761; uncertain in its s. 1559

successes are unhappy 1665; poorest in s. 1057

successful attempts 1345; businesses 563; crime 762; one 1814; relationship 1763

successfully exposing 1092; more s. 1558

succession of errors 553; of miracles 64

successor philosopher to any s. 645

such a margin 2050; a thing as truth 1044; a way that it catches you 1930

suck made for me to s. 212

suckled humanity 499

sudden deaths 1806

suddenly created s. 798

suffer the slavery 646; those who s. 76

suffered because of an evil man 746; in it unless it has all been suffering 1764; like themselves 1782

suffering as such 1771; full of s. 1766; inflicted by whites 1463; is the substance of life 1767; isn't ennobling 1770; knocks at

your door 1769; together 1765

suffers not at the hands 460; the mysteries 1576; truth s. 474

sufficiently alone 1172

suggest it with a brief gesture 1931

suggesting and guiding action 48

suggestion that life in the past 1347

suggestions accept her s. 1340

suit along with his s. 1363; suit lounge s. 1753

summed up in dealing justly 1035

summer school 574; television 1833

sun of the dead 400; shadow in the s. 387; worship the s. 485

sundry all and s. 105

sunshine of the light 1693

superficial invariably s. 1909

superfluities only 2063

superfluous wealth 2063

superior man is easy to serve 1273; sensitivity and morality 1988; to his fellows 538; wise patient s. 461

superiority kind of s. 1768; sign of s. 136; to the sleeping world 1711; without it 1259

superiors with our s. 536

supernatural source of evil 765

supersedes all other forms 2000

superstition is belief 584; judgment is s. 326; kind of s. 2031; source of s. 634; to insist 676

superstitions end as s. 1917

supplement to the reality of nature 140

supplied well s. 307

supplies fresh s. 2042

supply has always been in excess 1952; their deficiency 1788

support from their associates. 813; in misfortune 1308; the artist 160

suppose that there is no knowledge 1617

a t. 55; profound t. 1848;
seas of t. 1862; system of
t. 1639; talent for t. 1860;
that went into the action
62; the ebb was 1834; to
signify 530; was as physical 1007; were ours 216;
which does not result 55
thoughtful fears grow t.
637
thoughtless deludes the t.
121
thoughts accompaniment
of our t. 824; and opin-
ions 1761; are the shadows
1852; feelings and t. 28;
have a ridiculous begin-
ning 812; have tremen-
dous energy 1866; ideas
sounds t. 160; in simple
and clear language 1860;
look anything but imbe-
cile fools 1851; misleading
t. 2090; of a man 1846; of
man 1690; of others 1859;
on thought 1866; one's t.
1858; our own t. 1845; rejected t. 1850; subtle t.
1410; their models 385
thousand times a day 416
thousands of interactions
1491; of years 18
thread on which we string
1087
threads which sew people
together 1246
threat constitute a t. 530;
of two equally fearful 442;
to freedom 247
threatening far more t.
1178
threats to national security
1653
three things that can kill
90; times removed 1866
thrift but generosity 2006
thrilling lie 1520
throbs of pain 1615
throes of profound transition 1089
transition profound t. 1089
throne of bayonets 1610
through and through 898;
asceticism 1664; it all I
still know 1159; passed t.
502; sexual happiness
1664; silence is a link
1690; words 1140
throughout human history
2054; its course 325

throw our weight 718; up
his job 1239
thrown back upon routine
827; out of their life's
course 1440
thudding heart 1007
thunder of electoral combat 1455
thunder-cloud and the rain
1339
thwarted in the open fields
of life 1474; sensation
1865
tie of sympathy 1783
ties at all 618
tigers which they dare not
dismount 1972
tiger's heart 641
tight-rope see it on the t.
1922
time a long t. 883; all the t.
303; and effort 1688; and
mediocrity 738; and soci-
ety 1627; best t. 919; by
that t. 2041; by this t.
1245; can find t. 193;
comes 924; course of t.
762; dissolves in t. 156;
doesn't matter 1396; every
t. they occur 41; first t.
865; for organized think-
ing 919; genius of its t.
251; given t. 1627; half of
the t. 433; hands of t. 460;
in earlier t. 135; in little t.
181; in our t. 941; in their
own t. 484; inopportune
t. 2014; long t. 930; makes
all grief decay 819; makes
more converts 1555; man
spends his t. 377; measure
t. 1615; much of the t.
1402; of the rack 1833; of
war 1095, 1384; or taste
301; pass the t. 651; popular in our t. 740; proper t.
403; right t. 814; same
given t. 1789; sections of
t. 267; shallow as t. 1677;
societies in t. 1713; supposed to benefit 1131; that
of t. 601; there came a t.
221; to cultivate modesty
1299; to fill t. 2058; to
time 364; vice of our t.
1279; wake up one more t.
224; waste your t. 2057;
when every scientist 1644;
when for every addition
1058; you think 1834

time-consuming things 531
timeliness in t. 2064
timely death 411
times bad t. 567; earlier t.
1161; from their taste
2075; I wondered 20;
nothing in our t. 2007; of
disorder and stress 610; of
peace 610; revolutionary
t. 1596; thousand t. 416;
twenty t. 1749
timid to lock doors 875;
weak or the t. 857
tingling currents of
thought 1854
tinglings of a merited
shame 1674
tiny tablets 1019; threads
1246
tire of the importance 969
tired of sleep 2025; of the
effort 1760; of the role 382
tires power t. 1493
tiresome for children 1256
titanic features 1339
title and rank 1287
tobacco-pipes of those who
diffuse 779
today Americans are overcome 1715; I happen to
have a headache 347; in
the world t. 1885; life t.
1347; movie industry t.
1837; there's more fellowship 92; to help us get
there 1831
toes tramps on his t. 1563
together go very well t.
1671; than separately 1962;
through the years 1246;
working t. 523
toil and trouble 492; to
pleasure 1419
toilsome trouble 1501
told about desire 438;
bravely t. 1140; in silence
1136; somebody 561;
something that is t. 1945
tolerance consists 1867; is a
very dull virtue 1869; is
composed of nine parts
1868; is most readily
achieved 1870
tolerant of the evil 764;
wonderfully t. 733
toleration of each 1867
tomorrow be demonstrated
1932
tone assuming a loud t.
170

ments 1103; but you can never imagine 646; so hard 1804; their luck 1234; to control thought 1863; to find reasons to trust 1896; to govern the world 565; to ignore it 383; to picture 1831; to think before I talk 1885

trying on one face 2115; to defend yourself 777; to experiment 269; to get away from it 1777; to keep his hand in 1428; to know 1642; to prove 434; to set up 118

tube test t. 1836

tumult of men and events 839

tumultuous conquerors 860

turmoil means t. 1502

turn against him 1967; bloom in their t. 245; in his tongue 1363; into an idea 928; one's back 167; the inevitable 1123; to dust or magic 1811

turned against ourselves 130; back 1638; into television 1258; out the way I was 1981

turning point in the process 1736

turns to pleasing pain 1420

twentieth century 416

twice and three times removed 1866; read t. 1010

two plus two makes four 711

two edged virtue 159

tyrannical it is likely to be 1976

tyrannies inevitably produce t. 1451

tyranny evils of t. 1969; exhibit their t. 1527; is always better organized 1973; is always mild at first 1963; like hell 1965; milder fate than t. 394; of his culture 161; unnecessary t. 1534

tyranny's disease 1888

tyrant grinds down his slaves 1967; or martyr 609; to be a t. 1964; weak t. 1528

tyrants seldom want pre-

texts 1966; worst of t. 1960

tyrant's heart 1961

ugly and base 39; and the stupid 429; fact 1842; first with an u. woman 192; not so u. 39; nothing is u. 1029; realities are so u. 195; serpent 1003; things 186

ulterior motives 850

ultimate affront 421; aim of the human mind 1915; ends 790

ultimately consists in what it can do 1336; the danger 700

unacceptable thoroughly u. 61

unanswered questions 300

unattainable perfection 1406; truth 553

unattractive as virtue 2007

unavailing star 1406

unaware of the absurdity 7

unbalance which is u. 1947

unbelief in denying 202

unbridled desire 439

uncertain in its success 1559; of its distractions 167

uncertainty and expectation 253; of every circumstance 2050

uncomfortable dangerous and u. 2001

uncommon strength 2060

unconditionally given as u. 242

unconscious something u. 973

unconsciously almost u. 645

uncorking the imagination 1190

uncover a hitherto unknown segment 1075

undecided breeze 919

undefeatable strength u. 1155

undeniable existence 964

under all speech 1677; an ancient obsolete vesture 1338; every aspect 1921; every stone 1433; ground 625; his feet 270; modern conditions 788; one's nose 1807; other circumstances 1738; the dear deceit 185;

the illusion 1130; the impression 1137; the obligation 1625

undergo the fatigue 1027

underrating the achievements 1506

understand a good many things 1231; a man 1979; able to u. 163; anything 1256; cannot u. 1271, 1978; failure to u. 806; more 655; others 38; that memory 1271; that sexuality 1673; the bureaucracy 241; the causes of war 1535; the grief 985; they do not u. 1977; things we do not u. 256; wisdom 2078; yourself 205

understandable this is u. 1176

understanding beyond their own u. 1260; enemy of u. 2067; is at its weakest 1356; of her 654; of myth or religion 1576; reach an u. 1716; that we boldly defend 1146; what is subversive 1199; without u. 504

understands even a fool u. 679; them dispassionately 850

undervalues himself 1298

underwent athletes u. 1547

undeserved than at deserved 534

uneasy lies the head 1606

uneducated government by the u. 133

unemployed or journalists 1220

unexciting truth 1520

unexpected perform u. 163

unfamiliar and complex 474

unfit to rule 434

unfolding among our valued friends 271; of his creative powers 1664

unfortunately invented for itself 2094

unfreedom of the human will 1057

unfurls it in another 1987; the range 1713

ungarnished truth 1217

ungrateful animal 341

unhabitual way 732

unhappier creature 545